Psychoanalysis in Social Re

The use of psychoanalytic ideas to explore social and political questions is not new. Freud began this work himself and social research has consistently drawn on his ideas. This makes perfect sense. Social and political theory must find ways to conceptualise the relation between human subjects and our social environment; and the distinctive and intense observation of individual psychical structuring afforded within clinical psychoanalysis has given rise to rich theoretical and methodological resources for doing just this. However, psychoanalytic concepts do not remain the same when they are rearticulated in the context of research.

This book traces the reiteration and transformation of concepts in the psychoanalytic theory of Freud, Klein and Lacan, the social theory of Butler, Derrida, Foucault, Laclau and Zizek, and case studies of empirical research ranging from the classic Tavistock Institute studies to contemporary work in politics, gender studies, cultural studies and education. Each chapter explores one cluster of concepts:

- Melancholia, loss and subjectivity
- Overdetermination and free association
- Resistance, reflexivity and the compulsion to repeat
- Repression, disavowal and foreclosure
- Psychic defenses and social defenses

Arguing against the reification of psychoanalytic concepts, Claudia Lapping suggests the need for a reflexive understanding of the play of attachments and substitutions as concepts are reframed in the contrasting activities of psychoanalysis and research. This book will be invaluable for students and researchers interested in psychoanalytic ideas, social theory and processes of interpretive analysis in empirical research.

Claudia Lapping is Senior Lecturer at the Institute of Education, University of London, where she teaches on the doctoral programme and on the MA Psychosocial Studies and Education. She is interested in the development of psychosocial methodologies and her research draws on sociological and psychoanalytic approaches to explore knowledge practices in higher education.

Psychoanalysis in Social Research

Shifting theories and reframing concepts

Claudia Lapping

Routledge
Taylor & Francis Group

LONDON AND NEW YORK

First published 2011
by Routledge
2 Park Square, Milton Park, Abingdon, Oxon, OX14 4RN

Simultaneously published in the USA and Canada
by Routledge
711 Third Avenue, New York, NY 10017

Routledge is an imprint of the Taylor & Francis Group, an informa business

First issued in paperback 2012

British Library Cataloguing in Publication Data
A catalogue record for this book is available from the British Library

Library of Congress Cataloging in Publication Data
Lapping, Claudia.
Psychoanalysis in social research : shifting theories and reframing
concepts / by Claudia Lapping.
p. cm.
Includes bibliographical references.
1. Social sciences and psychoanalysis. 2. Social sciences–Research.
I. Title.
BF175.4.S65L37 2011
150.19'5–dc22
2010043086

ISBN: 978-0-415-47925-7 (hbk)
ISBN: 978-0-203-88282-5 (ebk)
ISBN: 978-0-415-65686-3 (pbk)

Typeset in Sabon
by Wearset Ltd, Boldon, Tyne and Wear

Contents

Acknowledgments

I did not write this book on my own. I find it difficult to express the extent of my gratitude for the kindness, support and inspiration I have received from friends and colleagues over the last three years of thinking, reading, sitting down to write and getting up again. Alex Moore, Tamara Bibby, Deborah Chinn, Jaamia Galant, Jenny Parkes and Olivia Sagan acted as my 'reflecting team' on the research project that ran alongside the writing of this book. They have accompanied me through complicated methodological quandaries, and contributed very directly to the development of the data analysis in chapter four. In addition, Alex's circumspect, encouraging comments on early drafts provided important reassurance, and guided me towards significant revisions, particularly in chapter five; and Jenny's wisdom, friendship and critical reading cheered me along, as well as inspiring improvements to chapter one and the conclusion. Natasha Whiteman helped me to untangle several chapters and, more importantly, truly shared the burden of the various stages of writing and failing to write. Gabrielle Ivinson, Tim Diggins, Paul Dowling and John Adlam gave me kind and precise feedback on various versions of chapter five; and Ann Phoenix was similarly generous in relation to chapter two. Stephen Frosh read the complete manuscript and made suggestions for clarifications and revisions, which I have attempted to respond to in the final edit. I would like to thank Russell Dudley Smith for recommending Steinmetz' article on Bourdieu and one of my anonymous research participants for suggesting Spivak's chapter on Foucault.

I am also grateful to colleagues at the Institute of Education who gave me feedback on early versions of chapters or encouraged me in the early stages of writing: Annette Braun, Sheryl Clarke, Sam Duncan, David Halpin, Roger Hutchins, Adam Lefstein, Jo Metivier, Caroline Pelletier, Jessica Ringrose, Sue Rogers and David Scott. Many ideas in the book were also originally formulated in my discussions with students on the Ed.D courses 'Methods of Enquiry 1' and 'Using psychoanalytic approaches in educational research', and on my MA module 'Theorizing subjectivity, discourse and ideology'. Much love and thanks also to the participants in my project for helping me more than they can know; and to my friends, my sisters and my nephews, who have distracted me over the last three years with the things that are more important than this research. And, finally, if sections of the book are relatively clearly written, credit is due to my parents, who have always been strict about words and syntax. I apologize to them for unwieldy sentences and redundant neologisms. I honestly could not have written this book without the friendship, encouragement and substantive contributions I received from of all of these people. The errors, omissions and inadequacies that remain are all my own.

My thanks to Routledge for permission to reuse sections of chapter five that first appeared in *Knowledge and Identity: Concepts and Applications in Bernstein's Sociology*, edited by Gabrielle Ivinson, Brian Davies and John Fitz.

The ESRC funded 'The development of a psychosocial methodology for exploring knowledge practices in higher education', an empirical research project which ran alongside, benefiting from and informing, the writing of this book. Data from the project forms the basis for the discussion in chapter four, and this analysis contributed to the argument in chapter five.

I dedicate this book, with love and thanks, to my peculiar parents, for always being there.

Introduction
Reframing psychoanalytic concepts, or bricolage decomposed

The central concern of this book is to explore what happens to concepts when they are deployed in contrasting contexts and used in the analysis of new objects of study. More specifically, the book explores the way psychoanalytic concepts are used within empirical social scientific research. The broad, underlying argument, or perhaps presumption, of the book is that concepts are necessarily reiterated and transformed in the process of research and analysis. We can either try to police the use of established terminologies, or else we can explore the transformations brought about in new instantiations of old concepts. My preference is for the second of these alternatives. Rather than arguing for or against the use of psychoanalytic concepts within social research, this book is an attempt to look closely at the ways in which different aspects of psychoanalytic ideas are repeated and transformed when they are articulated in the context of social theory and research. Each chapter traces the instantiation of one concept in instances of both psychoanalytic and social scientific analysis. The book aims to develop a picture of concepts as constituted in a cluster of ideas that are connected in chains of meaning, but that tug in different directions, with some chains well established and some threads hanging loose, waiting to be extended, or knotted into a relation with threads from elsewhere in the tangle of conceptual frameworks and ideas.

The use of psychoanalytic ideas to construct new ways of understanding social and political questions is, clearly, not new. Freud began this work himself, and social and political theory has consistently drawn on his ideas. This makes perfect sense to me. Social and political theory must find ways to conceptualize the relation between human subjects and our social environment; and the distinctive and intense observation of individual psychical structuring afforded within clinical psychoanalysis has given rise to rich theoretical and methodological resources for doing just this. The use of psychoanalytic approaches within *empirical* social research might be justified in a similar way: if psychoanalysis can help us to understand the mechanisms by which the subject is constituted in relation to the social fabric, surely it will be productive to draw on these ideas in the production and analysis of empirical research data? Some of the earliest empirical studies using psychoanalytic approaches to explore social and political contexts emerged in the 1950s and 1960s (Trist and Murray, 1951; Mitscherlich and Mitscherlich, 1967 [1975]) and the production of psychoanalytically informed empirical social research has continued more or less consistently ever since. Within the UK there have recently been moves to institutionalize this work in journals, conferences and academic departments, under the heading 'psychosocial studies'. This attempt to bring together a diverse body of research has given rise to heated debates over legitimate ways of using psychoanalytic ideas in empirical work outside the clinical context. These debates sometimes seem to me to close down the meanings of psychoanalysis, claiming one school or another as the legitimate version, and reifying the clinic as an originary point of reference for an understanding of psychoanalytic concepts. Nevertheless, they are a useful starting point for marking out some key conceptual distinctions that constitute the field.

In the recent flurry of writing about the status of psychoanalysis in 'psychosocial' research, there seems to be a tussle over meanings and practices and a policing of 'correct' usage in ways that sometimes conflict with the broader theoretical or epistemological positioning of the authors. Discussions have tended to focus on particular concepts and pieces of research as the basis for more generalized claims about the potential for recontextualizing psychoanalysis into non-clinical contexts. There have been particularly heated interventions over the possibility of using notions of 'transference' and 'counter-transference' outside the clinical setting. This discussion is inflected by contrasting epistemological orientations in relation to psychoanalytic concepts. More constructionist perspectives foreground the dangers of claims to authoritative expert knowledge and the distinctiveness of the clinical setting (Frosh and Baraitser, 2008; Parker, 2010). The constructionist sensibility draws attention to the inevitability of the relation between knowledge and power: Foucault's claim that 'there is no power relation without the correlative constitution of a field of knowledge' (1977, p. 27). Constructionism also foregrounds the context of production of knowledge and evinces scepticism about the possibility of replicating psychoanalytic technologies outside this context of production. Frosh and Baraitser note:

> The phenomena of the psychosocial are produced through the actions of analyst and analysand, researcher and researched. This means that cherished psychoanalytic ideas have to be rethought for the different context of investigation and expression: transference and countertransference, for example, are simply not the same in and out of the consulting room.
>
> (2008, p. 363)

This extract might be read as articulating an interest in the way psychoanalytic concepts and 'the phenomena of the psychosocial' are produced within specific contexts. However the delineation of these contexts as either 'in' or 'out' of the consulting room constitutes a slightly problematic binary. There is a tension between the authors' understanding of the way concepts need to be rethought in relation to the specificities of the context, their elision of multiple consulting rooms into one entity, and their concern about the risk of 'distorting' psychoanalytic ideas (ibid., p. 347). This kind of tension is inherent to the constructionist position: we want to explore the constructed nature of knowledge, but at the same time we find it difficult to relax allegiances to 'cherished' ideas within our own practice. In contrast, those who own to 'a phobic revulsion to constructionists' (Hoggett, 2008, p. 380, Rustin, 2008) articulate a more naturalized, universal conceptualization of psychical processes, and seem less edgy about both the status of the expert and the use of psychoanalytic concepts in non-clinical settings. Thus epistemological differences within the field of psychoanalytic theory and practice are carried over into debates about the use of psychoanalysis in the field of social research.

In order to clarify some elements of these oppositional positions I want to explore the conceptualization of transference and counter-transference in a little more detail, and I will try to suggest why this might have become the focus for epistemological debates about the relation between clinical practice and research. The conceptualization of affect and language is of central importance here. Within psychoanalytic theory significant positions are marked out in relation to the status of affect, understood either as directly accessible knowledge, or as an experience that is always already mediated by language. A key methodological question for either practitioner or researcher is: Can we trust our experiences of affect? Or must we set our affective responses aside in the process of interpretation? Is language the more appropriate object of our interpretive work?

Transference might be defined as the way in which feelings, relationships, signifiers or discursive categories are repeated within present interactions: so our responses in the present can be understood as repetitions of significant relations or discourses. Counter-transference refers to feelings evoked in the analyst/other in response to the transferences of the patient/subject. Understood in this way, there is no reason why instances of both transference and counter-transference should be limited to the clinical psychoanalytic context. However, psychoanalysis offers several more specific theorizations of the concept in relation to the particular objectives and experiences of the clinic.[1] Laplanche, for example, delineates a distinction between the transference of experiences and feelings from childhood and the transference of the original relation between the child and adult, which he describes as 'the originary infantile situation' (1999, p. 229). He suggests that in the therapeutic psychoanalytic relation the former may be a preliminary stage to be worked through before the latter is able to emerge (ibid., p. 214, n. 1). Similar kinds of distinctions are made in the theorization of the 'counter-transference'. Racker distinguishes counter-transferential feelings that result from the analyst's identification with different aspects of the patient: the analyst might identify with the patient's ego, or with an internal object that is not incorporated into the ego. Racker suggests that these contrasting aspects of the counter-transference should be dealt with in different ways by the analyst (Racker, 1982, p. 61). These kinds of conceptual distinctions embed notions of transference and counter-transference within the clinical relationship in a way that may or may not be of relevance in the context of research. An awareness of these ideas might help a researcher to develop sensitivity to material that arises in empirical research; and perhaps to articulate similar conceptual distinctions that are more pertinent to the encounter between researcher and participant.[2] Why might there be such controversy about the potential of using conceptualizations of transference and counter-transference to analyse relations outside the clinic?

One answer to this question relates to the way psychoanalytic techniques are specifically designed to facilitate the emergence of the transference. Freud argues that in psychoanalysis 'the decisive part of the work is achieved by creating in the patient's relation to the doctor – in the "transference" – new editions of old conflicts' (Freud, cited in Racker, 1982, p. 46). He suggests that it is when persistent patterns, 'old conflicts', are repeated in the context of the clinical relation that they may be shifted and transformed (Freud, 1920). 'Free association', which Christopher Bollas has described as not the method, but the very goal of psychoanalysis (1999, p. 62), is the means for eliciting the transference which is required for this psychoanalytic work to take place. However, it is not easy for the patient to comply with the instruction to 'free associate'. This injunction requires us to speak aloud ideas as they arise, without selection, censorship or an attempt to construct coherence, and this goes against all normal conventions for social interaction. One important obstacle in the attempt to dispense with self-censorship is the presence of the analyst, and the patient's anticipation of their judgement, approval or disapproval. Psychoanalytic technique is designed to minimize this obstacle. However, different schools of practice suggest different ways in which this might be achieved.

All schools of psychoanalysis require the analyst to create a space in which significant patterns and repetitions are likely to emerge. This is why it is necessary for the practitioner to restrict the comments they make within a session to a distinctive psychoanalytic mode of interpretation of what the patient has said; and to avoid giving away personal information that the patient will use to construct an image of their analyst and to censor their own words within the sessions. The creation of an enigmatic space through a distinctive, concentrated mode of listening is intended to facilitate the articulation and interpretation of significant transferences. The contrasting emphases of different schools of psychoanalysis suggest different techniques for achieving this distinctive space, and these relate to conceptualizations of the epistemological status of language and affect.

Lacanian technique guides towards the production of 'the position of the analyst' which is distinct from the personal responses and desires of the practitioner (Fink, 1997; Parker, 2010). Bruce Fink suggests that when the practitioner occupies 'the position of the analyst' the patient will stop thinking about the analyst as another human being, and that when this happens 'the analyst begins to operate as pure function' (ibid., p. 14). This is achieved through a very specific technique: the analyst only intervenes to direct the patient's attention to connotative, symbolic aspects of their speech. Even in the later stages of analysis, interpretations must always be based on linguistic or symbolic aspects of the interaction with the patient, and the analyst must put aside their own affective responses. The Lacanian epistemological premise is that we must mistrust our experiences of affect; and that it is the materiality of language and signifiers that provides a basis for the act of interpretation that, in Juan David Nasio's words, 'produces the unconscious' and 'causes it to exist' (Nasio, cited in Frosh and Baraitser, 2008, p. 356). Importantly, when the analyst restricts their comments to linguistic ambiguities, slips and disjuncture, rather than the intentional narrative trajectory of what is being said, the patient will learn that they are not being judged in the ways they might normally anticipate, and this will facilitate processes of transference and free association.

Other schools of psychoanalysis suggest alternative modes of interpretation that might facilitate the patient's free associations. Bollas describes the Kleinian way of listening as emphasizing the need for the analyst to offer frequent interpretations of the patient's projections. He suggests that one purpose of these interpretations is to correct the patient's assumptions about the silence of the analyst: if the analyst failed to intervene, the patient 'would assume the analyst was silent for innumerable wrong reasons' (Bollas, 1999, p. 188). In addition, it is considered legitimate for practitioners to make use of their own experiences of affect in the process of interpretation. Rather than focusing on the evisceration of the analyst as an affective presence – the production of the analyst as pure function – they will try to understand how both participants in an analytic relation might be unconsciously communicating emotions which might help in the development of an interpretation (Hoggett, 2008, p. 380). Thus while Lacanian approaches suggest that the communication of feeling is inherently suspect, other traditions consider this a useful source of information about the patient. Underlying these different positions are significant contrasts in beliefs about the status of affect as natural or constructed, available to interpretation or unknowable. All schools of psychoanalysis advocate great care in the interpretation of affective responses, but some admit the possibility that affect might be communicated between two subjects, while others suggest that any assumption of a direct understanding of the other is to be avoided. These contrasting epistemological positions can be mapped onto positions taken in the current debates about the use of psychoanalysis within empirical research.

From current debates on the use of notions of 'transference' and 'counter-transference' in the interpretation of research interviews it would appear that practitioners and researchers who tend towards a more Lacanian perspective are more likely to be suspicious of researchers' interpretations of transferential and counter-transferential processes (Frosh and Baraitser, 2008; Parker 2010); while those who are less sceptical about the possibility of working with affect in clinical relations are also less suspicious of researchers who claim to do so (Hoggett, 2008; Rustin, 2008). This is only partially explained, it seems to me, by their contrasting epistemological positions: the foregrounding of context on the part of the constructionists; a naturalizing or universalizing of psychical processes by non-constructionists. It is possible that the articulation of these contrasting positions is also contingent on the particular instances of research that are taken as exemplars within these commentaries. There has been significant focus on pieces of research that do not sufficiently problematize the researcher's access to the affect of their participants (Frosh and Baraitser, 2008, p. 363). This is clearly going to be more serious a misdemeanor for those who are already sceptical about the direct communication of affect than it is for those who accept this as an inherent and not necessarily problematic aspect of human relations. If more Lacanian exemplars had been used as the basis for debating the potential of psychoanalysis as a source for the construction and analysis of the research interview, the positions might have been reversed: the Lacanians might have been less critical – less inclined to use words such as 'distortion' (ibid., p. 347) and 'misapplication' (Parker, 2010, p. 2); and those who prioritize the affective realm might have criticized the evisceration of empathetic and affective sensibilities that for them are central to the psychoanalytic treatment of suffering. Thus far it seems to me that the debate, while interesting, informative, productive and at times entertaining, has been little more than a replaying of established epistemological alliances and oppositions.

This book attempts to construct a different position. Rather than arguing *for* a version of psychoanalysis I am arguing *against* the reification of psychoanalytic concepts. Psychoanalytic concepts are not unitary objects that exist outside a particular analysis. They are constituted in the process of analysis, in the discontinuous elements of discourse; they are signifying elements that are only temporarily ordered or fixed within a particular social and historical context. We might think of any particular articulation of a concept as an element of practice, brought into being within a specific act of interpretation and hovering on the edge between an established theoretical framework and the abyss of non meaning. I am interested in the way that multiple acts of interpretation might bring a concept into being in different ways.

So, this book is an attempt to explore the instantiation of psychoanalytic concepts within empirical social research. In attempting this I have in mind work within the sociology of knowledge, and, in particular, the notion of 'recontextualization', which provides a framework for thinking about the way concepts and discourses emerge in different forms when they are articulated in contrasting settings (Bernstein, 2000; Dowling, 2009). Basil Bernstein suggests that any articulation 'is constructed by a recontextualising principle that selectively appropriates, relocates, refocuses and relates other discourses to constitute its own order' (ibid., p. 33), while Paul Dowling argues against the 'fetishising' of knowledge as an entity that has an existence that is independent of the practices or activities in which it is articulated (Dowling, 2009, p. 105). I am also reminded of Derrida's discussion of the concept of structure, where he argues against the notion of a fixed origin or centre, and comments: 'Since these concepts are not elements or atoms and since they are taken from a syntax and a system, every particular borrowing drags along with it the whole of metaphysics' (Derrida, 1978, pp. 355–356). He argues that it is a linguistic necessity that we repeat the ideas we are trying to avoid. In some sense, he suggests, we might understand all discourse as bricoleur: 'If one calls *bricolage* the necessity of borrowing one's concept from the text of a heritage which is more or less coherent or ruined, it must be said that every discourse is *bricoleur*' (ibid., p. 360). From this perspective, though, he concludes 'the very idea of *bricolage* is menaced and the difference in which it took on its meaning decomposes' (ibid., p. 361). Where Levi Strauss had opposed the bricoleur to the engineer, who 'should be one to construct the totality of his language, syntax and lexicon' (ibid., p. 361), Derrida's proposition decomposes the possibility of this distinction. He suggests that if all discourse is limited by a linguistic or textual heritage from which it must borrow its terms, it is also this linguistic heritage that provides the possibility of play and substitution: 'This field is in fact that of *freeplay*, that is to say, a field of infinite substitutions in the closure of a finite ensemble' (ibid., p. 365). My brief appropriation of Derrida here is certainly in the spirit of *bricolage*, but one thing I want to take from his account is this sense of play, which I think is useful in understanding the formation and reformation of concepts within and across the contrasting activities of psychoanalysis and research.

One way of explaining the book is in relation to an understanding of concepts as structures without origin that both permit and set a limit on the freeplay of articulations. I want to try to think about the articulation of psychoanalytic concepts within research as instances of decomposed bricolage, a 'freeplay' of ideas or signifiers. The chapters explore articulations of conceptual structures within canonical psychoanalytic texts, social theory and empirical research. The analysis traces different elements that are brought together under the signifiers 'melancholia', 'overdetermination', 'resistance', 'libidinal types' and 'psychic defences'; and looks at the way these elements are either reiterated or suppressed in examples of empirical research. In some instances I also try to note the way conceptual structures are tied into other theoretical, political and methodological discourses. At the same time, the book acts as an introduction to a series of key psychoanalytic ideas and presents, in some detail, a number of pieces of psychoanalytically informed empirical social research.

The book originated in concerns arising from my own use of psychoanalytic concepts to interpret research data, and my desire to clarify exactly what it meant to use these concepts in this way. I was also occasionally frustrated by an assumption of a shared understanding when signifiers of psychoanalytic concepts were deployed, but not fully explained, in other authors' accounts of empirical research. The book is therefore designed, first, to open up the different meanings that are hidden or congealed within individual signifiers that act as placeholders for complex theoretical languages, and second, to explore the way these meanings are reiterated and transformed in examples of empirical work. Writing each chapter involved constantly moving between more theoretical texts and accounts of empirical research in order to develop my own account of the relation between these two modes of methodological practice. The rationale for the selection of empirical examples was not consistent. In some instances I was keen to include seminal works or works that are widely referenced within psychoanalytic or psychosocial literature. In other cases I have included less well known, or less substantial, pieces of research that seem to me to constitute an interesting or distinctive instantiation of a particular concept. My presentation of each of the empirical cases is intended to foreground the ways in which they rearticulate aspects of a psychoanalytic concept, and in order to maintain this focus I have kept to a minimum other critical commentary on the methodology of each example.

Finally, before presenting an outline of the book as a whole, I want to offer a brief account of the range of disciplinary fields represented in the examples of empirical projects I have selected to examine here. Most of my research has been in the sociology of education, but my explicit aim in writing the book was to explore studies from a wider range of disciplinary fields. So, while several of the examples of empirical research used in the book are drawn from education studies, I have also explored work from other fields including politics, organization studies, literary studies, gender studies and cultural studies; as well as social scientific studies carried out by practising psychotherapists. Of the work taken from education studies, the majority of examples are from the sociology of higher education/the sociology of knowledge. This foregrounding of empirical studies of knowledge in higher education seems to me to be appropriate in relation to the reflexive aspect of my argument. As well as tracing the use of psychoanalytic concepts in social research, the book is also an exploration of the limits of methodology, and the analysis throughout the book attempts to foreground social and psychical aspects of methodological practice that are traditionally hidden or suppressed in accounts of research methodology. Empirical studies of knowledge within higher education have contributed to our understanding of these aspects of research practice and can support the development of reflexive approaches within research.[3] This conceptualization of methodological practice as broader than traditional accounts of research methodology runs throughout the book. It is developed most explicitly in the final two chapters, which present an initial theorization of psychical relations within processes of recontextualization, based on my current research into knowledge practices in the humanities and social sciences.

The first chapter of the book explores the conceptual structure of melancholia. It begins with the initial analogy Freud drew between mourning and melancholia as a basis for his theorization of the presence of a lost object in instances of melancholia. Freud describes melancholia as the subject's failure to separate from the lost object, the subject's incorporation of the lost object; and his account articulates several possible versions of this incorporation. In his initial version, it is the object itself that is incorporated by the subject. In his later account, the subject incorporates the social prohibition on the relation to the lost object, and uses this as a means of self-regulation. The chapter looks at Klein's reformulation of Freud's account, which takes up his notion of the incorporation of the lost object, but foregrounds the loss of the mother and the notion of reparation as key to the formation of the ego. This is contrasted with the work of Judith Butler, which follows a contrasting strand of Freud's ideas, exploring the way the incorporation of social prohibitions can act as a foreclosure on possible sexual identities. The chapter then presents four studies that rearticulate different elements within this cluster of conceptualizations of loss: the Mitscherlichs' (1975) study of national identity in post-war Germany; David Eng and Shinhee Han's (2003) development of a notion of 'racial melancholia' in their analysis of Asian American identities; Adam Jukes' (1993a) study of the relation between male violence and infant loss; and Jessica Ringrose's (2008) analysis of the repetitive, melancholic invocation of heteronormative discourse in the constitution of young women's subjectivity. My interpretation of these studies draws attention to the different modes of loss, or negation, of the object: repression, disavowal and foreclosure. This is important, as it also suggests that 'loss' cannot be understood as a single entity, that 'melancholia' should not be understood as one unified idea, but rather as a conceptual structure that permits many articulations.

The second and third chapters trace the relationship between conceptualizations of discourse and conceptualizations of the unconscious. Chapter 2 looks at the way Freud's articulation of the concept of overdetermination in the *Interpretation of Dreams* (1958) re-emerges in Laclau and Mouffe's theory of discourse (2001). Freud understands the elements of the dream as produced through symbolic associations that condense multiple meanings within 'nodal points', words or visual images. This approach reemerges in Laclau and Mouffe's account of discourse as constituted in the symbolic mechanisms of synonymy, metonymy and metaphor. The chapter aligns this conceptualization of discourse with a particular, Lacanian, understanding of the practice of free association and of the analyst's technique of 'evenly hovering attentiveness'. The Lacanian prioritization of symbolic associations between linguistic elements breaks down the distinction between the interpretation of associations produced within the clinic and the interpretation of associations between discursive elements in other contexts. This argument revisits some of the discussion of affect, language, transference and counter-transference outlined here in the introduction. The chapter looks at the way a more Lacanian conceptualization of discourse has been used in studies of the Black Consciousness Movement in South Africa (Howarth, 1997, 2004) and of international policies on higher education curricula (Burgos, 1999), and suggests that these empirical studies rearticulate the significance of the nodal point, and of the constitution of chains of associations across political and institutional settings. The chapter also articulates some contrasts between the role of the researcher and the role of the psychoanalyst, and suggests the potential for multiple instantiations of free association and 'evenly hovering attentiveness', both in clinical relations and in the practice of empirical research.

Chapter 3 looks at the conceptualization of resistance, and explores possible connections between Freud's theorization of the unconscious compulsion to repeat and Foucault's account of resistance as a repetition within discourse. The analysis suggests that while Foucault's explicit theorization of resistance does not refer to a notion of the unconscious, the opposition that this implies between 'discourse' and 'psyche' might be interpreted with an element of playfulness. It is possible to interpret Foucault's conceptualization of resistance as imbued with a suppressed, psychoanalytic understanding of the force that drives the repetition of discursive categories. 'Discourse' and 'psyche' might be seen as different textures it is possible to explore, or perspectives it is possible to constitute, in the interpretation of empirical data, rather than as fixed and opposed epistemological positions. The chapter takes Alex Moore's study of teachers' responses to new policy initiatives (2004, 2006) to illustrate how a Foucauldian understanding of resistance as repetition within discourse and a psychoanalytic understanding of the compulsion to repeat can be used to foreground different aspects of empirical data.

The final section of Chapter 3 examines Lacan's suggestion that 'there is only one resistance, the resistance of the analyst' (Lacan, 1991, p. 228); and explores the productivity of this idea in the development of reflexive processes within the interpretation of research data. Lacan is critical of the way psychoanalysts reiterate psychoanalytic dogma rather than waiting for an interpretation to emerge in the process of analysis. In a sense Lacan's argument here articulates some of the broader questions raised throughout the book: In what sense do interpretations inevitably repeat existing conceptual vocabularies? What do we gain from these identifications with authoritative disciplinary discourses? Is it the case that each act of interpretation must, or should, in some way both repeat *and* transform the terms of its linguistic heritage? In their book *Knowing Nothing, Staying Stupid* (2005), Dany Nobus and Malcolm Quinn suggest that it is this in between-ness – the recognition that the terms of knowledge are precisely what stands in the way of knowledge – that is the distinctive characteristic of psychoanalytic knowledge:

> within a properly psychoanalytic economy of labour, working-through implies neither the institutionalization nor the evacuation, neither the hierarchization nor the destruction of knowedge, but its recognition as an edifice built on the foundations of ignorance, a fantasmatic construct designed to control the stupidity of the drive. The corollary of this rec-ognition is that psychoanalysis cannot be employed as a fully finished doctrine, either within or outside the treatment. And if the psychoana-lyst needs to learn that 'his knowledge is but a symptom of his own ignorance', as Lacan put it ... other disciplines may use their confronta-tion with psychoanalysis to adopt a similar stance vis-à-vis their own knowledge and methodologies ... If there is anything to be learnt from psychoanalysis it is that the most advanced form of learning is learning how to acknowledge the unknown dimension of one's own knowledge.
>
> (ibid., p. 209)

If we apply this way of thinking about knowledge to a consideration of the use of psychoanalysis in empirical social research, or to a consideration of the nature of academic practice more generally, we might ask: What kinds of ignorance are hidden within our methodologies and our edifices of knowledge? What are the unknown dimensions of this knowledge?

I have attempted to address these questions through a reflexive presen-tation of interpretations within my current research project, and it is perhaps worth clarifying here two contrasting strands within conceptuali-zations of reflexivity. For Bourdieu, reflexivity is a means of accounting for the social construction of science while maintaining a realist epistemology (2004, p. 88). He says:

> Understood as the effort whereby social science, taking itself for its object, uses its own weapons to understand and check itself, it [reflex-ivity] is a particularly effective means of increasing the chances of attaining truth by increasing the cross-controls and providing the prin-ciples of a technical critique, which makes it possible to keep closer watch over the factors capable of biasing research. It is not a matter of pursuing a new form of absolute knowledge, but of exercising a spe-cific form of epistemological vigilance, the very form that this vigilance must take in an area where the epistemological obstacles are first and foremost social obstacles.
>
> (ibid., p. 89)

This understanding of reflexivity appears to differ in two significant ways from the more Lacanian version articulated by Nobus and Quinn (above). First, while Bourdieu holds onto a realist ideal of truth, Lacan points to the importance of foregrounding ignorance. And second, while Lacan suggests that the impediments to understanding ignorance are psychical resistances, Bourdieu suggests that scientific knowledge is limited by 'social obstacles'. However, the language Bourdieu uses to describe the object of reflexive processes is imbued with psychoanalytic ideas. As George Steinmetz has pointed out (2006), Bourdieu frequently appears troubled by the relation between sociology and psychoanalysis, attempting to keep them apart and disavowing the centrality of psychoanalytic concepts within his own theories. Without referencing psychoanalysis, Bourdieu talks about bringing to light what is hidden in the 'transcendental unconscious' of the scientist (Bourdieu, 2004, p. 86), and suggests that the coding systems used by researchers 'may belong to the common anthropological unconscious' (ibid., p. 90). So it may be that while the goals of reflexivity, truth or ignorance, seem to diverge significantly across the two perspectives, the techniques of reflexivity that they propose may not be that different.

Chapter 4 explores the productivity of a Lacanian conceptualization of repression, disavowal and foreclosure as a tool in the development of a reflexive understanding of the research process. The chapter includes two levels of analysis. First, an analysis of data produced in my recent interview-based research project exploring knowledge practices in higher education, in the fields of cultural studies, literary studies and political science. The analysis traces psychical relations to signifiers of affect, politics and disciplinary methodologies within participants' accounts of their practice and suggests that these relations can be understood in terms of the psychical processes of repression, disavowal and foreclosure. At the same time, I try to note moments where this argument is punctuated by alternative possible interpretations, and to explore how my own attachment to particular methodological principles constitutes resistances within the interpretive process. Just as my participants' practice is characterized by repression and disavowal, so too is my own, and by drawing attention to this, and to the imaginary identifications that also constitute a part of the interpretive process, I hope to maintain a sense of the fragility and incompleteness of my analysis. Interpretation of data relating to socially situated human subjects must always remain in a sense provisional, but the process of developing interpretations, perhaps inevitably, closes down our sense of the provisional aspects of our work. It is here that Lacan's critique of the tendency to impose the terms of knowledge can, perhaps, help us to draw back from a position of untenable authority in relation to the subjects of our research.

The provisionality of academic interpretation can also be understood in terms of the social and psychical relations constituted in processes of recontextualization. Theories of recontextualization within the sociology of knowledge construct disciplinary concepts and fields of knowledge as social objects that are neither unified nor separate from the contexts in relation to which they are articulated. These theories explore the way aspects of one discourse are repeated and transformed in a new setting. The articulation or suppression of different aspects of disciplinary concepts can be conceptualized as strategic social activity that constitutes discursive alliances and oppositions. From this perspective, interpretations are always provisional, not just because of the individualized resistances of the researcher, but because of the resistance and mutability of the discursive contexts within which they are produced. Chapter 5 explores the recontextualization of Melanie Klein's theory of ego development and also develops an account of the psychical aspect of recontextualising strategies. The chapter distinguishes two aspects of Klein's work: first her narrative of ego development from the paranoid schizoid to the depressive position; and second her specification of different instantiations of the psychic defences of splitting, projection and introjection. It traces the way these different signifying elements are repeated or transformed in three pieces of social research: Elliott Jaques' (1951) study of industrial relations; Isabel Menzies Lyth's (1959) study of a nursing service in a large teaching hospital; and Basil Bernstein's (2000) exploration of disciplinary knowledge formations within higher education. The analysis suggests that these three studies constitute contrasting recontextualizing strategies in relation to Klein's terminology, the content of her ideas, and the acknowledgment of psychoanalytic authorities. In addition, I argue that Bernstein's cheerfully unacknowledged and unelaborated invocation of the vocabulary of the psychic defences, in his account of the ongoing exchange between fields of knowledge within education and external fields of economic and professional practice, provides a starting point for the conceptualization of a psychical relation within processes of recontextualisation.

The sociology of knowledge and theories of recontextualization constitute a position that, initially at least, stands a little outside debates over uses of psychoanalysis within research. My argument for the conceptualization of a psychical relation within processes of recontextualization reintroduces a relation to different versions of psychoanalysis that I have, slightly disingenuously, attempted to suppress in my account of the objectives of the book. In relation to Bernstein's work, I argue that his decapitation of Klein's concepts suggests that the psychical relations connoted in his account may be closer to Lacanian theory than to Klein. In a similar way, other sections of the book tend to prioritize Lacanian ideas and arguments over other versions of psychoanalysis. It is still the case that my primary interest is an exploration of the ways in which psychoanalytic concepts are repeated and transformed in different settings, but it is not possible to completely disentangle my account of these processes from my own epistemological attachments.

1 Melancholia

Lost objects of national, ethnic, classed, gendered and sexual identities

Introduction: political discourse as a form of mourning?

Writing about post-Communist political discourse twenty years after the fall of the Berlin Wall, and noting a strand that is turning from anti-communism to a sense of nostalgia for 'the "good old days" of Communism', Slavoj Zizek comments: 'The nostalgia for communism shouldn't be taken too seriously: far from expressing an actual wish to return to a grey Socialist reality, it is a form of mourning, of gently getting rid of the past' (2009). What might it mean to interpret nostalgic political discourses in terms of psychical processes of mourning? Just how little or how much of a clinical psychoanalytic account of mourning might we be able to trace in this kind of analysis? In 'Mourning and Melancholia' Freud explains that mourning can take place in response to the loss of a loved person, but also in response to 'the loss of some abstraction ... such as one's country, liberty, an ideal, and so on' (1957, p. 243). He suggests that in mourning: 'Each single one of the memories and expectations in which the libido is bound to the object is brought up and hypercathected and detachment of the libido is accomplished in respect of it' (p. 245).

The fall of the Communist regimes in Eastern Europe can, then, be understood as a loss that requires a period of mourning during which the subject might be expected to revisit different aspects of the lost object. Eventually, when this work of revisiting and detaching from the lost object is achieved, Freud suggests, 'the ego becomes free and uninhibited again' (p. 245). Zizek's interpretation implies that contemporary nostalgia for Communism should be understood as an instance of revisiting of memories of a lost object, and that this strand of political discourse will naturally be left behind when the process of mourning is completed. However, the intense and painful sorrow that is also associated with mourning is not directly apparent in Zizek's example. For me, his interpretation is at once insightful and puzzling: insightful because it makes sense that the people who grew up under Communism need in some way to engage with the traces of the lost regime; and puzzling because I can't quite work out what this interpretation leaves out, or what kinds of accounts might add depth to an interpretation of nostalgic political discourse as a form of mourning for a lost aspect of national identity. How is Zizek's speculative interpretation different from the interpretation of mourning in the clinical context? How is it similar? What principles are being used to distinguish this as an instance of mourning rather than melancholia? Is there additional data that might perhaps help to elaborate Zizek's interpretation?

Freud's conceptualization of melancholia and Klein's development of his ideas in her account of processes of mourning have provided an enormously productive structure for interpretation within both psychoanalysis and more sociologically orientated research. Adam Phillips explains:

> Without mourning for primary objects there is no way out of the magic circle of the family. Indeed, partly through the work of Klein, mourning has provided the foundation for development in most versions of psychoanalysis; so much so, in fact, that mourning has acquired the status of a quasi-religious concept in psychoanalysis. Analysts believe in mourning; if a patient were to claim, as Emerson once did, that mourning was 'shallow' he or she would be considered to be 'out of touch' with something or other.
>
> (1997, p. 153)

There are, as Phillips suggests, potential dangers when a conceptual structure gains a hegemonic grip on practice, taking on a 'quasi-religious' status that limits interpretive strategies. But the productivity of the concept also suggests the potential for enriched understandings of melancholia to be developed in the construction of analyses that reactivate naturalized theoretical categories. Freud initially developed his conception of melancholia through his observations of similarities between patients mourning a death and those with no evident object of their apparent mourning. What is so enticing about his articulation of this analogy as a way of understanding social as well as purely psychical relations? And in what ways might uses of the concept within social analysis constitute either productive reactivations or dogmatic sedimentations[1] of its psychoanalytic origins? This chapter explores a series of four studies that deploy the concepts of mourning and melancholia to interpret national, ethnic, gendered and classed social identities and suggests the productivity of these accounts. However, the broader aim of my presentation of these contrasting studies is to explore the idea that melancholia is a conceptual structure that permits diverse instantiations through a play of substitutions, none of which constitutes an essential, immutable core. Even the notion of 'loss' cannot be constituted as a fixed centre, since the meaning of loss itself shifts across the various instantiations explored in the chapter. The concept of melancholia is thus not an entity that exists outside a particular instance of analysis: rather, melancholia is a cluster of ideas and conceptual structures that can be taken up, shifted and transformed in the process of articulating an interpretation.

The studies explored in this chapter have been selected to illustrate the range of conceptual and methodological threads taken up in the re-articulation of notions of melancholia. Some of the examples combine clinical and speculative analysis, while others bring psychoanalytic conceptions of melancholia to bear in the interpretation of cultural or sociological data. I am interested both in the methodological processes suggested in these analyses and also in the ways in which they foreground or suppress different elements within psychoanalytic theorizations of mourning and melancholia. Psychoanalytic theorizations specify the symptoms associated with mourning and melancholia and construct speculative accounts of the psychical or subjective aspects of these processes. Freud's initial account tends to foreground distinctions between the processes of mourning and melancholia, while Melanie Klein's theory tends to foreground continuities between the two conditions. Both Freud and Klein theorize a relation between melancholic processes and the establishment of the ego, or the initiation of the subject. Judith Butler develops this account of the loss that instantiates the subject to conceptualize gender as a melancholic effect of entry into a symbolic order that forecloses non-heterosexual identities.

The first section of the chapter sets out some elements of these theorizations of psychical responses to loss. The following sections explore the way different elements of these theories are used in four analyses that focus on loss as constitutive of social, rather than individualized identities. The studies range from Alexander and Margarete Mitscherlichs' (1975) account of post-war German identity, first published in 1967, to David Eng and Shinhee Han's exploration of Asian American subjectivity, published in *Loss*, a collection of essays exploring experiences of loss within the socio-political contexts of the twentieth century (Eng and Kanzanjian, 2003); and from Adam Jukes, (1993a) analysis of violence and male sexuality written in the context of the women's movement in the late eighties and early nineties to Jessica Ringrose's study of girls' friendships within the regulative, heterosexualized context of early twenty first-century popular culture (2008).

Throughout the chapter I am also trying to maintain a sense of the social relations instantiated within methodological practice: an understanding of methodology as embodied within specific historical and professional contexts (Bourdieu, 2004). The authors of the studies discussed in this chapter have varied political and professional affiliations, ranging, for example, from those with clinical training, such as the Mitscherlichs, Shinhee Han and Adam Jukes, to those positioned within university departments of the humanities and social sciences, such as Judith Butler, David Eng and Jessica Ringrose. Contrasting embodiments of theory are constituted through the recontextualization of discursive features or aspects of theory from one context to another: the new context will recognize and value aspects of the existing discourse or theory, and will ignore or reject others (Bernstein, 2000, Lacan, 2007). The foregounding or suppression of aspects of the concept of melancholia cannot, therefore, be abstracted from the particular context and embodiment of the theorist.

Theorizations of mourning and melancholia: Freud, Klein and Butler

Freud's conceptualization of melancholia is based on an analogy he constructs between patients mourning bereavement and patients exhibiting symptoms of melancholy. He notes the similarity in the 'painful frame of mind', 'loss of interest in the outside world' and the 'loss of the capacity to love' (1957, p. 244) that characterizes both 'normal' mourning and the melancholic condition that is considered pathological. However, where in mourning this 'grave departure from the normal attitude to life' (p. 243) is an understandable and temporary response to a visible loss, the prolonged distress experienced in cases of melancholia is less easy to explain. Freud suggests that the analogy with mourning can help to make instances of melancholia more intelligible: the comparison allows us to construct the idea of a 'lost object' within processes of melancholy. The metaphor of the 'lost object' can help us to account for cases where the 'mourning' is not for someone who has died, and also for cases where 'one cannot clearly see what it is that has been lost'. He suggests, in addition, that in cases where this 'loss' is ideal rather than actual, 'it is all the more reasonable to suppose that the patient cannot consciously perceive what he has lost either' (p. 245). For Freud this unperceived or unconscious loss suggests a certain emptiness of the ego. He says: 'In mourning it is the world which has become poor and empty; in melancholia it is the ego itself' (p. 246).

Freud suggests that in mourning the ego is able to detach itself from the lost object while in melancholia the lost object is internalized and becomes a constitutive element of the ego. He describes melancholia as an acutely painful and unresolved form of mourning, associated with 'self reproaches', 'self revilings' and 'a delusional expectation of punishment'. This attack on the self distinguishes melancholia from mourning in which, he says, 'the disturbance of self regard is absent' (p. 244). The self-reproaches associated with melancholia, Freud says, can frequently be understood as identifications with the loved object:

> If one listens patiently to a melancholic's many and various self-accusations, one cannot in the end avoid the impression that often the most violent of them are hardly at all applicable to the patient himself, but that with insignificant modifications they do fit someone else, someone whom the patient loves, or has loved, or should love.
>
> (p. 248)

He concludes, 'the self reproaches are reproaches against a loved object which have been shifted away from it on to the patient's own ego'. Through these identifications, the features associated with the lost object are internalized by the ego, and the emotions directed at the object are turned inwards, creating a split within the ego between the internalized object and the critical emotions the ego directs at it. Freud suggests an ongoing struggle in which the ego fights both to detach from the object and also to maintain the strong emotional attachment. The ambiguity in the loved/hated nature of the lost object, and the failure to detach from the object cause of melancholia thus creates a visceral ambivalence in the relation between the object and the ego; or, to be more precise, the ambivalence persists in the relation between the internalization of the object and the other elements of the ego.

Freud summarizes this account at the end of 'Mourning and Melancholia', suggesting three preconditions for melancholia: 'loss of the object, ambivalence, and regression of libido into the ego' (p. 258). In *The Ego and the Id* (1923), however, Freud develops a slightly different version of the conceptual structure. He first repeats the structure he had developed in his earlier paper: 'an object which was lost has been set up again inside the ego – that is, that an object-cathexis has been replaced by an identification' (ibid., p. 28). Freud suggests this response to loss is far more significant than he had originally suggested. He now argues that melancholic processes play a part in the construction of the super-ego, which is instantiated in the first identifications of the subject. This simultaneous formation of the subject and the super-ego takes place during the Oedipus conflict, in which the child is forced to give up their polymorphous desire for the mother and to identify with (one of) their parents, thus taking on a sexual identity (p. 34). These identifications instantiate the influence of the parents and of wider social and moral obligations within the child: 'The child's parents, and especially his father, were perceived as the obstacle to a realization of his Oedipus wishes; so his infantile ego fortified itself for the carrying out of the repression by erecting the same obstacle within itself,' (p. 34). Freud notes that this formulation constitutes a slight alteration in the conceptual structure of melancholia: 'these identifications', he says, 'are not what we would have expected' (p. 32). Instead of an internalization of the object, there is an internalisation of the prohibition of the object, and this is the basis of the super ego. This development, Freud says, begins to suggest the 'full significance' (p. 28) of melancholic processes and of the role they play in the formation of the ego.

There are several significant distinctions within Freud's account. There is the distinction between a process in which the subject is able to detach from the lost object and a process in which the relation to the object is sustained, in some form, within the ego. There is the distinction between the internalization of the lost object within the ego and the internalization of the prohibition of the object. And there is the distinction between melancholia as a pathological process and melancholia as the common basis for the formation of the subject. I am drawing attention to these distinctions because it seems to me that they mark out aspects that are either foregrounded or left out when the concept of melancholia is referenced in the analysis of social identities. It is also the case that Klein's reconceptualization of mourning/melancholia foregrounds the internalization of the object and pays less attention to the internalization of social prohibitions. Judith Butler's account of melancholic gender, in contrast, foregrounds the relation between cultural prohibition and the simultaneous incorporation and disavowal of the lost object of homosexual love. Butler's discussion raises questions about the finality of the social prohibition and the distinctions between the psychical mechanisms of repression, disavowal and foreclosure.

As well as developing Freud's conceptualization of the internalization of the object, Klein introduces significant new aspects to the conceptual structure of melancholia: an earlier first instantiation of the ego, related to the absence of the mother rather than the intervention of the father; the role of the present object (the mother) in the process of production of internal objects; and the potentially reparative nature of this process. Also central to Klein's account is the prioritization of affect and her conceptualization of the processes of internalization.

What comes first for Klein is an intensely affective primary encounter with an external world. The infant's experiences of this world are internalized, gradually building up a parallel world of inner objects. However, this inner world is, in Klein's words, 'inaccessible to the child's accurate observation and judgment', it is the product of unconscious fantasy, 'phantasmatic', giving rise to 'doubts, uncertainties and anxieties' (1940, p. 149). The phantasmatic inner objects are overwhelming for the child, so that, for Klein, 'every infant experiences anxieties which are psychotic in content' (p. 150). These anxieties are dealt with by reference to the external world, which can 'disprove anxieties' (p. 149) and enable the child to establish 'good' internal objects. Thus, through a gradual process of reality checking, the infant begins to establish a less persecutory and terrifying internal world. In Klein's terms this is the shift from the need to preserve the ego in the early, paranoid schizoid position, to the depressive position in which the infant recognizes and identifies with good aspects of the object and feels the need to preserve them.

Melanie Klein's reinterpretation of mourning in her account of the infant depressive position foregrounds feelings of destruction and peril related to the ego's fragile sense of its own survivability in addition to the self-reproaches, sadness and lack of self-regard given prominence in Freud's account. Klein suggests that the depressive feelings associated with melancholia are first experienced in early infancy:

the baby experiences depressive feelings which reach a climax just before, during and after weaning. This is the state of mind in the baby which I termed the 'depressive position', and I suggested that it is a melancholia in *statu nascendi*. The object which is being mourned is the mother's breast and all that the breast and the milk have come to stand for in the infant's mind: namely, love, goodness and security.

(p. 148)

Pitted against these symbols of love, goodness and security are the extreme chaos and vulnerability of the infant's world and their uncontrollable, violent and destructive anxieties. As soon as the object that represents what is good is withdrawn, it becomes the object of the infant's fears and aggression, at the same time giving rise to guilt that the loss is a result of the infant's own greedy and destructive impulses. Thus, the ambivalent feelings that Freud described in the relation to the object are rearticulated in Klein's account.

The key moment for Klein is the withdrawal of the loved object, the breast, symbol of 'love, goodness and security'. This traumatic moment is a crystallization of the child's chaotic inner world and of the potential to develop a more ambivalent relation towards its objects: the depressive position. According to Klein, the ongoing encounters with the loved object, the mother, gradually reduce the extremities of ambivalence and develop a more stable inner representation:

All the enjoyments which the baby lives through in relation to his mother are so many proofs to him that the loved object *inside as well as outside* is not injured, is not turned into a vengeful person. The increase of love and trust, and the diminishing of fears through happy experiences, help the baby step by step to overcome his depression and feeling of loss (mourning).

(p. 149)

In contrast to Freud's suggestion that we internalise the lost object, Klein's emphasis is on the importance of the mother, a present object, in the construction of the good internal objects (see Mitchell, cited in Jukes, 1993a, p. 36). Within this process Klein also introduces the concept of reparation: the construction of the good internal object through experiences of love and trust in relation to a present, external object, allows the infant to make reparation and to overcome their own guilt for the initial destruction of the object (Klein, 1940, p. 163).

For Klein, the infant's experience of 'early psychotic anxieties' and the resolution of these anxieties through the establishment of relatively stable internal 'good' objects, the depressive position, are evoked in processes of mourning in adulthood (pp. 156–157). She argues that when, as Freud has suggested, mourning is resolved by the ego's identification with the lost object, this identification also re-establishes the stability of earlier internal objects that have been threatened with destruction as the ego experiences a new loss:

> We know that the loss of a loved person leads to an impulse in the mourner to reinstate the lost loved object in the ego (Freud and Abraham). In my view, however, he not only takes into himself (re-incorporates) the person whom he has just lost, but also reinstates his internalized good objects (ultimately his loved parents), who became part of his inner world from the earliest stages of his development onwards.
>
> (p. 156, see also pp. 165–166)

Her emphasis here is on the persistence of the early good objects within the ego and the feelings of ambivalence, fear and destructiveness associated with them, which are re-evoked in later instances of loss. The foregrounding of this link between internalized objects established in infancy and adult loss of a loved object is reiterated in Adam Jukes' (1993a) exploration of violence and male sexuality.

Klein's explicit referencing of Freud allows her to signal both allegiance and innovation in relation to his ideas. We might understand Klein as subjectively positioned within and constitutive of a particular discursive practice. Her theorization performatively re-inscribes melancholia in a way that both reconstructs the field of psychoanalytic practice but also maintains the connection with Freud. Thus while she asserts that her ideas are 'therapeutically of an importance so great it cannot yet be fully estimated' (1940, p. 167) she also explicitly draws attention to continuities with Freud's work, and it was also important for later 'Kleinians' to 'repeatedly assert her derivation from Freud's thinking' (Bollas, 1999, p. 181). As Bourdieu has suggested, the materialization of theory in the body of the scientist/ therapist must be 'constantly adjusted to the expectations inscribed within the field' (2004, p. 41) and the recontextualizing principle within the field of legitimate psychoanalysis appears to have required the reiteration of a relation with the inventor of the practice. While it is clearly possible to engage in a debate over the precise relationship between Klein's analysis and Freud's conceptualization of mourning, my point here is to briefly draw attention to her account as constituted in relation to the social conventions and conditions of its production rather than in relation to intrinsic theoretical or practical innovations.[2]

Unlike Klein, Butler is working outside the clinical context. Throughout *The Psychic Life of Power* (1997) she engages with psychoanalytic ideas in order to explore the tantalizing question left open in Althusser's theory of ideology (1971): Why does the subject turn to meet the hail of the law? In her exploration of this question, Butler keeps returning to Freud and his discussion of melancholia. In particular she returns to Freud's articulation of melancholy as the failure of mourning, the failure to separate from the lost object, and as the internalization of the prohibited object, which binds the subject to the social structures that instantiate the law. Freud's formulation points the way to a conceptualization of the subject as itself containing that which is in excess of the law. This provides a basis for Butler's reconceptualization of gender as a form of melancholy: the gendered subject of the heterosexual regime containing the loss of foreclosed homosexual attachment.

Butler describes her approach as a speculative extension of psychoanalytic logic, saying:

> I make no empirical claims, nor attempt a survey of current psychoanalytic scholarship on gender, sexuality or melancholy. I want merely to suggest what I take to be some productive convergences between Freud's thinking on ungrieved and ungrievable loss and the predicament of living in a culture which can mourn the loss of homosexual attachment only with great difficulty.
>
> (1997, p. 138)

Her speculative reconceptualization of melancholia is constituted as an elaboration of her performative theory of gender, and more specifically as an analysis of queer political responses to the homophobia that proliferated within public policy and media discourses around AIDS. She suggests that both the homophobic stigmatization 'not only of AIDS but also of queerness' (1993, p. 233) and also the resistance to this stigmatization in the politicization of practices of mourning to recognize those who have died of AIDS, can be understood as symptoms of a cultural melancholia. She argues:

> It is precisely to counter the pervasive cultural risk of gay melancholia (what the newspapers generalize as 'depression') that there has been an insistent publicisation and politicization of grief over those who have died of AIDS. The Names Project Quilt is exemplary, ritualizing and repeating the name itself as a way of publicly avowing limitless loss.
>
> (1997, p. 148)

These symptoms taken together conform to the accounts of 'uncompleted grief' (ibid., p. 23) narrated by Freud and Klein: the ambivalence towards the lost object, the repudiating attack on the lost object, and the attempt to reinstantiate the lost object within processes of mourning.

Butler's analysis foregrounds two aspects of Freud's account of melancholia, suggesting that both discursive prohibitions on homosexuality and the internalization of the lost object of homosexual love are central components in the constitution of compulsory heterosexuality. 'Heterosexuality', she says, 'is cultivated through prohibitions, and these prohibitions take as one of their objects homosexual attachments, thereby forcing the loss of these attachments' (pp. 136–137). Within the heterosexual matrix, Butler suggests, this loss is instituted as a preemptive foreclosure of possible sexual identities: the force of the cultural prohibition means that becoming a heterosexual girl or a heterosexual boy involves the repudiation in advance of homosexual attachment. This attachment is then internalized, and 'continues to haunt and inhabit the ego as one of its constitutive identifications' (p. 134). This account of gender as produced through the melancholic incorporation of prohibited sexual attachments disturbs hegemonic notions of sexual division, suggesting homosexual attachment as a constitutive element of heterosexual identities.

I think it is useful to think a little more about Butler's use of the Lacanian conception of 'foreclosure' in relation to sexual attachment. For Lacan, foreclosure constitutes an absolute exclusion from the social or symbolic order (see Fink, 1995, pp. 74, 112). Foreclosure is sometimes associated with psychosis, the failure to be constituted as a recognizable subject; however it might also reference an idea or a sexual identity that can not be thought. Butler distinguishes foreclosure from repression, 'an action by an already formed subject'. Foreclosure, in contrast, is defined as 'an act of negation that founds and forms the subject' (1997, pp. 211–212, n. 13). There is, then, something foundational and absolute about the notion of foreclosure, a definitive exclusion that forms the basis or failure of subjectivity. In Butler's discussion of homosexual attachment, it is not the idea of homosexuality that is foreclosed, but rather, Butler argues, the possibility of acknowledging homosexual attachment is foreclosed within certain rigid heterosexual practices and identities. What is lost is not a particular loved object, but the possibility of homosexual attachment; and this foreclosed attachment remains within the ego as a ghostly and disavowed threat to the heterosexual subject.

The force of the foreclosure suggested in Butler's account gives a Lacanian emphasis to Freud's original account of the lost object and the formation of the subject. However, she does not elaborate the precise relation between the remnants of the foreclosed attachment that persist within an individual ego and the symbolic category 'homosexuality' that is not foreclosed. Instead, she suggests the contingency of this foreclosure, arguing that 'phenomenologically there are many ways of experiencing gender and sexuality that do not reduce to this equation' (1997, p. 136). It is, she says, 'rigid forms of gender and sexual identifications, whether homosexual or heterosexual, [that] appear to spawn forms of melancholy' (p. 144). She is thus just as critical of the denial of a relation to heterosexuality within the gay or lesbian subject as she is of the denial of homosexuality as a presence within heterosexual subjectivity. The strategy of denial, she says, 'misses the political opportunity to work on the weakness in heterosexual subjectivation and to refute the logic of mutual exclusion by which heterosexism proceeds' (p. 148). However, it is not the individual subject but the socially pervasive prohibition, 'repeated and ritualized throughout the culture' (p. 140) that constitutes and enforces this denial through 'the absence of cultural conventions for avowing the loss of homosexual love' (p. 147).[3]

Butler's reconceptualisation of melancholia as constitutive of gender foregrounds or extends several aspects of Freud's initial account. Her conceptualization of loss as instantiated in the foreclosure that 'founds and forms' the subject might be thought of as a crystallization of Freud's observation of the poverty and emptiness of the ego in instances of melancholia. The emphasis on foreclosure also, perhaps, extends Freud's account of the melancholic loss as 'withdrawn from consciousness' (1957, p. 245). Foreclosure suggests a loss that cannot be withdrawn from consciousness as it was never first admitted as an element of conscious subjectivity: it is a loss that is always already disavowed. In Butler's words, homosexual attachment 'becomes subject to a double disavowal, a never having loved and a never having lost' (1997 p. 140). Her account binds the internalization of the object into the internalization of the cultural prohibition of the object, since both subject and object are brought into being through the act of foreclosure. In this move Butler explicitly distinguishes herself from more Kleinian conceptual frameworks that seem to understand love 'within a psychic economy that carries no socially significant residue' (p. 25). In contrast, for Butler: 'The "institution" of the ego cannot fully overcome its social residue, given that its "voice" is from the start borrowed from elsewhere, a recasting of a social plaint as psychic self judgement' (p. 198).

This also constitutes a reformulation of Althusser's description of the subject turning towards the hail of the law. The subject comes into being precisely through the 'voice borrowed from elsewhere'; is inscribed from the beginning within the law; and thus in turning towards the law is seeking and reaffirming its being as a subject.

The melancholic production of social identities: repression, disavowal and foreclosure

While the core elements of loss and internalization are present in processes of mourning for all three theorists, Klein and Butler develop very different strands in Freud's account. Klein focuses on the nature of the internalization and the relation to a present (m)other in the construction of the internal object; while Butler's work explores the relation between the prohibited attachment and the cultural law. Butler's account also foregrounds the mechanisms of foreclosure and disavowal of loss inherent in the melancholic production of gender. These different instantiations of loss, alongside the closely related notion of repression, may perhaps be useful as a conceptual frame for the following discussion of social analyses deploying psychoanalytic concept of melancholia. The opposition between the Freudian sense of emptiness within the ego and the more Kleinian understanding of reparative processes that might restore the internal good object is also useful to bear in mind in relation to the selected examples.

The Mitscherlichs' (1975) study of German identity in post-war Germany suggests ways in which social and cultural practices constitute melancholic mechanism of denial that forestall recognition and mourning for the atrocities of the war. David Eng and Shinhee Han (2003) explore the multi-faceted losses constituted in the production of the Asian American subject to conceptualize a 'racial melancholia'. They use a Kleinian framework to suggest the possibility for these melancholic remains to form the basis of a reparative political language within which loss can be acknowledged. Adam Jukes (1993a) also references aspects of Klein's framework to develop an account of gendered violence emerging when a present object re-evokes the sense of peril and vulnerability within a temporarily 'encapsulated' internal object. Finally, Jessica Ringrose (2008) traces the repetitive melancholic invocation of heteronormative discourse in the constitution of young women's subjectivity. It is also interesting to note the contrasting methodological orientations – speculative, psychoanalytic, cultural, sociological – that constitute each study. The following sections explore the way each of these studies, in turn, rearticulates the conceptual structure of melancholia in the analysis of social identities.

Denial and derealization: the inability to mourn and post-war German identity

In *The Inability to Mourn* (1975), first published in German in 1967, psychoanalysts Alexander and Margarete Mitscherlich explore post-war German culture and identity. They begin with the observation that despite the mass involvement in the Nazi movement, from membership of Hitler Youth to active service in the SS or the German army, there was little evidence of guilt or depression following the defeat of Hitler and the exposure of the extent of the Nazi atrocities. They argue: 'That so few signs of melancholia or even of mourning are to be seen among the great masses of the population can be attributed only to a collective denial of the past' (1975, p. 28). Their study traces the different mechanisms of denial within economic and cultural activity as well as within case studies of patients in clinical psychoanalytic practice. Their conceptualization draws on Freud, but also has analogies with Butler's account of the lack of cultural practices by which to mourn lost homosexual attachments (p. 29). Although their theorization is not consistent with Butler's they, like her, draw attention to the effects of cultural rather than individualized aspects of psychical processes. 'It makes a great deal of difference', they argue, whether a massive clinical persecution mania develops in a single individual because of conflicts in his childhood and in his later personal life, or whether within a society a compulsion to conform leads to a similarly massive delusional projection onto a persecutor ostensibly equipped with mysterious powers.' (pp. 32–33).

Indeed, their account of German denial of the war echoes quite precisely Butler's account of the double disavowal of homosexual attachment:

> In view of the meagerness of any outward signs of an inner burden that could not be managed by normal means, one might have gathered that Germany had never been Nazi and that in 1945 it had at most lost a group of Nazi, that is to say foreign, 'occupiers'.
>
> (p. 32)

However, the Mitscherlichs' analysis suggests that this disavowal of Nazi identity is achieved not through the absolutist, exclusionary mechanism of symbolic foreclosure, but through multiple cultural, political and personalized mechanisms of denial.

As evidence of cultural denial the Mitscherlichs cite the commemoration of German losses in the bombings of Dresden and Frankfurt, but the lack of any comparable memorial of the victims of the concentration camps (p. 30); they note the sustained readership for 'books and newspaper articles claiming that what was done was done under pressure from evil persecutors' (p. 16); they contrast a newspaper notice celebrating the birthday of a professor who served in the Nazi government with the continuing negative reactions to the few who resisted the regime (pp. 51–53); and they point to the lack of historical studies of the Nazi period by West German scholars (p. 53). They suggest that these cultural mechanisms constitute a collective denial of national culpability.[4]

In the sphere of political and economic activity the Mitscherlichs argue that the refusal of West Germany to give up its claims to the territories of East Germany constituted a denial of the realities of their defeat: 'Germans remain incapable of acknowledging that Russian demands were a logical consequence of the war. They behave as if the whole conflict had been some insignificant skirmish, and not an ideological crusade' (p. 5). They suggest that there is also a diversion of libidinal energy from the field of politics to the field of industry and consumerism. Describing 'the problem of political apathy' and 'an increasingly intense stimulation of feeling in the consumer field' (pp. 8–9) they argue:

> Germans have shown a minimum of psychological interest in trying to find out why they became followers of a man who led them into the greatest material and moral catastrophe in their history. They have also shown a minimum of interest in the new ordering of their society. Instead, with a spirit of enterprise that arouses general admiration and envy, they concentrated all their energies on the restora-

tion of what had been destroyed, and on the extension and modernization of their industrial potential – down to and including their kitchen utensils.

(p. 9)

The Mitscherlichs suggest this industrious diversion of energy constitutes a 'manic defense' by means of which to 'obliterate the past' (p. 15). This redirection of libidinal energy appears to keep at bay the more painful response to loss whereby the object is internalized and guilt and self-reproach are turned inwards. As a corollary of this process, the Mitscherlichs point to the 'theory of enforced obedience' whereby 'suddenly the leaders ... were alone responsible for putting genocide into practice' (p. 15). This projection of responsibility onto the leaders required a rapid withdrawal of attachment from the regime and its leader: 'The most important collectively practiced defense was to withdraw cathecting energies from all the circumstances related to former enthusiasm for the Third Reich, idealization of the Fuhrer and his doctrine, and of course, actual criminal acts' (ibid., p. 20). The energies previously invested in identification with the Nazi regime are thus redirected into industrial activity and feelings of guilt, shame and responsibility are externalized onto 'the leaders'. These mechanisms together, the Mitscherlichs suggest, constitute a 'de-realisation' of the past whereby 'the memory of the twelve years of Nazi rule' became 'increasingly dim and ghostlike' (p. 20) allowing Germans to 'ward off the experience of a melancholy impoverishment of the self' (p. 24).

Alongside their analysis of the cultural and political landscape the Mitscherlichs present three case studies of patients in clinical psycho-analysis. The first two patients identified themselves, in different ways, as the victim in relation to the war. The first patient, who had served for seven years in the SS, felt no guilt, but rather that he had been unjustly treated, and that 'all the crimes and destruction committed by the Germans are ... merely the necessary consequence of the far graver wrongs to which the German people were subjected' (p. 38). The second had not been a member of any Nazi organization but 'spent a great deal of time expressing his hatred of his fellow-countrymen, who had robbed him of his pride as a German' (p. 42). The third patient said he 'had never been a convinced Nazi'. However, he had served as an officer in the army during the war, and had several gaps in his memory of that time. During analysis, some of these memories came back to him. The Mitscherlichs report:

In spite of his very religious and respectable bourgeois upbringing [the patient] had one day caused a violent scene in a café in a Danish town. Some Danish relatives of his were making derogatory remarks about the Nazis; in response, he had loudly declared that he could not permit such statements and had threatened to denounce them to the German authorities.

(p. 34)

Another forgotten memory that this patient recalled during his analysis was of requisitioning a house belonging to a Jewish family. These two memories 'made it oppressively clear to him ... how much more he had shared the collective beliefs of that time than he had previously been willing to admit to himself' (p. 34). Nevertheless, the authors report, the recollection of these incidents 'evoked hardly any feeling' (p. 35). They note: 'In view of his normally acute sensibility, this seemed very striking ... the treatment was no longer dealing with the patient's individual resistance to the appearance of feelings of unpleasure, but with a *collectively approved* resistance' (italics in original, p. 35).

In relation to methodology it is worth noting that this patient's treatment lasted for more than a year and it is on this basis, perhaps, that it is possible for the Mitscherlichs to suggest a distinction between 'the patient's individual resistance' and 'a *collectively approved* resistance'. The opportunity to observe repeated patterns and deviations from these patterns is one of the distinctive features of psychoanalytic methodology that, arguably, tends not to be replicated in traditional forms of the qualitative research interview. The authors conclude:

> None of the three mourns over lost ideals in the sense of grappling with the urgent problem of how all this came about and was allowed to run its course unchecked. Above all, not one of the three summoned up any real sympathy for the victims of Nazi ideology.
>
> (p. 43).

The consistency of the denials of guilt or responsibility across the cultural, political and clinical instances presented in the Mitscherlichs' analysis constitutes a persuasive picture of a collective inability to acknowledge either the loss of the powerful Nazi regime or the loss of its victims. The urgent tone of their account, which can perhaps at times feel self-righteous, reminds us of the extent to which, at the time of their writing in particular, 'German nationalistic feeling remains inextricably connected with memories of Auschwitz and Lidice' (p. 16); and they evoke the fear and uncertainty often associated with the potential re-emergence of German nationalism. They argue for the need to engage with memories of the war, to enable mourning to replace the 'manic' processes of denial.

Encountering their work more than thirty years on, and twenty years after German reunification, it is possible to suggest that the Mitscherlichs' assumption that Germany should 'get over' its attachment to a unified national identity might have been a little naive or idealistic. With hindsight, the inability to acknowledge the loss of territory to the East might better be understood in terms of a Lacanian foreclosure of subjectivity rather than a temporary denial of political reality. Stavrakakis and Chrysoloras (2006) have suggested that Lacanian theory 'can substantially improve our understanding of national identity, since it explains in a novel way the force, the salience and the longevity of national identifications' (p. 159). Thus the denial of the possibility that the division of Germany is just and irrevocable might be understood, in Butler's terms, 'less as a refusal to grieve (the Mitscherlich formulation that accents the choice involved) than a preemption of grief' (Butler, 1997, p. 147). The force of national identity might, somewhat scarily, be said to foreclose the possibility of contemplating its loss.

Preservation of loved lost objects of racial melancholia

In their essay 'A Dialogue on Racial Melancholia' (2003) David Eng (a professor in the humanities) and Shinhee Han (a psychotherapist) argue for a conceptualization of racial melancholia that can account for processes of immigration and the production of assimilated identities. They draw an analogy between the notion of finite mourning, in relation to assimilation into white America, and the myth of the melting pot:

> To the extent that ideals of whiteness for Asian Americans (and other groups of color) remain unattainable, processes of assimilation are suspended, conflicted, and unresolved. The irresolution of this process places the concept of assimilation within a melancholic framework. Put otherwise, mourning describes a finite process that might be reasonably aligned with the popular American myth of immigration, assimilation, and the melting pot for dominant white ethnic groups. In contrast, melancholia delineates an unresolved process that might usefully describe the unstable immigration and suspended assimilation of Asian Americans into the national fabric.
>
> (p. 345)

More specifically, they argue that the lost objects of Asian American subjectivity include both stereotypes of the 'model minority' and identifications with an 'original' Asian culture. They combine cultural and clinical analysis to develop a politicized conceptualization of intergenerational melancholia and language as a lost object. They argue against pathologizing understandings of a melancholic immigrant subjectivity, arguing instead for its 'productive political potentials' (p. 365).

Eng and Han's analysis suggests that the stereotype of Asian Americans as a 'model minority' – 'economically or academically successful with no personal or familial problems to speak of' (p. 347) – works in several ways. At a cultural level it facilitates the 'democratic myths of liberty and inclusion', the erasure from memory of exclusion laws disqualifying Asians from US citizenship (p. 347), and a loss of memory about Asian contributions to the development of the nation. This forgetting, they suggest, is symptomatic of both white and Asian American subjectivity. They cite Maxine Hong Kingston's novel *China Men*, in which the narrator speculates about the elusive figure of her grandfather, one of the Chinese workers who built the American railway, but whose contribution is not recognized either in American cultural history or in the memories of his family (Kingston, 1989). In addition, the focus on academic or economic achievement rules the model Asian American subject out of realms of activity that might constitute a 'well rounded' white American identity and, they argue, 'the "success" of the model minority myth comes to mask our lack of political and cultural representation' (Eng and Han, 2003, p. 351). At an individual level this requires a form of disavowal: 'a psychic splitting on the part of the Asian American subject, who knows and does not know, at once, that he or she is part of the larger group' (p. 348). Eng and Han suggest that ideals of assimilated or 'model minority' identities force a mimicry that is destined to fail:

> Asian Americans are forced to mimic the model minority stereotype in order to be recognized by mainstream society – in order *to be* at all. To the extent, however, that this mimicry of the model minority stereotype functions only to estrange Asian Americans from mainstream norms and ideals (as well as from themselves), mimicry can operate only as a melancholic process.
>
> (p. 350)

Eng and Han suggest that these processes might be interpreted in a similar way to Butler's account of melancholia in which 'the ego constitutively emerges in relation to a superego that admonishes and judges it to be lacking' (p. 361). Ideals of both Asian identity and mainstream American identity, whether repressed or disavowed,[5] are unavailable to the Asian American subject.

While arguing for a non-pathological understanding of racial melancholia, Eng and Han foreground the pain involved in these losses, and the way the experience of such loss can persist across generations. They explore two instances in which, they suggest, 'daughters have absorbed and been saturated by their mothers' losses' (p. 355). The first of these is a clinical example. Elaine, a US-born Korean American student whose father is a professor, was at risk of failing her first year in college. In therapy she told Han:

> My parents have sacrificed everything to raise me here. If my parents had stayed in Korea, my mom would be so much happier and not depressed. She would have friends to speak Korean with, my father would be a famous professor, and we would be better off socially and

economically. I wouldn't be so pressured to succeed. They sacrificed everything for me, and now it's up to me to please them and to do well in school.

(p. 353)

Han suggests that the loss Elaine's mother has suffered in moving to the US has been 'transferred onto and incorporated by Elaine'. They interpret Elaine's depression as 'the result of internalized guilt and residual anger that she not only feels towards but also identifies with in her mother' (p. 353). Eng and Han note resonances between Elaine's identifications and a video by Rea Tajiri about a young Japanese American girl whose parents were interned during the war. In the video, the girl's mother has no memories of her wartime experience, while the daughter has nightmares which turn out to be images of the mother's experiences in the camp. Eng and Han suggest that in both instances 'the mothers' voices haunt the daughters': the losses imposed in an exclusionary US polity are passed through the generations. They argue that the melancholic instantiation of this exclusion as internalized loss 'threatens to erase the *political* bases of melancholia' (p. 355) so that cases like Elaine's are perceived as familial conflicts, rather than as a symptom of social exclusion and inequity.

There is perhaps scope here for clarification of the differential affordances of the two forms of data that Eng and Han draw on in their analysis. An account produced by a patient within a therapeutic relation provides a direct basis for the analysis of melancholic processes. Similarly, the video might be interpreted as an artefact that reiterates a melancholic loss. However, the presumably fictional account of the daughter's nightmares containing images of her mother's forgotten experiences has a different status: it is already constituted through the interpretive work of the film maker, and is thus a more complicated and indirect instantiation of the effects of intergenerational racial melancholia.

The second clinical case study discussed in Eng and Han's essay explores the losses instantiated for Nelson, a young Japanese boy, in his acquisition of English after immigrating to America. The authors describe how the boy's mother, who was not fluent in the language, was advised to speak English at home to support her son's development at school. During his therapy with Han, Nelson described an incident at school where he had mispronounced a word, and, in front of his classmates, his teacher had asked him who had taught him this error. Nelson had responded that he'd learnt his pronunciation from his mother. He associated this memory with a sense of embarrassment and of being ridiculed by his classmates. Eng and Han's interpretation suggests that in learning English Nelson experienced a double loss of nurturing relations: he lost both his mother tongue and his attachment to his mother. In addition, there is a loss of the ideal of native fluency in English. They suggest:

'Nelson's analytic situation reveals how on two fronts ideals of white-ness and ideals of Asianness are lost and unresolved for the Asian American subject. In both instances, language is the privileged vehicle by which standards of successful assimilation and failed imitation are measured'.

(p. 357).

Drawing on a Kleinian framework, Eng and Han suggest that the incident at school damaged Nelson's internalization of his mother as a good object. They use this instance to develop an understanding of the racial aspect of Klein's internal objects: 'Nelson's case history emphatically under-scores the way in which good attachments to a primary object can be threatened and transformed into bad attachments *specifically through the axis of race*' (p. 360, italics in original). They suggest that Nelson's concern to perfect his English can be understood as an attempt to reinstate his mother as a good object, but they conclude: 'the racial melancholia that underwrites Nelson's unresolved loss of the Japanese mother renders any attempt to reinstate this loved object extraordinarily tenuous' (p. 361). Nevertheless, they also invoke the reparative aspect of Klein's theory, raising the possibility that 'certain losses are grieved because they are not, perhaps, even seen as losses but are seen as social gains' (p. 362). This suggests, perhaps, an essential ambivalence in the relation to the internalized loss of Japanese or of Japanese-ness, and the potential for change in the relation to the internalized object. Eng and Han argue: 'The crucial point to investigate, then, is the social and psychic status of that lost object, idealized or deval-ued, and the ways in which that lost object can or cannot be reinstated into the psychic life of the individual in order to rebuild an internal world'; and they suggest that this conceptualization of racial melancholia 'removes Asian Americans from the position of solipsistic "victim"' (p. 363).

In attempting to invert what they interpret as Freud's vision of melancho-lia as a 'destructive force', Eng and Han argue for the productivity of 'the aggressive and militant preservation of the loved and lost object' (p. 363). Thus, they suggest, melancholic practices might eventually reconstitute the social legitimacy of the disavowed object. However, taking their earlier point about the dangers of the individualized aspects of melancholia, I wonder whether this kind of productive potential might require an externalization in the production of cultural artefacts or practices, such as the rituals of mourn-ing for AIDS victims cited by Butler. Indeed, the texts they cite within the essay – I've mentioned Tajiri's video, but also they also discuss autobio-graphical fiction by Maxine Hong Kingston (1976, 1989), Gish Jen (1991) and Monique T.-D. Truong (1991), amongst others – might be interpreted as examples of the productive refusal to 'get over' melancholic loss

Valerie Hey's paper, 'Getting over it? Reflections on the melancholia of reclassified identities' (2006) makes a similar point. She suggests that the autobiographically inflected theorizations of class by 'ex' working class feminist academics might be understood as textual instantiations of a melancholic attachment to a lost working class identity. She argues that the act of becoming an academic involves 'defeating the working class self' and suggests that the preservation of the autobiographical voice within sociological writing about class might be a way to 'appease the guilt' for this destructive act (p. 303). Responding to the suggestion that she should 'get over it', Hey defends this type of personal writing as 'the angry refusal to forget one's history' (p. 301) and as 'an offensive defensive formation' that might work not only as a solipsistic relief for the author but also 'on others' behalf' (p. 305). In a similar vein to Eng and Han, Hey argues there is a need to develop 'a more social understanding of melancholia to prise open the meanings of grievance in a way that avoids the dead end excesses of identity politics' (p. 302).

The present object and the absent object: male sexuality, violence and loss

Adam Jukes' (1993a, 1993b) exploration of male sexuality and male violence against women is an interesting contrast to Judith Butler's work. Both constitute explicitly politicized developments of the conceptual structure of melancholia in the analysis of problematic gender relations. However, where Butler uses the concept of melancholia to reconfigure notions of heterosexual subjectivity, Jukes separates out his analysis of loss from an account of girls' and boys' socialization into patriarchal norms, and, in contrast to Butler's work, Jukes' analysis references aspects of the Kleinian framework. While Jukes' account has quite rightly been criticized for reiterating, rather than troubling, the binary, heterosexual division of gender (e.g. Frosh, 2007), his work is of interest as a recontextualization of a Kleinian conceptualization of the relation between the emotions evoked by an object present in adulthood and the originary loss of the (m)other.

Jukes' study is based on his therapeutic work with men who are violent towards their female partners. He argues that orthodox psychoanalytic approaches, with their intense focus on relations within the family, implicitly implicate women in the violence of which they are the object. In contrast, he attempts to construct a link between 'a culture which is founded firmly and essentially on gender' (1993a, p. 37) and the infant's association of peril with the loss of the mother. His account is based on the sense of fear, peril and profound vulnerability reported by the men he works with when they are describing their violence towards their female partners:

> Most men insist – at least during the early phase of the programme – that they do not feel hatred or even anger before the violent attack on their partner. All they are aware of is their profound vulnerability, and the fact that their life is under threat.
>
> (p. 34)

Jukes relates the sense of threat the men report to the peril experienced by the infant at the withdrawal of the breast, when they first become aware of their vulnerability and their dependency on the (m)other. He continues: 'What is the nature of this threat? It will become clear that I believe it derives from the natural link between the separate, frustrating object and the absent or abandoning, and therefore persecuting, object' (p. 34).

Jukes is drawing on a Kleinian conception of the absent or abandoning object as the breast, withdrawn from the infant, while the separate frustrating object, for these violent men, is the female partner who challenges the man's authority or control. Where for Klein it is the emotions associated with adult mourning that re-evoke the peril of the infant's loss of the mother, here the evocation of infant loss is initiated by a female challenge to masculine authority. Jukes argues that the shared feminine identification of the present object, the man's female partner, and the absent object, the mother, is a primary factor in the psychical connection between these two experiences.

In order to make this argument, Jukes reconceptualizes the contents of the internalization associated with the experience of loss. Whereas for Klein, the good internal object is formed through an experience of love and trust with a present object (the mother), Jukes suggests that 'the encapsulated psychosis is formed by the absent object' (p. 36). He suggests that the ego reconstitutes the absent object through fantasy and delusion and this internalization thus retains the terrifying psychotic contents that, for Klein, are overcome through the relation with the mother. For Jukes, the present object does not overcome the psychosis, but rather contains or 'encapsulates' it. As such, rather than constituting a stable or reparative relation to the lost object, the internalization is simply a temporary containment of 'the terror of the fundamentally ruptured subject' (p. 36):

> The real terror is not of losing something but of falling into that place in which there is nothing to lose. This chaos made carnate (what Jones called aphanisis) is the helplessness and vulnerability. The peril is not simply a loss of life, but a loss of self.
>
> (p. 36)

This account evokes the internalization of the object as a potentially overwhelming force, kept at bay through a temporary 'encapsulation'. He continues:

> The encapsulated psychosis contains ineffable fear, rage and frustration. I have said that this becomes structured in relation to fantasies of deprivation by the primary, feminine object. The hatred of women (and its mild oedipal derivative, normal contempt for women) as the source of the rupture is inevitable.
>
> (p. 37)

In order to develop this account of the relation between primary loss and 'hatred of women' Jukes' suggests that the infant's experience is structured by the pre-existing codes of a culture that is 'predicated on male dominance and female inferiority and subordination' (p. 30). He asks: 'Is it questionable to assert that emotional, physical and psychological deprivation is associated with mothering as a gender based activity performed by women?'; and asserts 'It is inevitable, for the vast heterosexual majority, that frustration will come to be associated with the absent female Other'. From this he extrapolates: 'The primary object, woman (and the inheritors of the transference – wives, girlfriends) assumes its sadistic qualities when she behaves in ways which frustrate the man/child's socially constructed, socially legitimated expectations of servicing and authority' (pp. 37–38). This formulation suggests that the formation of the gendered subject pre-dates the loss of the mother and that the repudiation of the mother relates to her failure to fulfil her legitimated feminine role. While Jukes is concerned to foreground the cultural constitution of male sexuality, in doing so he also produces a slightly reductive and rigid account of the relation between femininity and mothering. Alternative accounts of the relation to the mother foreground the fluidity of an ongoing construction of masculinity through the repudiation of feminine identifications *within* the masculine subject (Frosh, 1994, ch. 5).

It is also worth noting the relation between the rigidity of Jukes' account of gender socialization and the unreliability of figures on the gender differentials in domestic abuse. Jukes' study is premised on the assumption that male violence against women is significantly more prevalent than female violence against men, and he cites a range of statistics to support this claim. One statistic suggests, for example, that 'over 99 percent of violent abuse between heterosexual couples is by men against their female partners' (1993a, p. 29). Stephen Frosh's account (1994, pp. 94–95) suggests a similar disparity in the statistics on sexual abuse. However, the ManKind Initiative (2009) reports a Home Office survey on intimate violence that gives a very different picture, suggesting that 40 per cent of victims of domestic abuse are men. While figures confirming the predominance of men as abusers are intuitively persuasive, the Home Office survey coupled with the argument that men significantly under-report experiences of abuse constitutes a very different starting point for an analysis of the relation between male sexuality and partner violence.

Jukes' assertion of the 'inevitability' of destructive gender relations can, perhaps, be contextualised in his account of his own position within the field of therapeutic practice and feminist politics.[6] His therapeutic practice is informed by his own experience of analysis within which he explored his own 'intense feelings of hatred for women' (1993b, p. xxi). He explains how his understanding of this hatred developed further both through his therapeutic work with violent men at the London Men's Centre, and through his engagement with the work and writing of feminists in the women's refuge movement. He suggests:

the 'speaking bitterness' of women's writing simply could not be ignored. Their experience and understanding of male violence towards women presented me with concepts and tools which – simply – were much more effective in confronting men's behaviour than anything possible within an analytic approach or understanding.

(1993b, p. xxii)

Thus his appropriation of feminist theory is very much oriented towards practice and embedded within his committed engagement to supporting his own and other men's struggle with their hatred of women. This activist orientation may perhaps influence his methodology and writing. In his book, dramatically entitled *Why Men Hate Women* with the cover slogan 'A book written for men that every woman should read', he admits not only that this may be a shocking book, but that it is part of his intention to shock (1993b, p. xxxii). Thus the rhetorical tone to some of his writing constitutes, perhaps, the embodiment of his positioning across therapeutic, political and academic contexts.

Melancholic self-regulation within heteronormative discourse

Jessica Ringrose's account of the production of young women's subjectivities (2008) traces discourses of femininity and heterosexual competition from media and popular music to her participants' accounts of their peers in groups and individual interviews. Her analysis suggests that the production of gendered subjectivities within these discourses involves repetitive, melancholic regulation of both self and others. These processes do not involve a simple injunction to be heterosexual: the injunction is rather to construct a heterosexual identity within a complex web of competing discursive regulations and at the same time to recognize the differential effects of these regulations in relation to hierarchical codes of class and ethnicity. In relation to the conceptualization of melancholia, most of Ringrose's discussion focuses on the ways in which these multifarious prohibitions are reiterated in the girls' talk, but hanging over this melancholic self-regulation is the threatened loss of their current friendships as they enter the heterosexual regime.

One organizing theme of Ringrose's analysis is a discourse of competitive sexual aggression that she identifies within contemporary popular and celebrity culture. An exemplary instance of this discourse is Avril Lavigne's hit single 'Girlfriend', the lyrics of which address a boy with the words: 'I don't like your girlfriend/I think you need a new one/I could be your girlfriend … I'm the mother fucking princess/I can tell you like me and you know I'm right' (p, 34). Ringrose interprets the boyfriend-stealing image celebrated in the song as threatening female friendship by 'aggressively displaying the self who desires the delicious boy' (p. 36); but, she suggests, it can also be interpreted as a form of alienated desire, since what the girl in the song desires is in fact 'the desiring gaze of one wanted by another' (p. 36). Ringrose traces how this hypersexualized aggression is instantiated both by other celebrities – 'Christina Aguilera can be "dirty", and Paris Hilton can perform sexy slut in her porn video with more to gain than to lose' (p. 54) – and in other media, with Lavigne 'posing nude on the cover of Blender music magazine save the slogan "Hell Yeah I'm Hot!" brandished across her breasts' (p. 55, n. 2). This discourse re-emerges in complicated ways in Ringrose's interview data.

The empirical base of Ringrose's study comprises two focus group interviews followed by individual interviews with a friendship group of five racially and economically marginalized girls aged between twelve and fourteen. In the focus groups the girls discussed their peer group at school and described the complexities of their relations with other girls. Ringrose reports: 'much energy in the focus group interviews was spent disciplining those girls who were viewed as sexually aggressive' (p. 41). They describe such girls as both 'slut' and 'stunning', re-invoking the contradictory demand that they be sexually attractive but within strict regulatory boundaries that they themselves police within their talk. This evokes Freud's description of the re-establishment of regulatory norms within the ego. The norms that insist that the girls prioritize heterosexual relations over female friendship are incorporated within the ego and re-emerge in their negotiation of relationships within their peer group. Their criticism of others as 'sluts', 'a girl that tries too hard', 'a girl that shows too much of herself', 'wears skirts about that big' or 'lets boys come up to her and touch her bum' (pp. 41, 42, 43), can be read as a pre-emptive form of the self-beratement that is symptomatic of melancholia.

Ringrose reads this complicated invocation and resistance of the sexually aggressive yet compliant girl as inflected with codes of class. She notes that 'working class girls/women have been positioned as hyper-sexual and in need of regulation and sanitation'. Because of this there's an imperative for working class girls to construct themselves as 'respectable' and to distance themselves from sexualized identifications (Skeggs, 1997; Hey, 1997; Walkerdine, 1990). Ringrose explains: 'These classed discourses set up contradictory and painful dynamics since girls are called up on to perform as sexually aggressive to be desirable, and yet are open to constant recuperation into the position of slut' (2008, p. 43).

The paper also traces psychological, educational and media discourses on girls' aggression as constitutive elements of gendered identities. These discourses, she suggests, 'position girls as covert, mean and incapable of expressing direct rational (masculine) forms of aggression' (p. 37). They pathologize girls' aggression and fail to take into account the social context – 'the heterosexual, raced and classed dynamics' – within which conflicts arise. A conflict described by the girls in Ringrose's study illustrates both of these aspects of dominant understandings of girls' aggression.

The girls described how they had fallen out with Katie, who had previously been one of their friends. Their account suggests the dispute was rooted in the heterosexual politics of the group: 'She thought she was better than us... like, oh who fancies you, no one, oh well I guess they all fancy me then'; 'she would say really horrible stuff to me and Elizabeth like, make us feel small'; and finally, Elizabeth says 'because when me and Luke were boyfriend and girlfriend, she said that she would kiss Luke even though I was going out with him' (pp. 45–46). Eventually, they had decided to talk to Katie about the way she'd been acting, and the argument had escalated. Katie told her mother about what had happened and the school authorities were brought in. Ringrose reports: 'the girls were sanctioned under an anti-bully provision at the school, where the girls were positioned as bullies. The head teacher's (highly astute) advice during the disciplinary meeting with all the girls was to "Just be friends"'(p. 46).

Ringrose suggests that labelling the girls as bullies both pathologizes the incident and 'trivialises and obscures the competitive heterosexualised economy of the school' (p. 46). In addition, at times within the interviews the girls themselves seemed to reiterate this pathologizing discourse of girls' aggression, saying: 'girls can be really nice and then they can be really like horrible'; 'all girls are two faced'; 'yeah ... like everyone slags someone off behind their back' (p. 47). Again, this can be seen as a form of melancholic self-reproach, an internalization of dominant, pathologizing images of girls' aggression.[7]

What is mourned in this continual, melancholic regulation of girls' sexuality is the legitimacy and centrality of their existing friendships, under threat as the demands of the adult heterosexual economy begin to encroach. We get a sense of the girls' intimacy in Ringrose's description of the bodily arrangement of the friends during one of the interviews: 'It is in a living room, with the girls squeezed onto a small sofa and on the floor. The girls' bodies are pressed close upon one another, hugging, touching, pushing, poking and jostling one another...'(p. 43). She also reports a conversation where they fantasized about the future, developing a scenario in which they would have children, adopt perhaps, but not get married, and they would live in a house together, working as doctors or lawyers. Ringrose contrasts this fantasy with the sexually competitive image of stealing someone else's boyfriend in the song by Avril Lavigne. She suggests:

> Avril's song/video presents us with a (post-feminist/pre-feminist?) version of violently fighting for and winning the boy to become the 'motherfucking princess'. But something quite different is presented in these extracts. Faced with the demands to embrace competitive success at every level ... We see a passionate desire to prolong the bonds of friendship ... and the idea of compulsory heterosexuality/marriage is undermined in these desires for the future. These potent fantasies

illustrate how friendships can offer spaces for radical dissent, which jar against the dominant regulative heterosexualised context through which girls must stake out their relationships and their lives.

(p. 53)

As in Eng and Han's analysis, Ringrose is speculating about a possibility for a recuperative form of melancholia in which a refusal to let go of the lost object might in some way rupture or shift the regulative framework. However, she also acknowledges that these are tenuous, vulnerable spaces in a complex discursive network within which the refusal of an injunction to conform to heterosexualized images of femininity is constituted by naming others as 'sluts', a denigration of the other that can simultaneously be read in relation to codes regulating the classed and economic positioning of the subject. This analysis suggests the complexity of melancholic processes in the ongoing production of young women's sexual identities.

Finally, it may be useful to consider some contrasts between Butler's account of homosexual attachment and Ringrose's analysis of girls' friendships, in order to clarify notions of foreclosure, repression and disavowal as melancholic mechanisms. The notion of foreclosure has two aspects: it involves the absolute rejection of an idea or subjectivity from symbolization and is, at the same time, the basis for the constitution of the subject (see Fink, 1997). Thus Butler argues the very possibility of homosexual attachment is radically ruled out in rigid heterosexual practices and subjectivities. Repression, in contrast, involves the covering over of an already present impulse or attachment. Ringrose's account suggests how the discourses of the heterosexual economy call on girls to repress their existing attachments to their friends. This less radical mechanism might permit the more fluid instantiations of gender that, as Butler notes (1997, p. 136), exist alongside hyperbolic disavowals of homosexual love. The distinction between disavowal and repression is also helpful here. Where foreclosure refers to an idea that can never be formulated, and repression refers to the subject's suppression of their own impulse or attachment, disavowal is process whereby a symbolic category is both recognized and at the same time rejected or denied (See chapter 5). So that, in Butler's account, there is a foreclosure of the subject's own homosexual attachment and a disavowal of the legitimacy of homosexuality as a social category. In contrast, the girls in Ringrose's study are contemplating what it might mean for them to repress their intimacy in order to constitute themselves as subjects in the aggressive terms of prevailing discourses of heterosexuality.

Conclusion: loss and politics

The studies explored in the chapter extend psychoanalytic accounts of melancholia in significant ways. They suggest how specific social practices such as the positioning of English within the American school system or heterosexualised media discourses constitute racialized and sexualized losses within social subjectivities. In doing this, they might shift our attention away from individualized aspects of melancholic processes and towards the many ways in which the social bond infiltrates the ego. This might have practical implications for political and therapeutic practice. Eng and Han suggest 'the pressing need to consider carefully methods by which a more speculative approach to psychoanalysis might enhance clinical applications' (2003, p. 344). Adam Phillips has also noted the productivity of the engagement between psychoanalysis and more speculative or sociological work, suggesting that the constraints of the clinic can block out the social and political dimensions of psychotherapeutic practice. He notes: 'It is fortunate that writers are interested in psychoanalysis because, unlike analysts, they are free to think up thoughts unconstrained by the hypnotic effect of clinical practice' (1997, p. 157).

In addition, however, each of the studies described here reconstitutes the conceptual structure of melancholia: some ideas or signifiers are reasserted, others are suppressed, and new associations are made, linking the conceptual structure of melancholia into contrasting theorizations of loss and politics. So when Eng and Han invoke Klein's notion of reparation, this might be understood as an attempt to carve a positive political vision and to distance themselves from the negativity associated with more intransigent, pathological understandings of melancholia. The Kleinian conceptualization of the ego's drive to repair in order to overcome its guilt and anxiety for attacks on the lost object has been used to support positive political agendas, as opposed to Butler's more anarchic notion of the refusal to give up the object as a way of disrupting the prevailing cultural or symbolic order. Although they reference Klein, it is possible to interpret Eng and Han's argument for the 'militant preservation of the loved and lost object' (2003, p. 363) as more consistent with a Butlerian conception of politics. More concretely, we might ask: Is the notion of Japanese-ness mourned because of guilt associated with the gains made through the rejection of Japanese-ness? Does the preservation of a notion of Japanese-ness constitute reparation for the enjoyment gained in the moment of loss? Or, alternatively, does the preservation of Japanese-ness constitute an uncertain refusal of a painful cultural prohibition that cannot ever be repaired? These interpretations are not necessarily mutually exclusive, but they are not the same: they constitute versions of melancholia that instantiate, I think, quite different notions of loss and politics. Within a Kleinian framework the development of the ego involves loss, but also guilt and reparation for the ego's destructive response to that loss. Within a more Butlerian framework the subject is formed in relation to the prohibitions of the cultural law, a loss that cannot be recuperated.

Methodologically it is important to note the dispersion of these different versions of loss within the conceptual structure of melancholia. Foreclosure, repression and disavowal are very different, distinct ways of understanding loss. In the same way, loss of the breast does not equate to loss of pre-discursive, polyvalent sexuality, and loss of racial identity does not equate to loss of an imaginary sense of omnipotence. The concept 'melancholia' temporarily binds these dispersed moments together, enables us to articulate them as loss, and gives us a frame within which these contrasting elements can substitute for one another. This temporary alliance might produce shifts in meanings or practices further down the chain of signification, in psychotherapeutic or political practice. Importantly, though, the productivity of these substitutions should not lead to the reification of melancholia as a unified entity that stands outside the process of interpretation: melancholia is a signifier that is always articulated within an existing web of psychoanalytic, political and sociological discourse.

Further than this, the binding of different moments within the conceptual structure of melancholia might be understood as a sedimentation of the Oedipal myth as universal origin of identity: there is always an attachment, there is always a prohibition, there is always a loss. Is it possible to maintain elements of the structure of melancholia without also reiterating the oppressive diagnosis of Oedipus to all of every culture? In Lacan's theorization of the four discourses (2007), for example, he talks about going 'beyond oedipus' and reduces the Oedipus complex to the barest disembodied structure. But nevertheless, his discourses have attachment, loss and prohibition embedded within them. This kind of re-articulation of melancholia might be interpreted as a subversion that enables us to diagnose the phallocentric structuring of subjectivity. Alternatively, as a Deleuzian or feminist critique might suggest (Braidotti, 2002; Holland, 1999; Goodchild, 1996), Lacan's theory, like all other interpretations of melancholic loss, might be merely another instance of the proliferation of the oppressive law of psychoanalysis.

2 Overdetermination
The conceptualization of dreams and discourse

Introduction: the unconscious and discourse

This is the first of two chapters exploring the relation between conceptualizations of the unconscious and conceptualizations of discourse. Taken together these chapters constitute a comparison between a Foucaultian understanding of discourse and the meaning of discourse in recent work by more Lacanian theorists such as Zizek (1989) and Laclau and Mouffe (2001). More Lacanian conceptualizations of discourse, which can be seen as a development of the Freudian/Althusserian idea of overdetermination, seem to take the notion of the unconscious for granted. Laclau has explicitly stated: 'I think that the psychoanalytic discovery of the unconscious is one of these epoch- making events whose ontological dimensions we are only starting to glimpse' (2004, p. 315). He goes on to clarify this, suggesting that for him the concepts associated with a Lacanian understanding of the relation between the subject and discourse cannot be limited to a 'particular region of human reality'. Rather, he suggests, 'when one realizes their full ontological implications they transform any field, the political field included' (ibid., p. 316). For Laclau, the category of 'discourse' must incorporate these psychoanalytic understandings of the subject and the unconscious. In contrast, Foucault's account of discourse seems to suppress a relation to a psychoanalytic conception of the unconscious. In his account of resistance, discussed in the next chapter, this allows him to foreground the potential of regional, diverse instantiations of discourse, in a way that contrasts with Laclau's more universalizing, ontologizing move. For Laclau, it seems to me, discourse is essentially related to a notion of the unconscious; for Foucault, discourse is plural and irregular. In both cases, I find it interesting to think about the relation between empirical analysis and speculative theorization: the speculative impulse to constitute a notion of the unconscious, or some alternative to the unconscious (power for example), to account for something that is probably empirically unaccountable, emerges in very different ways, it seems to me, in these two conceptualizations of discourse.

This chapter, then, traces the position of the unconscious within a conceptualization of discourse. To do this it explores the way Freud's (1958) articulation of the concept of overdetermination in *The Interpretation of Dreams* re-emerges in Laclau and Mouffe's theory of discourse. Freud understands dreams as overdetermined, produced in multiple chains of symbolic associations that condense dispersed meanings into individual elements of the dream, and that displace or invert the feelings associated with these meanings. This understanding of overdetermination re-emerges in Laclau and Mouffe's account of discourse as constituted in symbolic relations that organize social formations around 'nodal points', signifiers that are able to contain diverse social interests. Methodologically, I will argue, the analysis of instances of overdetermination in specific social and political discursive formations can be interpreted as an extension of Lacanian versions of the Freudian techniques of free association and the analyst's 'evenly hovering attentiveness'. The Lacanian prioritization of symbolic associations between linguistic elements enables us to break down the distinction between the interpretation of associations produced in the clinic and the interpretation of associations between discursive elements in other social and political contexts. This argument revisits some of the ideas set out in the introduction, relating to the conceptualization of affect and language, and the method of free association. The methodological questions underlying contrasting interpretations of free association relate to the status of affect and language: the possibility of making use of the analyst's experiences of affect within the interpretive process versus the requirement to limit interpretations to symbolic associations of language. The signifiers 'free association' and 'evenly hovering attentiveness' contain both of these possible interpretations. From the perspective of discourse theory, however, affect is understood as always already articulated within, or mediated by, language; a psychoanalytic approach to interpretation is not restricted to clinical relations; and symbolic associations between elements in diverse discursive artefacts can be interpreted in a similar way to the patient's associations to the elements of a dream.

I will begin the chapter by outlining Freud's understanding of the dream and his conceptualization of overdetermination, drawing links with the conceptualization of language and discourse in the work of Laclau and Mouffe. In order to think about the methodological implications of these theorizations of dreams and discourse, the following section explores contrasting interpretations of 'free association' and the technique of the analyst. The second half of the chapter explores interpretations of overdetermination and symbolic relations in three examples of empirical analysis. Freud's analysis of 'The May-Beetle Dream' (1958) is used to illustrate the interpretation of symbolic relations within a patient's associations, and, specifically, to clarify the processes of condensation and displacement and the constitution of 'nodal points'. David Howarth's (2000a, 2004) analysis of the Black Consciousness Movement and South African political discourse explores the conditions under which it is possible for a signifier to become established as a nodal point that can shape the political terrain. Finally, Rosa Burgos' (1999) analysis of the position of 'theory' as a signifier in higher education policy and curricula suggests how an empirical instance can be used to explore the symbolic relations condensing meanings within chains of signification traced across international policy, institutional politics and intellectual traditions.

Overdetermination: symbolic relations and psychical force

For Freud, a dream is constituted in the associations produced within the analysis of the dream. The process of interpretation constructs a relation between the elements the patient describes in their narration of the dream and the associations that follow the narration, as well as associations and themes that emerged earlier in the analysis. This process of interpretation reveals the dream thoughts, meanings that are not evident in the manifest content of the dream. The symbolic and psychical processes that are traced between all of these elements during the analysis are what Freud calls the dreamwork: the mechanisms that produced the content of the dream as it was experienced during sleep. Thus, the dream should be understood to include both the manifest content of the dream and the associations surrounding this experience of the dream; while the dreamwork is the process by which the elements of the dream are determined by their potential to express the multiple hidden dream thoughts.

The conceptualization of the dreamwork as the process that constitutes the symbolic/psychical relations that connect the manifest content of the dream to the dream thoughts, is at the core of Freud's account and interpretation of dreams. The dream thoughts are identified in the analysis of free associations, while the dreamwork is the construction of those associations by means of the condensation and displacement of ideas and feelings into the words, images and narratives that are elements of the dream content. Condensation refers to the process whereby one element or signifier comes to express the meaning of multiple dream thoughts, constituting a point of articulation for many diverse chains of associations. Displacement refers to the way that as meanings shift in chains of associations there is also a movement of psychical intensity, so that the significance or affect attached to an idea may be hidden or suppressed when the idea is expressed through an associated element or signifier. These processes will be illustrated in the empirical examples presented in the second half of the chapter.

Freud's account of dream analysis suggests that each element of the manifest content of a dream may be associated with several dream thoughts, and, in parallel, each of the dream thoughts can be traced through chains of associations to several elements of the dream:

Not only are the elements of a dream determined by the dream-thoughts many times over, but the individual dream-thoughts are represented in the dream by several elements. Associative paths lead from one element of the dream to several dream-thoughts and from one dream-thought to several elements of a dream ...

(1958, p. 389)

This constitutes one of the main ideas connoted by the concept of overdetermination: the production of elements within multiple interconnecting chains of associations, rather than through a linear determining cause. In his interpretations, Freud traces these symbolic relations or 'associative paths'. Any contextual or visual element may play a part in the construction of these paths of meaning, but Freud frequently foregrounds linguistic aspects of associative processes: the phonological, etymological and semantic associations of particular words within the analysis. Although the elements of the dream are constituted in a variety of different means of representation, Freud articulates the linguistic nature of these different verbal and non-verbal media. He makes an analogy between the visual 'script' of the dream content and the linguistic nature of the dream thoughts, arguing that the symbolic relations between these are essential to an understanding of the dream:

the dream content is expressed as it were in a pictographic script, the characters of which have to be transposed individually into the language of the dream thoughts. If we attempted to read these characters according to their pictorial value instead of according to their symbolic relation, we should clearly be led into error.

(ibid., pp. 381–382)

How might we interpret the distinction Freud is suggesting between 'pictorial value' and 'symbolic relation'? If we take an image of a brick, for example, he seems to suggest that its 'pictorial value' does not account for potential symbolic connections to other ideas. However, if we consider the image as constituted in a network of associations, in the way that words are connected within language, the ambiguities or symbolic relations that might punctuate the image become more apparent: a brick – a good bloke; shitting bricks – frightened; another brick in the wall – one in a multitude; brick by brick – methodical progress. Or alternatively, the image of a brick might be expressed as a colour, which would connote a relation to other objects of the same/different colour. In this way, an image within a dream can contain all the ambiguities and associations of a linguistic unit.

It is this network of associations that constitutes the 'language' of the dream thoughts. This is what Freud means when he suggests that we should interpret non-verbal elements according to their linguistic aspects. He explains further:

There is no need to be astonished at the part played by words in dream-formation. Words, since they are the nodal points of numerous ideas, may be regarded as predestined to ambiguity; and the neuroses (e.g. in framing obsessions and phobias), no less than dreams, make unashamed use of the advantages thus offered by words for purposes of condensation and disguise.

(ibid., p. 456)

This understanding of the productivity of words, and of their role as 'nodal points', is replicated in Lacanian and post-Lacanian theory (Lacan, 1957; Zizek, 1989; Laclau and Mouffe, 2001; Laclau, 1996). The nodal point is a word or a signifier that is able to hold within it several different meanings. In dreams, this potential for symbolic ambiguity allows a word or image to contain several of the ideas present in the dream thoughts. Condensed within one element of the dream, the ideas are both expressed and kept hidden. Within post-Lacanian social analysis similar kinds of interpretations are applied to political contexts: political signifiers – 'democracy', 'freedom', 'choice', 'the environment' – constitute nodal points that, through their ability to connote several meanings, come to represent a range of contrasting social or political interests. Once several contrasting meanings are attached to one element, this signifier becomes a powerful mechanism in the organization of the discourse.

Lacan develops Freud's account of the associative potential of language, conceptualizing discourse as constituted from the material of the symbolic order, an open network of signifiers that exist in their differential symbolic relations to other signifying elements (see Evans, 1996, p. 202). Lacan describes these signifiers as 'that material support that concrete discourse borrows from language' (1957, p. 163), thus distinguishing between the articulated signifying chains of discourse and the universe of linguistic units that are not in a fixed relation to other elements of language. He says: 'There is in effect no signifying chain that does not have, as if attached to the punctuation of each of its units, a whole articulation of relevant contexts suspended 'vertically', as it were, from that point' (Lacan 1957, p. 170). The 'units' that constitute a signifying chain are 'punctuated' by potential symbolic relations to other linguistic elements of the symbolic order. Lacan's interpretation foregrounds the potential Freud has discovered for language to 'signify *something quite other* than what it says' (ibid., p. 172, italics in original). This 'other' is present in the unarticulated symbolic relations to elements of the symbolic order.

Laclau and Mouffe's conceptualization of discourse is imitative of Lacan's account of discourse, signifying chains and the symbolic order. In their account they describe the process of articulation of disassociated 'elements' into 'moments' within discourse:

The structured totality resulting from the articulatory practice, we will call *discourse*. The differential positions, insofar as they appear articulated within a discourse, we will call *moments*. By contrast, we will call *element* any difference that is not discursively articulated.

(2001, p. 105)

As in Lacan's account of the relation between the symbolic order and the signifying chain, for Laclau and Mouffe there is a field of discursivity that is the excessive material from which discourse is articulated. The description of elements articulated within discourse as 'moments' foregrounds the openness and contingency of any discursive formation: 'no discursive formation is a sutured totality and the transformation of the elements into moments is never complete' (p. 107). It is this openness that constitutes their theory of discourse as a radial challenge to hegemonic conceptions of politics and society. However, while talking about the 'impossibility of an ultimate fixity of meaning', they draw on the Freudian notion of the 'nodal point' to explain the appearance of fixity in institutionalized social meanings:

The impossibility of an ultimate fixity of meaning implies that there have to be partial fixations – otherwise the very flow of differences would be impossible. Even in order to differ, to subvert meaning, there has to be *a* meaning. If the social does not manage to fix itself in the intelligible and instituted forms of a *society*, the social only exists, however, as an effort to construct that impossible object. Any discourse is constituted as an attempt to dominate the field of discursivity, to arrest the flow of differences, to construct a centre. We will call the privileged discursive points of this partial fixation, *nodal points*.

(p. 112)

The ambiguity of the nodal point has two aspects: it is that which enables it to contain diverse meanings in a point of temporary fixation, but it is also that which keeps open the possibility for meaning to be subverted:

since ... all discourse is subverted by a field of discursivity which overflows it, the transition from 'elements' to 'moments' can never be complete. The status of the 'elements' is that of floating signifiers, incapable of being wholly articulated to a discursive chain. And this floating character finally penetrates every discursive (i.e. social) identity. But if we accept the non-complete character of all discursive fixation and, at the same time, affirm the relational character of every identity, the ambiguous character of the signifier, its non-fixation to any signified, can only exist insofar as there is a proliferation of signifieds. It is not the poverty of signfieds but, on the contrary, polysemy that disarticulates a discursive structure. That is what establishes the over-determined, symbolic relation of every social identity. Society never manages to be identical to itself, as every nodal point is constituted within an intertextuality that overflows it. *The practice of articulation therefore, consists in the construction of nodal points which partially fix meaning; and the partial character of this fixation proceeds from the openness of the social, a result, in its turn, of the constant over-flowing of every discourse by the infinitude of the field of discursivity.*

(p. 113, emphasis in original)

Laclau and Mouffe's conceptualization of discourse as produced within an overflowing field of discursivity reorients methodological practice for political and social science. Empirical work in the field of discourse theory explores social events as overdetermined within shifting chains of significa-tion produced through complex networks of overflowing symbolic associ-ations. Just as there is no one, linear cause of an element of a dream, so there is no one linear explanation of social change (see also Althusser, 1962). Instead, complex symbolic paths of associations overdetermine the elements both of dreams and of history.

This understanding of the dream or the social terrain as constituted within a complex web of symbolic relations is one aspect of Freud's account. However, the picture of meanings sliding across paths of associ-ations, of condensed elements within a network of signifiers, invites, for Freud, a further question about the determination of elements within the dream. Why do meanings take one associative path rather than another? What drives the churning of meaning within the network of elements? To answer this question, Freud conceptualizes a 'psychical force', which he distinguishes from the other aspects of the dream thoughts that contribute to the complex overdetermination of the dream content:

> We shall be led to conclude that the multiple determination which decides what shall be included in a dream is not always a primary factor in dream-construction but is often the secondary product of a psychical force which is still unknown to us.
>
> (1958, p. 417)

He relates this force to the displacement of psychical intensity that occurs as meanings shift from one signifying element to another:

> It thus seems plausible to suppose that in the dream-work a psychical force is operating which on the one hand strips the elements which have a high psychical value of their intensity, and on the other, *by means of overdetermination*, creates from elements of low psychical value new values, which afterwards find their way into the dream-content.
>
> (p. 417, emphasis in original)

This additional, primary aspect of dreams is necessary to explain not only the symbolic production of the meaning of the dream, but the work of the dream in relation to what we might perhaps initially think of as something like affect, or desire: what Freud calls, 'psychical intensity'. As meanings shift from element to element along the associative chain, so the psychical intensities attached to the meanings are transformed, disguised or inverted. Freud suggests that these displacements of psychical intensity are driven by something other than mere symbolic associations: 'a psychical force which is still unknown to us'.

This suggestion raises significant methodological questions: how might we come to understand this 'psychical force' which is 'still unknown to us'? How does it relate to the symbolic associations between the dream content and the dream thoughts? Freud's suggestion is that the psychical force is manifest in the displacements enacted in the dreamwork (ibid., p. 417). The psychical force is thus a speculative inference based on the observation of the condensation and displacement of meanings and psychical intensities across elements in a signifying chain. We might, perhaps, think of this force as the unconscious. For Freud, at some points at least, it can be conceptualized as 'a psychical agency in the mind' (pp. 417–418), but within other theoretical frameworks the 'psychical force', or the unconscious, might be thought of in terms of an unknown or unknowable within language (e.g. Fink, 1995, p. 42). For Lacan, this relation to language is necessary to the unconscious: 'Language is the condition of the unconscious – that's what I say' (Lacan, 2007, p. 41). This enigmatic statement suggests many possible relations, both between language and the unconscious and between what Lacan says and what Lacan means. However, perhaps, it is possible to interpret the description of language as the 'condition' of the unconscious as something close to a methodological claim about how we come to conceptualize the unconscious via the linguistic associations of symbolic relations. And from this perspective Lacan's claim is not dissimilar to Freud's suggestion that the force we do not yet know is made visible through processes of condensation and displacement, the mechanisms that constitute the dream.

It might also be possible to distinguish the 'psychical force' that Freud refers to from 'economic' or 'material', 'linguistic' or 'cultural' forces, which might be constituted as 'determining' in the analysis of the objects of other fields of enquiry. However, the sustainability of these distinctions is put into question in debates around Althusser's proposition that the economic is determining 'in the last instance' in processes of historical change (Althusser, 1962; Laclau and Mouffe, 2001; Glynos and Stavrakakis, 2004). Within these debates, post-Althusserian, Lacanian influenced social theorists have rearticulated the significance of the psychical force that drives and sustains ideological and discursive phenomena (e.g. Zizek, 1989, Laclau, 2004) and Ernesto Laclau argues forcefully against separating out the linguistic and affective aspects of discourse (2004, p. 303). He makes the link back to Freud explicit in his account:

> What rhetoric can explain is the *form* that an overdetermining invest-ment takes, but not the *force* that explains the investment as such and its perdurability. Here something else has to be brought into the picture. Any overdetermination requires not only metaphorical con-densations but also cathectic investments. That is, something belong-ing to the order of *affect* has a primary role in discursively constructing the social. Freud already knew it: the social link is a libidinal link.
>
> (2004, p. 326, emphasis in original)

The psychical or affective force, then, emerges for both Freud and Laclau in the theorization of the complex symbolic relations that overdetermine social or psychological symptoms. However, as I have suggested, the posi-tion of this force can be interpreted in various ways. Laclau seems to make a strong claim for an identification between the affective force and the process of signification: 'affect', he says, 'is not something *added* to signification, but something consubstantial with it' (ibid., p. 326). 'Affect' here seems to refer not to emotion or feeling, but to a productive force within language. This again echoes Lacan's conceptualization of the 'agency' of linguistic elements that constitute not only metaphorical or associative meanings, but also the discursive articulation of inarticulable desire (Lacan, 1989; Glynos and Stavrakakis, 2004, pp. 209–210). Zizek provides a useful illustration of this relation between desire and meaning. He explains how the image of the Marlboro man only takes on its meaning as an image of America when it is invested with the desire of 'real' Americans:

> Let us take the example of the famous advertisement for Marlboro: the picture of the bronzed cowboy, the wide prairie plains, and so on – all this 'connotes', of course, a certain image of America (the land of hard, honest people, of limitless horizons...) but the effect of 'quilting' occurs only when a certain inversion takes place; it does not occur until 'real' Americans start to identify themselves (in their ideological self-experience) with the image created by the Marlboro advertisement – until America itself is experienced as 'Marlboro country'.
>
> (Zizek, 1989, p. 96)

This example clarifies how the meaning of a signifier – the image of the Marlboro man – can only be fixed, quilted as a nodal point within dis-course, when the subjects of discourse identify with the image as an expres-sion of their desire.

This account of overdetermination as the discursive production of the social through complex symbolic processes that involve both metaphorical condensations and a psychical or affective force constructs a homology between dreams and the social terrain. These theorists suggest that we should perhaps learn to interpret the social terrain of everyday life a little bit more like we treat dreams. However, methodologically, this theoretical suggestion cannot be detached from the analysis of empirical instances: the site of displacements may be situated within the talk of a patient within the clinic or in the analysis of policy processes and social practices. These settings instantiate different kinds of data through which to interpret the constitution of overdetermining symbolic relations: condensed meanings, displacements of psychical intensities, and an unknown psychical force. The rest of this chapter explores how these differences are instantiated in contrasting empirical methodologies.

Free association and the body of the analyst: affect or symbolization as the technical apparatus for interpretation?

Christopher Bollas has suggested that free association is 'the only goal of psychoanalysis' (1999, p. 64). He argues:

> Psychoanalysis has only ever had one requirement, one aim, one goal of its own. There has only ever been one request. A request that Freud enunciated, often found difficult to follow, but which was realizable for each participant. In the name of psychoanalysis he asked the patient to speak whatever crossed his mind. The goal was free association.
>
> (ibid., p. 62)

This suggestion foregrounds the centrality of technique – the technique of free association – within psychoanalytic conceptions of both mind and therapy. The request to free associate, to talk without direction, runs counter to embedded cultural and epistemological practices. As Bollas points out, 'Few other intellectual traditions had been as linear and goal-directed as Western consciousness', and so: 'To ask Western man to discover truth by abandoning the effort to find it and adopting instead the leisurely task of simply stating what crosses the mind moment to moment is to undermine the entire structure of Western epistemology' (p. 63). The request to talk without direction is thus not only an intervention into the everyday selections and repressions of the individual, but also into the powerful ideological injunctions that control and direct both thought and speech. Because of this, the spontaneous articulation of ideas as they cross our mind is extremely difficult to achieve.

The idea, of course, is that free association allows us to move from the constraints of the conscious mind to enable us to observe the constraints of the unconscious. However, the injunction to dispense with self-censorship requires the subject to 'forget the anticipated judgment of the other'

(Bollas, 1999, p. 11). The psychoanalytic tradition suggests that the achievement of this forgetting also requires a skilled analyst/interviewer, able to generate an appropriate position from which to receive the patient's associations (see Kvale, 1999, Bollas, 1999). Freud described this position as one in which the analyst achieved a state of 'evenly suspended attention':

> Experience soon showed that the attitude which the analytic physician could most advantageously adopt was to surrender himself to his own unconscious mental activity, in a state of *evenly suspended attention*, to avoid so far as possible reflection and the construction of conscious expectations, not to try to fix anything that he heard particularly in his memory, and by these means to catch the drift of the patient's unconscious with his own unconscious.
>
> (Freud, cited in Bollas, 1999, pp. 63–64)

The ability of the analyst to embody an 'evenly suspended attention' has two significant effects. First, as already suggested, the embodiment of this state enables the analyst to support the process of free association on the part of the patient (see introduction). Second, and more controversially, 'evenly suspended attention' might be understood as an appropriately receptive state from which the analyst might be able to both receive and interpret these associations (Bollas, 1999; Racker, 1982).

This receptive state is in some ways similar to that demanded of the patient in free association: the analyst is attempting not to direct their thoughts as they listen; not to rush to interpret. Through this undirected yet attentive reception of the free associations produced by the patient, the analyst is able to notice the ways in which the unconscious interrupts the flow of talk and pushes it in ways that depart from the apparent direction of the narrative. Heinrich Racker has described this way of listening using the story of an old Chinese sage:

> One day this sage lost his pearls. He therefore sent his eyes to search for his pearls, but his eyes did not find them. Next he sent his ears to search for the pearls, but his ears did not find them either. Then he sent his hands to search for the pearls, but neither did his hands find them. And so he sent all of his senses to search for his pearls but none found them. Finally he sent his *not search* to look for his pearls. *And his not search found them.*
>
> (Racker, 1982, p. 17)

This parable might apply to all research, and to all researchers. We can all try to avoid directing our search so that we might notice the elements that tug in another direction. However, further claims are sometimes made about the quality of 'evenly suspended attention' within psychoanalysis.

These claims relate to the specialist training of the analyst so, it is suggested, an analyst's ability to listen is dependent on 'the degree to which
he himself is conscious of his own unconscious' (ibid., p. 18). This knowledge of one's own unconscious is assumed to be developed through the
analyst's own experience of analysis. Further claims still are sometimes
made about the ability of the analyst to receive, in some way, the thoughts
and feelings of the patient. Racker suggests: 'If the analyst is well identified with the patient, then the thoughts and feelings which emerge in him
will be, precisely, those which did not emerge in the patient, i.e. the
repressed and the unconscious' (p. 17). This appears to be a more radical,
or mystical interpretation of Freud's suggestion that the analyst might
'catch the drift of the patient's unconscious with his own unconscious'. It
seems to suggest some kind of 'emergence' of the patient's 'thoughts and
feelings' within the analyst, without explicating a material/symbolic basis
for this phenomenon.

The distinction between these ways of understanding the relation
between the analyst and the free associations produced by the patient
seems to me to be pertinent to an exploration of the contrasts between
Freud's dream interpretation and a discourse theoretical approach to
policy analysis. It affects the extent to which the interpretive activity might
be said to be the same in each case. If we understand the reception of affect
as primary to the interpretive process, it may be difficult to accept the
coherence of this type of analysis outside of the clinical setting, while if we
understand the interpretation of affect as secondary to the interpretation
of symbolic relations, then the recontextualization of ideas and methods
such as free association may be less problematic.

For Racker, and to differing extents for other psychoanalytic theorists,
the thoughts and feelings which 'emerge' in the analyst may be directly relevant to the interpretation of the thoughts and feelings of the patient. Feelings that emerge in the body of the analyst are thus understood as
'countertransferences': direct responses to feelings or unconscious patterns
of behaviour presented by the patient. Racker, like most other practitioners, emphasizes that the responses that emerge in the analyst's body need
to be treated with care: 'To become dominated or carried away by such
feelings would represent the above-mentioned "danger", or the "disturbance" of the treatment by the countertransference' (p. 19). Nevertheless,
he suggests it is possible, with careful analysis, to use these feelings to gain
a better understanding of the patient:

> To use the perception of these countertransference events, after having
> analysed their origin and their dynamics, as an indictor of what is hap-
> pening in the patient in his unconscious relation to the analyst, would
> be an example of the possibility of utilizing the countertransference as
> an instrument for understanding the transference.

(p. 19)

For Racker, the analytic training, which provides practitioners with a level of understanding of their own unconscious, enables them to use their own feelings productively within the analysis of another subject. The body of the trained analyst is thus viewed as a significant part of the technical apparatus for interpretation.

In the Lacanian tradition such a move is seen as more problematic. For Lacan, the dangers inherent in taking our own feelings as evidence of the feelings of an other are insurmountable. Bruce Fink suggests: 'Lacan's perspective is not that countertransferential feelings do not exit, but that they are always and inescapably situated at the imaginary level and thus must be set aside by the analyst' (Fink, 1995, p. 86). To say that these feelings are 'situated at the imaginary level' is to suggest that they are always a misrecognition, rather than an indication of the feelings or unconscious of the patient. For Lacan, the unconscious is revealed not through affect, but through symbolic relations. This distinction, then, has potentially significant methodological implications for the possibility of exploring the unconscious outside the clinical setting.

In simple terms, the theoretical conflict is over whether it is ever possible to know the thoughts and feelings of another person.[1] Outside the clinical or research contexts we may sometimes have the impression that we know what someone else is thinking or feeling: often this occurs when we know the other person well; and sometimes we have opportunities to 'confirm' our impressions with the object of our fantasy. Such confirmation is pleasurable: 'I *knew* you were thinking that too!', 'I *knew* you would be embarrassed!', 'I *knew* you were hating it!' At times the clinical relationship may mimic this apparent recognition between intimates. What is at issue is the status of this 'recognition'. Is it the result of some kind of a unconscious communication based on the technically skilled attention of the analyst? Or, alternatively, are teachings of psychoanalysis directly opposed to this mystical claim? Lacan teaches us that these moments of apparent knowledge of the other are situated at the level of the imaginary, a misrecognition or idealization of our relationship to an other; such an experience may be based on our everyday, identifiable experience of the other, and thus can be traced in the realm of the symbolic; but these feelings should never be understood as an ineffable or mystical connection, a transfer of unconscious affect between two subjects.

The emphasis on the analytic training, and the construction of Freud's 'evenly suspended attention' as a 'means to catch the drift of the patient's unconscious with his own unconscious' might be interpreted as a mystifying, exclusionary position, based more on the need to maintain the boundaries of a professional specialism than on a specificity of the practice. However, as Janet Malcolm has pointed out, psychoanalysis is no different from any other discipline in requiring training in order to develop fluency in its specialized vocabulary (Malcolm, 1986, pp. 25–26). The Lacanian perspective does not deny the importance of psychoanalytic training in constructing an appropriate relation between analyst and patient. But Lacan shifts the emphasis of the training from the analyst's receptiveness to affect to the analyst's duty to disrupt imaginary recognitions. This is achieved by focusing on symbolic relations, the associative aspects of language that are missed in rationalist, linear approaches to interpretive work. From this perspective, Freud's claim to be able to 'catch the drift of the patient's unconscious with his own unconscious' might be understood as a claim about leaving the rationalist confines of dominant discourse, rather than as some kind of mystical interchange between subjects. This interpretation seems to be consistent with Freud's foregrounding of symbolic relations in *The Interpretation of Dreams*.

The Lacanian shift of emphasis from the affective to the symbolic register, then, has significant implications for methodological practice, both within the clinic and within research. For Lacan, the prioritization of affect belongs in the imaginary order, an order of misrecognition of the subject as a complete, knowable entity, rather than an entity instantiated in a web of symbolic relations. In order to believe that I have direct access to some sort of truth, about myself or about another being, I must ignore the complex symbolic associations that structure every aspect of my being. The imaginary position, though, is very seductive: it allows us to cover over complex, difficult and irresoluble aspects of subjectivity. Rosa Burgos, whose work will be explored later in this chapter, describes the distinction between the symbolic and the imaginary in this way:

> The symbolic shares with the imaginary register the form of signification; however, it differs from the latter in that the imaginary operates as that which conceals the open-ended character of the symbolic. The imaginary compensates for the gap that forever shows that all symbolic registers are structured by a constitutive lack, something that is missing, and paradoxically exceeding the system, something escaping symbolization, that is, the real.
>
> (Burgos, 2000, p. 89)

From a Lacanian perspective, we are caught within the imaginary order when we fail to recognize the (in)significance of our position and the essential incompleteness of the symbolic order of discourse. Or, in Zizek's words, *'fantasy is a means for an ideology to take its own failure into account in advance'* (1989, p. 126, italics in original). This failure is the impossibility of representation, of knowing, of capturing the real within discourse. The real is the excess that escapes symbolization: that which constitutes a lack within our subjectivity, and also a lack in our knowledge of the other. Within this framework, any impression we might have that our feelings can provide us with knowledge of the other is necessarily a misrecognition.

The concept of overdetermination – central to both Freud's interpretation of dreams and Laclau and Mouffe's theory of discourse – foregrounds the role of symbolic relations in the production of social and psychical symptoms. Interpretation, then, must also foreground symbolic features. This suggests a need for scepticism with respect to the significance of affective experience as evidence of an unconscious, psychical force. However, it also suggests the need for some elaboration of what might constitute symbolic relations and perhaps an initial technical vocabulary to support the interpretation of associations between symbolic elements.

The interpretation of dreams, the construction of symbolic associations and the processes of condensation and displacement

For Freud, then, a dream is constituted in the associations produced within the analysis of the dream. At the same time he acknowledges the uncertainties surrounding the claim that all of the associations articulated in the analysis 'played a part in the formation of the dream'. He gives 'limited assent' to the suggestion that some associations produced in the analysis constitute 'new trains of thought' that weren't present in the original night-time instantiation of the dream. However, he suggests that this doubt can be overcome, and 'one can convince oneself' that all of the associations produced in the analysis, 'were already linked in some other way in the dream-thoughts':

> In view of the very great number of associations produced in analysis to each individual element of the content of a dream, some readers may be led to doubt whether, as a matter of principle, we are justified in regarding as part of the dream-thoughts all the associations that occur to us during the subsequent analysis – whether we are justified, that is, in supposing that all these thoughts were already active during the state of sleep and played a part in the formation of the dream. Is it not more probable that new trains of thought have arisen in the course of the analysis which had no share in forming the dream? I can only give limited assent to this argument. It is no doubt true that some trains of thought arise for the first time during the analysis. But one can convince oneself in all such cases that these new connections are only set up between thoughts which were already linked in some other way in the dream-thoughts. The new connections are, as it were, looplines or short-circuits, made possible by the existence of other and deeper-lying connecting paths. It must be allowed that the great bulk of the thoughts which are revealed in analysis were already active during the process of forming the dream; for, after working through a string of thoughts which seem to have no connection with the formation of a dream, one suddenly comes upon one which is represented in its content and is indispensable for its interpretation, but which could not have been reached except by this particular line of approach.
>
> (Freud, 1958, pp. 384–385)

In this extract, Freud appears to vacillate between confident assertion and methodological doubt. Perhaps it is simply rhetoric. Perhaps he is only conceding momentarily to pre-empt his critics. Nevertheless, there is an acknowledgement of an underlying methodological question about the status of free associations in relation to dreams. What are these associations instances of? Are they articulations of random thoughts, unrelated to the patient's dream? Or are they, as Freud suggests, 'new connections ... between thoughts which were already linked in some other way in the dream-thoughts', and, as such, suggestive of 'the existence of other deeper-lying connecting paths'? These are basic methodological questions that resonate beyond the conceptualization of dreams. They affect the theorization of overdetermination within psychoanalysis and also the recontextualization of the concept into social theory and discursive analysis. The familiar inversion which suggests that research is a process of construction rather than one of discovery offers a kind of instantly gratificatory way out of the methodological impasse (i.e. the analysis constructs an understanding of dreams as part of a complex symbolic system, rather than discovering this system as an entity that pre-exists the analysis) but does not help us to engage with the more complex question of what it is that constitutes a methodologically convincing construction.

The technical language Freud offers us to support his interpretation of separate elements as interconnected associations can be summarized as the processes of condensation and displacement. However, these processes incorporate the multiple complex instantiations of associations between symbolic elements. These include etymological features, geographical or historical contiguities, the linguistic tropes of synonymy, homonymy, metaphor and metonymy, and many other axes of similarity or opposition that might give rise to a psychical association between elements. These are conceptualized by Freud as processes by which meanings are attached to and transferred between different elements, instances or signifiers.

The example of 'The May-Beetle Dream', which Freud presents in *The Interpretation of Dreams*, can be used to illustrate the way in which Freud's account rearticulates associations produced in clinical sessions. The analysis suggests the complexity of the chains of meaning evoked in the associations, the nature of the condensation of these meanings within the dream content, and the ways in which elements which appear as central in the chains of associations are displaced in the apparently central images or narrative of the dream content.

The dream itself is quite brief:

> She called to mind that she had two may-beetles in a box and that she must set them free or they would suffocate. She opened the box and the may-beetles were in an exhausted state. One of them flew out of the open window; but the other was crushed by the casement while she was shutting it at someone's request. (Signs of disgust)
>
> (1958, p. 395)

Freud's account of his analysis of the dream presents a complex chain of associations moving from the events of the evening when the patient had the dream, when she had felt sorry for a moth that had fallen in a tumbler of water, to other incidents of cruelty to animals drawn from books she had read, from memories of her own childhood and from incidents when her daughter was younger and had been cruel to insects. These initial associations in turn lead to reflections on contradictions between appearance and character, and again Freud's patient moves between instances taken from novels and books to instances from her own life. Interwoven into these associations are several references to (the patient's) sexual desire and (masculine) sexual potency.

'The May-Beetle Dream'

Content of the dream:

> *She called to mind that she had two may-beetles in a box and that she must set them free or they would suffocate. She opened the box and the may-beetles were in an exhausted state. One of them flew out of the open window; but the other was crushed by the casement while she was shutting it at someone's request. (Signs of disgust)*

Analysis:
Her husband was temporarily away from home, and her fourteen-year-old daughter was sleeping in the bed beside her. The evening before, the girl had drawn her attention to a moth which had fallen into her tumbler of water; but she had not taken it out and felt sorry for the poor creature next morning. The book she had been reading during the evening had told how some boys had thrown a cat into boiling water, and had described the animal's convulsions. These were the two precipitating causes of the dreams – in themselves indifferent. She then pursued the subject of *cruelty to animals* further. Some years before, while they were spending the summer at a particular place, her daughter had been very cruel to animals. She was collecting butterflies and asked the patient for some *arsenic* to kill them with. On one occasion a moth with a pin through its body had gone on flying about the room for a long time; another time some caterpillars which the child was keeping to turn into chrysalises starved to death. At a still more tender age the same child used to tear the wings of *beetles* and butterflies. But to-day she would be horrified at all these cruel actions – she had grown so kindhearted.

The patient reflected over this contradiction. It reminded her of another contradiction, between *appearance* and character, as George Eliot displays it in *Adam Bede*: one girl who was pretty, but vain and stupid, and another who was ugly but of high character; a *nobleman* who seduced the silly girl, and a working man who felt and acted with true nobility. How impossible it was, she remarked, to recognize that sort of thing in people! Who would have guessed, to look at *her*, that she was tormented by sexual desires?

In the same year in which the little girl had begun collecting butterflies, the district they were in had suffered from a serious plague of *may-beetles*. The children were furious with the beetles and *crushed* them unmercifully. At that time my patient had seen a man who tore the wings off may-beetles and then ate their bodies. She herself had been born in *May* and had been married in *May*. Three days after her marriage she had written to her parents at home saying how happy she was. But it had been far from true.

The evening before the dream she had been rummaging among some old letters and had read some of them – some serious and some comic – aloud to her children. There had been a most amusing letter from a piano-teacher who had courted her when she was a girl, and another from an admirer *of noble birth*.

She blamed herself because one of her daughters had got hold of a 'bad' book by Maupassant. The *arsenic* that the girl had asked for reminded her of the *arsenic pills* which restored the Duc de Mora's youthful strength in [Daudet's] *Le Nabab*.

...

She was living in a perpetual worry about her absent husband. Her fear that something might happen to him on his journey was expressed in numerous waking phantasies. A short time before, in the course of her analysis, she had lighted among her unconscious thoughts upon a complaint about her husband 'growing senile'. The wishful thought concealed by her present dream will perhaps best be conjectured if I mention that some days before she dreamt it, she was horrified in the middle of her daily affairs, by a phrase in the imperative mood which came into her head and was aimed at her husband: 'Go and hang yourself!' It turned out that a few hours earlier she had read somewhere or other that when a man is hanged he gets a powerful erection. The wish for an erection was what had emerged from repression in this horrifying disguise. 'Go and hang yourself!' was equivalent to: 'Get yourself an erection at any price!' Dr Jenkins's arsenic pills in *Le Nabab* fitted in here. But my patient was also aware that the most powerful aphrodisiac, cantharides (commonly known as 'Spanish flies'), was prepared from *crushed beetles*. This was the drift of the principal part of the dream's content.

The opening and shutting of *windows* was one of the main subjects of dispute between her and her husband. She herself was aerophilic in her sleeping habits; her husband was aerophobic. *Exhaustion* was the chief symptom she complained of at the time of the dream.

[1958, pp. 395–398]

Freud does not precisely explain the source of the associations he presents in the analysis of 'The May-Beetle Dream', but it appears that his account reconstructs the main features of the patient's associations following from the dream, while also drawing on some instances from her analysis prior to the presentation of the dream. In his account he uses italics to indicate the 'points at which one of the elements of the dream-content reappears in the dream-thoughts' (ibid., p. 398). However, it is also possible to extract some of the chains of associations constructed within Freud's analysis and to explore the ways in which they instantiate instances of condensation of meanings within the dream content. I have extracted four chains of associations to explore in this way.

1   *Cruelty to animals and concerns about her husband's aging and sexual potency:* suffocation/crushing of may-beetle in the dream – daughter asking for arsenic to kill butterflies – arsenic pills in a Daudet story used to 'restore youthful strength' – a thought instructing her husband to 'Go and hang yourself!' – reading that 'when a man is hanged he gets a powerful erection'.

Here, the first association is from the dream to another instance of cruelty to animals. This association has the structure of metonymy: where the word for a part comes to represent the whole. The dreamer's memory of her daughter's action is represented in the dream by one feature of the event, her cruelty to animals. The second association is based on the word arsenic, deployed in two different contexts. This might be understood as a relation of homonymy, one word connoting two different meanings: arsenic meaning death to butterflies in the memory of her daughter, but 'youthful strength' or potency in the Daudet story. The final associations relate the meaning of arsenic in the context of the story to the dreamer's husband. Here there is a longer chain of associations from the image in the dream, through the connotations associated with 'arsenic' to the dreamer's thoughts about her husband and sexual potency. Freud's analysis suggests that all these meanings are condensed into the image of the may-beetles in the dream.

2   *Contradictions between appearance and reality:* daughter's cruelty to animals when she was younger, contradicting her (apparent) kind-heartedness now – contradictions between appearance and character in George Eliot novel – contradiction between the dreamer's own appearance and her sensual desires – contradiction between what she wrote to her parents just after her marriage and the true situation.

The associations in this chain are based on analogous instances of contradictions between appearance and reality. The contradiction is not just part of the dream thoughts, but is also present in several oppositions within the dream: the opposition between setting the beetles free and the danger that they may suffocate; the opposition between the freed beetle and the beetle that is crushed in the window; and perhaps in the opposition between the dreamer's own agency and her obedience to the unnamed voice requesting that she shut the window. There is, then, a metaphorical relation between these associations, in that they share the characteristic of contradiction between appearance and reality. The meanings elicited in the chain of associations are condensed into the contradictory images in the dream.

3 *May-beetles, 'crushing may-beetles' and sexuality:* two may-beetles in
   the dream – plague of may-beetles when her daughter was a little girl –
   children crushing may-beetles – man tearing wings of and eating may-
   beetles – aphrodisiac prepared from crushed beetles.

In this instance, associations are produced between the suggestions of
cruelty to may-beetles in the dream and earlier experiences of danger,
cruelty or disgust in relation to may-beetles. Again, there are metonymic
links between the elements, with the image of the crushed may-beetles in
the dream standing in for the dreamer's other memories. The final association produces another aspect of the image of the crushed may-beetle, its
potentially aphrodisiac qualities. This sensuously and affectively laden
element in the chain of associations is hidden, displaced in the process of
condensation that produces the dream content.

4 *Exhaustion:* the may beetles in the dream 'were in an exhausted state'
   – 'Exhaustion was the chief symptom which she complained of at the
   time of the dream'.

This shorter chain can nevertheless also be understood as an instance of
the condensation of meanings in a chain of associations. The dreamer's
exhaustion, which Freud suggests had been the object of her complaints at
the time of the dream, is projected onto the may-beetles, and thus condensed into the image of the may-beetles in the box. This condensation of
meaning into an element within the dream also allows for the displacement
of the psychical intensity attached to her discussion of 'exhaustion' within
her analysis.

Within Freud's account of 'The May-Beetle Dream', then, associations
are constructed through homonymy, metonymy, and analogy or metaphor,
and through the re-attribution of feelings to elements within the dream.
Through this process, meanings that appear significant in the chain of associations are displaced, and either disappear or appear insignificant within
the content of the dream. The direct reporting of affect is also a feature of
Freud's account: 'disgust', 'blame', 'worry', 'fear', 'horror' and 'torment'
all appear as descriptions of the patient's responses. References to sexual
desire also appear throughout Freud's narrative. These instances of affect
and desire are not methodologically significant on their own, but they take
on a significance when analysed as instances of displacement within the
construction of the dream. The key theoretical question does not concern
the nature of the affect reported in the associations, but rather the nature
of the force driving their displacement within the dream. What can we
infer about the nature of this powerful hidden force from our observation
of the displacement of affect in the chain of associations?

Perhaps all we can infer, in this instance at least, is the way the force
makes use of symbolic associations to produce the dream content. If we

invert this suggestion, we get something very close to Lacan's formulation: 'language is the condition of the unconscious' (Lacan, 2007, p. 41). The unconscious only exists insofar as it can be interpreted through the symbolic relations of language. The other aspect of the unconscious we may be able to infer is a relation to the position of affect within discourse, since the condensation of meanings through symbolic associations has a simultaneous effect of displacing or covering over affect. The unconscious or 'still unknown' psychical force impels the expression/suppression of affect by means of linguistic associations.

So, it might be possible to use Freud's account of his interpretation to develop a sense of the position of the psychical force within the processes of condensation and displacement that overdetermine the dream content. However, there are significant ethical and methodological questions about Freud's construction of specific chains of association in his analysis of 'The May-Beetle Dream'. The reflections or methodological doubts Freud articulated about the possibility of claiming that all of the associations produced by the patient are necessarily a part of the dream-work, are pertinent here. How can Freud be sure that each of the associations elicited in his patient's talk is related to the production of the dream content? It is difficult to disentangle the extent to which Freud may be listening attentively to his patient or, alternatively, imposing his own theories of dreams and sexuality onto the material that she produces, in order to construct an illustration of those theories. At the same time, the associations Freud's patient produces may also be a response to her expectations of what her doctor was likely to find of interest.[2] These are serious considerations, and are not dissimilar to issues related to the counter-transference, and the unconscious demands that each party to the analysis makes on the other.[3]

To reiterate, the aim of this chapter is to compare instantiations of concepts within contrasting methodological approaches. Research practice within the field of discourse theory foregrounds a conception of overdetermination that rearticulates the mechanisms of association that Freud develops in his analysis of the dreamwork to explore instances of social and political change. In discussing the work of David Howarth and Rosa Burgos in the following sections, I have tried to keep in mind a series of questions. What form do the mechanisms of condensation and displacement take in the interpretation of different kinds of question and in relation to different sources of data? What is the object of interpretation in each example? Why might it be productive to theorize something like a 'psychical force' to explain each instance? And also, since for Freud it is the observation of displacements of psychical intensity that suggests an unconscious psychical force, how might it be possible to infer some sense of 'psychical intensity' within contrasting instances of empirical data?

Empirical analyses of overdetermination within discourse theory

The 'nodal point' within discursive political analysis: 'blackness', 'democracy' and 'non-racialism' in South African political discourse

Laclau and Mouffe's theory of discourse conceptualizes symbolic relations as a material aspect of the social terrain. This brings the analysis of symbolic associations within the realm of social and political analysis: not simply as a rhetorical tool of political actors, but as an instantiation of the substantive political landscape and an articulation of complex political subjectivities. Empirical work in the field of discourse theory explores politics and political identities as constituted within shifting chains of signification produced through complex networks of symbolic associations. Political arguments and policy decisions are analysed as contextually situated discourses, rather than as abstracted rational processes, and discourses are understood as constitutive of concrete social practices and institutions, rather than as distinct thought processes external to the practices that they describe.

This shift to a methodological practice that explores the political field as a product of overdetermining symbolic relations can be seen in David Howarth's work on political movements in South Africa (1997, 2000a).[4] Howarth maps the discursive context of political movements in South Africa between the 1976 Soweto uprisings and the 1986 declaration of a national state of emergency. He explores the main political groupings of the time and asks why the Black Consciousness Movement failed to establish 'blackness' as a hegemonic signifier, a nodal point that might unite diverse elements of resistance against the Apartheid regime. His analysis suggests how it might be possible to refine the meaning of 'nodal point' or 'empty signifier'[5] in the context of political change.

Howarth's analysis has two stages. First, he sets out to challenge dominant, negative interpretations of the Black Consciousness Movement (BCM) in South Africa. This stage of his analysis establishes the BCM ideology as a coherent strategic response to a complex political moment. The second stage of Howarth's argument asks the question: given the coherence and subtlety of the BCM ideology, why did it fail to cohere a politics of resistance to the Apartheid regime? And in what significant ways did the discourse of the BCM differ from the more successful Charterist discourse of the African National Congress (ANC) and the United Democratic Front (UDF)?

In his article 'Complexities of identity/difference: Black Consciousness Ideology in South Africa' (1997), Howarth develops an interpretation of the Black Consciousness Movement (BCM) in South Africa as the enactment of a complex symbolic rearticulation of black identity within the specific discursive context of 1960s and 1970s South African politics.

He opposes this interpretation to dominant readings in accounts produced in both academic and activist literature. He suggests that these accounts decontextualize the ideas developed in the BCM, representing them as advocating a simplistic 'blacks only' ideology that can be traced to previous separatist ideologies developed within pan Africanism and the Black Power movement in the US; as an 'apolitical' identity politics that 'failed to address the material interests of its target constituencies' (p. 52); or as a form of 'inverse racism'. Howarth's alternative reading situates the writings of Steve Biko and the South African BCM as a strategic response to specific discursive moves within South African policy at the time: most notably, the moves to divide opposition to Apartheid by offering limited institutional positions within the political system to specified ethnic groups. Howarth suggests:

> Biko's opposition to the 'working within the system' strategy centres on the immediate political dangers of being differentially incorporated into the institutions of domination, thus dividing black resistance to the system as a whole and forcing it into 'sectional politics'.
>
> (p. 57)

Thus separatist vocabulary within the South African BCM should be understood not as an abstracted, universal claim but as a strategic response to 'immediate political dangers'. In addition, Howarth traces within the writings of Biko and other BCM activists a complex reconceptualization of 'blackness', 'integration', 'non-racialism' and a 'true humanity' that counters liberal simplifications of the concrete experience of racial difference. This analysis challenges representations of Black Consciousness ideology as decontextualized rhetoric, naive identity politics or 'simple inverse racism'.

What this does is to establish the coherence of the BCM ideology, and its apparent appropriateness as a response to the specific political conditions within which it emerged. Howarth's detailed analysis of the writings of Biko and other BCM leaders demonstrates that theirs was a conscious discursive strategy aiming to shift the meaning of 'blackness', 'integration' and 'non-racialism' within South African politics. However, this conscious strategy failed, and Howarth uses this failure as an instance through which to explore the hegemonizing function of political signifiers, their potential to act as empty signifiers that are able to 'perform the totalizing function of linking together the elements of the system' (Howarth, 2004, p. 268). He says:

> We need now to account for the fact that the BCM, which was the leading political force at the time, was unable to reinscribe the Soweto dislocation in its own terms, thus failing to become the major opponent of the new order of domination.
>
> (2000a, p. 172)

The empirically oriented question is: why did the Black Consciousness Movement fail to hegemonize political resistance in South Africa? The theoretically oriented question is: What drives the establishment of an empty signifier capable of hegemonizing a political field? Or, as Howarth puts it 'a question is raised as to *how* the empty signifier can perform this function' (2004, pp. 268–269).

In his later paper 'The difficult emergence of a democratic imaginary: Black Consciousness and non-racial democracy in South Africa' (2000a), Howarth provides a detailed account of the interrelating contextual forces surrounding the failure of the BCM ideology after the Soweto uprisings. These include structural constraints, strategic conflicts and the failure of the BCM discourse to cover over conflictual cultural and psychological identifications. At the structural level Howarth identifies: 'the BCM's inability to incorporate working class interests and demands' (p. 172); 'leadership difficulties'; and 'structural weaknesses in the BCM's organizational infrastructure' (p. 173). These organizational difficulties were exacerbated by state repression and 'extensive implementation of apartheid by a powerful regime intent on eradicating any radical resistance to its programme' (p. 178). However, these failures at a structural and organizational level might be said to illustrate, rather then to explain, the failure of the BCM discourse to take hold politically. Howarth suggests we need to look further for an explanation of 'the movement's failure to become a surface of inscription able to register a series of demands and interests much broader than its initial form of articulation' (p. 173).

Howarth argues that the BCM was successful in constituting a positive, mythical image of blackness: 'a mythical image of black unity and identity that was rooted in a retrospective construction of a black historical past unsullied by the arrival of white settlers with their dominating logics of colonialism'. However, a difficulty with this construction was that 'the signifier of blackness in the philosophy and discourse of Black Consciousness could not conceal its manifest ambiguities' (p. 175). Howarth elaborates:

> It was not clear whether blackness referred to a common experience of racial oppression under white domination, or whether it designated a peculiarly African consciousness and sensibility … or whether it signified a more general Third-Worldist rejection of Western imperialism and colonialism.

> (p. 175)

Howarth suggests that none of these meanings articulated with the complex political and psychological subjectivity of Coloureds under Apartheid. It was suggested by sympathetic Coloured activists that to identify with the Black consciousness as '"merely" a political movement' was not sufficient 'to provide the psychological identity they sought' (Gerwel, cited in Howarth, 2000a, p. 176), while the demand to identify with 'a peculiarly African consciousness' was interpreted as 'demanding a shedding of all coloured, that is White, Western or European values and customs' (Gerwel, cited in Howarth). Howarth suggests that: 'To become 'black' for Coloureds in South Africa meant the renunciation of an ethnic, cultural or even national identity and a consequent experience of loss and dislocation not compensated for by the new discourse' (p. 176).

Similar difficulties were encountered in the attempt to address some Indian groups. Conflicts arose that were, Howarth suggests, 'testimony to the continued salience of ethnic identification, as well as the difficulties of erasing particularistic forms of identification, and replacing them with new forms of "universality"' (p. 176). In addition, the exclusion of whites caused strategic and ethical difficulties for the BCM: they could not make use of strategically positioned white supporters of resistance, and they opened themselves to the charge of inverse racism.

This combination of structural and discursive weaknesses overdetermined the failure of the BCM resignification of 'blackness' in unifying a politics of resistance. Howarth's data reveals political and cultural identities that could not cohere under the BCM discourse. In addition, the analysis suggests that the articulatory strategies proposed by the BCM were not sufficient to displace the complex emotions relating to particularistic subjective identitifications. Perhaps it might be possible to suggest that, in relation to the BCM signifier 'blackness', the psychical intensities attached to elements or identities within the discursive chain stayed put.

In contrast, the political discourse articulated in support of the ANC's 'Freedom Charter' by the United Democratic Front (UDF) was successful in mobilizing a popular democratic movement against the Apartheid regime. While the UDF, like the BCM, was criticized for failing to properly represent the interests of the working class (Howarth, 2000a, p. 180), it managed to engage the support of the unions and avoided oppositional exclusions of other established political groupings. While this drew the criticism that 'the UDF was nothing more than an "ad hoc organization consisting of many ad hoc committees and organizations reacting to one thing and another"' (ibid., p. 183), it proved an effective hegemonising strategy. The Charterist reactivation of an idea of 'non-racialism', placed alongside calls for a movement of 'the people' for 'national democracy', provided signifiers that were able to articulate the dispersed demands of different groupings. Howarth concludes:

> While Black Consciousness was ambiguous about who constituted the South African nation and people, the UDF stressed that *all* South Africans who were against apartheid could be part of the South African nation, and they drew a set of equivalences along these lines. Moreover, while Black Consciousness was unclear about its over-all political programme, the signifier 'democracy' in Charterist discourse was

able to include all social classes, and was able to accommodate numerous concrete interpretations of the nature of democracy itself.

(p. 185)

The interesting theoretical question raised by the contrasting fortunes of
these two political discourses is how the UDF signifiers of 'democracy' and
'non-racialism' came to function as nodal points, able to congeal a political
movement, while the BCM discourse of 'blackness' failed to achieve this.
Neither discourse addressed contentious class antagonisms, while the key
signifiers in both discourses connote an abstract, utopian unity that might
act to conceal subjective and political divisions, and to displace affective
intensities. Howarth's analysis suggests that structural and organizational
factors are not sufficient to account for the ability of a discourse to hegemonize a political field. It was the extent to which each discourse was able to
contain the ambiguities inherent within dispersed signifiers that determined
their potential as a hegemonic site of political identification.

In order for a signifier to constitute a nodal point, to cover over the structural incompleteness of a symbolic system, its potential for ambiguity must
match the contingent elements of the discourse it will initiate. The same, of
course, must be true of the nodal points within a dream. A hegemonic political discourse is constituted, like a dream, through a complex network of
symbolic relations to express a dispersed collection of interests and ideas.

The overdetermination of 'theory' as a signifier in educational policy and curricula

In an article in the *International Review of Education* (1999) Rosa Burgos
explores the changing position of 'theory' as a signifier in educational
policy and curricula. To do this she traces the condensation of meanings
across international policy, educational research and higher education curricula, presenting a series of instances that, she suggests, illustrate a tendency to 'underplay the significance of theoretical work' in official policy
documents, funding recommendations and curriculum guidance (p. 463).
Her analysis suggests that the meanings of 'theory' within these instances
can be understood as produced through processes analogous to the dreamwork: the significance of certain ideas is displaced through processes which
condense multiple, dispersed chains of meanings into the signifier of
'theory'. The signifier 'theory', she argues, comes to be permeated with
meanings such as 'not getting your hands dirty', 'not being real', 'ideological', 'indirect' and 'distant' from real educational problems. The 'non-
theoretical', cleansed of these meanings, appears as 'natural' and able to
offer 'the "direct" exploration and solution of "immediate and imperative
educational needs." ' (p. 463).

Burgos maps this discursive context through a series of instances
produced through psychical and symbolic processes analogous to the

dreamwork. For example, she describes a schooling plan developed for Latin American countries, which presents precise models for curriculum content and teaching methods. Underlying the plan, Burgos suggests, is an adherence to behaviourist theories of learning, a highly contentious and affectively laden area of debate within educational theory. However, the antagonisms associated with this theoretical approach were not made explicit within the plan, the contents of which were presented as 'the *natural* discourse of the field' (p. 463). An analogy can be drawn with processes of displacement in the production of a dream, where significant elements within the dream thoughts are hidden from view in the dream content. Here, as in dreams, it may be argued that details that appear as insignificant or as having little psychic intensity may in fact be covering over the most intense psychical or political forces: the plan presents curricula and teaching methods as uncontroversial, covering over heated professional and academic debates surrounding these practices.

Three further instances are drawn from the contrasting contexts of international organizations, Mexican national policy and an academic congress. Burgos points out that since the 1970s the agenda of international organizations has prioritized 'cost–benefit analyses, planning and taxonomies of objectives' over serious consideration of educational research. She quotes a UNESCO report that dismisses social theories as 'abstract schema' and recommends abandoning such theories in order to concentrate on 'real problems' (p. 463). A similar sentiment is traced in Mexican national policy on research funding. Burgos describes how funding bodies 'drastically reduced grants for graduate studies in the humanities' and simultaneously promoted positivistic, quantitative and statistical research in the social sciences. Perhaps more surprisingly, the final contextual example Burgos cites is the Mexican National Congress on Educational Research. She quotes from documentation for the 1992 event where it was suggested that 'theory ought to be postponed for the educational graduate curricula'. She also notes that the 1997 Congress Proceedings did not include any papers relating to the philosophy or theory of education. These instances map out a discursive context within which theory is repeatedly displaced and there is an assumption that knowledge about education should be transparent and pragmatic.

In addition, Burgos suggests that this discursive tendency resonates with a shift within the field of educational research. Where early studies in education and pedagogy were closely associated with philosophy, she suggests that 'at some point, speculation became degraded' (p. 468). She suggests that a new epistemological framework emerged within which 'education' was seen as the object of quantitative research aiming at 'reliable levels of predictability'. She relates this shift to a 'yearning for an education utopia' (p. 468) and an 'illusion of immediacy and transparency' (p. 470), both of which can be associated with the ideals of the Enlightenment:

I consider pedagogy and/or educational theories as a field that has been disturbed both by the very failure of the early Enlightenment project and paradoxically, by the predominance achieved by the positivistic tradition in the social sciences, which appeared as the very solution to the loss of legitimacy the field was undergoing.

(p. 469)

This depiction of the ongoing resonance of Enlightenment ideals and the promise of positivistic solutions constitutes a link between the dispersed instances Burgos has described, which, taken together, comprise the discursive context for a more localized case study.

This case study, the instance Burgos explores in most detail, traces the development of the curriculum for doctoral students in an education department of a Mexican university from 1975 to 1998. She describes the shift in the position of theory within the curriculum for research students. This shift was instantiated in several ways: in the reformulation of course aims from prioritizing the attainment of 'theoretical competence' to 'research competence' and finally to 'empirical research competence'; in the increase in time allotted to activities for apprenticing students into research practice, as opposed to theoretical and methodological seminars; and in the movement of theoretical seminars from compulsory to the optional components of the taught doctoral programme. As a result, Burgos suggests, 'a course in epistemology was no longer considered a basic qualification for becoming a researcher working in the area of knowledge production' (p. 467).

A bizarre element of this story is that these changes took place in the education department of an eminent university, whose staff represented a wide range of theoretically grounded research practices, including specialisms in Piagetian psycholinguistics, Bourdieu's sociology, psychoanalysis, ethnography, historical research and discourse analysis. Burgos reports that the decisions that resulted in the marginalization of theory within the curriculum were preceded by 'interesting and well informed collegial discussions' (p. 467). The withdrawal of theory from the core curriculum juxtaposed against a body of theoretically oriented academic staff is, perhaps, similar to the anomalous juxtapositions to be found in the content of dreams.

The discursive processes involved in the constitution of this apparently anomalous curriculum development within the education department can be traced, Burgos argues, in the wider discursive context of international and national policy. However, they can also be traced in more localized institutional pressures within the university over the length of time doctoral students were taking to complete their studies:

Overshadowing these discussions, however, were intense 'official' pressures. For example, one cannot overlook the pressure exercised by the educational hierarchy in the department – and other authorities within the university – to reduce the time between the completion of the taught-course portion of the programme (two years) and the completion of the thesis. Nor should one underestimate national and regional process which characterized theoretical interests as a waste of time.

(p. 467)

Burgos' analysis suggests that the identification of the departmental concern over completion rates with the need to reduce the theoretical component of the courses is an instance in a discursive chain that produces 'theory' as a signifier loaded with negative associations. 'Theory' thus comes to carry the burden of departmental problems that might have been dealt with through alternative means:

> Other possibilities could have been explored such as examining why students were taking so long to finish their dissertations (perhaps the overwhelming standards imposed by the department); organizing collegial discussions concerning the different 'uses' of theory and whose responsibility was the fact that 'students got lost in a theoretical stratosphere' (could it be the responsibility of theory?); and exercising alternative ways to bridge the gap between theoretical tools and educational demands.
>
> (p. 472)

These 'other possibilities', it seems, were not explored. The act of selection, Burgos argues, is thus obscured, and the withdrawal of theory as a core component of research training is 'represented as a necessary outcome of a course of action' (p. 471).

Burgos' account thus traces symbolic resonances across dispersed instances of policy and curricula, to show how meanings associated with 'practical solutions to immediate educational problems' congeal with a notion of 'direct engagement with practice', while notions of 'time wasting', 'obscurity' and 'irrelevance' are deposited onto the signifier 'theory'. These chains of meaning intersect with institutional discourses of accountability and the imperative for students to complete their theses more quickly, so that the solution that emerges is not to develop new approaches to supporting students or to reconsider the standards expected of doctoral work, but rather to displace theory from its central position in the production of new knowledge. 'Theory' thus emerges as a nodal point of dis-identification for a range of political interests that require immediate solutions to institutional and educational problems. Underlying this, Burgos' analysis suggests, is a desire to shed uncertain and ambivalent aspects of the policy process and to distance the process from explicit affiliations, theoretical or ideological commitments, which seem to bear particularly vulnerable aspects of responsibility and potential failure. 'Theory', from the perspective of Zizek or of Laclau and Mouffe, comes to stand in for the structural lack in the symbolic system, the impossibility of finding policy solutions to interminable social antagonisms. This allows the construction of a fantasy of policy as 'practical', 'direct' and potentially able to cure social ills.

In Lacanian terminology we might suggest that an ideal of a pragmatic, direct, policy solution is constituted as the object cause of desire, the *objet petit a*. This is not desire itself, but the representation of desire within language: the object that promises satisfaction but is destined to disappoint. As Glynos and Stavrakakis explain:

> The harmony, however, promised by fantasy cannot be realized; the *objet petit a* can function as the object-cause of desire only insofar as it is lacking. As soon as we buy the product we find out that the enjoyment that we get is partial, that it has nothing to do with what we have been promised: ' "That's not it!' is the very cry by which the *jouissance* obtained is distinguished from the *jouissance* expected'.
>
> (2004, p. 210)

This disappointment, Lacan suggests, specifies the limits of language (Lacan, 1998, p. 111). Desire appears as a force beyond language that drives the flow of meaning across the elements in the signifying chain, but that cannot be captured within language. The nodal point temporarily covers over this gap, concealing the openness of the symbolic order and the inadequacy of language to articulate desire. It is worth noting that there is a shift in the conceptualization of the nodal point here, from the Freudian emphasis on the expressive, or 'articulating' function of key signifiers to a more Lacanian emphasis on the essential lack within language, and the 'empty' aspect of the signifier (Laclau, 2004, p. 322). In its expressive aspect, 'theory' articulates a series of political and institutional interests; in its empty aspect, the signifier 'theory' covers over the impossibility of the desire articulated in idealised political and managerial objectives.

Conclusions: methodological continuities and discontinuities

I have suggested that Freud's conceptualization of the analyst's 'evenly hovering attention' might be understood as a way of attending to elements that connote symbolic relations outside the linear narratives of a dominant discourse. The work of both Burgos and Howarth might be understood in this way, as attending to associative tugs against dominant narratives. Howarth pays attention to a sense of something missing in dominant readings of the BCM that construct the movement's failure as a result of internal weaknesses in its ideology. Burgos notes dissonant elements within a trend that foregrounds the negative aspects of theory in policy and curricula, displacing its more positive connotations. Both draw attention to the way in which apparently coherent accounts cover over a set of more complicated relations, and they pose questions that invert the obviousness of what they are seeing.

In both cases, the dominant discourse is unsettled by the construction of a symbolic juxtaposition. Howarth juxtaposes the discourses of two organizations in the same political moment, and asks: how is it that they had such divergent historical trajectories? Burgos juxtaposes policy discourse with an instance of curriculum development and asks: how is it that the moves within these contrasting discursive settings seem so similar? In posing these questions, they are following threads that lead away from a taken for granted narrative, in a way that is at least partially continuous with Freud's method of dream analysis. However, where Freud's analysis of dreams traces these threads through a chain of elements in the analysand's talk within the clinic, Burgos and Howarth both construct chains of associations through historical, biographical and policy related documents. This constitutes a limit on the empirical basis for the theorization of symbolic connections within the discursive chain. It is worth pausing to consider the contrasting affordances of these methodological approaches.

As a starting point, it is possible to note three related shifts in the move from the clinical interpretation of the dream to the discursive interpretation of policy: there is a shift in what constitutes an association; there is an adjustment in the role of the analyst/researcher in setting a limit on what counts as an association, or what constitutes data that it is possible to interpret as an association; and there is a narrowing of the focus of the interpretive work. In his methodological reflections in the interpretation of dreams Freud asserted that it is possible to regard all of the associations that occur during the analysis as active in the production of the dream (1958, p. 384). This position takes the judgement of the individual analyst out of the decision of what can or cannot be counted as an association. Of course, this is not completely the case: as we saw in 'the May-Beetle Dream', the analyst makes judgements about which associations from earlier sessions are pertinent in the interpretation of the dream under consideration; and the clinical context in which the free associations emerge is produced through the professional knowledge and judgement of the analyst. Nevertheless, there is a relatively contained set of associations that are the object of the analyst's interpretive work. In contrast, it is the work of the discourse theorists to compile the set of material from which they are going to interpret discursive associations. In both these cases there is an ambiguity about the extent to which the association is understood to exist prior to the analysis. It seems slightly clearer in Freud's case: he understands the associations to have been 'already active during the state of sleep' and to have 'played a part in the formation of the dream' (1958, p. 384). In the case of the discourse analysts, the relation between the associations traced in documentary data and the object of enquiry – for Howarth the failure of the BCM; for Burgos the change in the doctoral curriculum – seems slightly less direct. It might be possible to say that the understanding of these discursive elements as associations is produced within the analysis, rather than being a characteristic inherent to the data prior to the analysis. Thus, in discourse analysis the role of the analyst/ researcher appears, in some specific ways, to be more active in constituting and conceptualizing the data as a set of associated discursive elements. This shifts the nature, and the timing, of the constraints in the interpretive process. While Freud's patients' accounts initiate multiple associative chains and leave many threads hanging loose, both Burgos and Howarth focus in on the nodal points within a pre specified discursive formation. This may in part relate to the mode of presentation: academic articles are necessarily tidy articulations of messy interpretive processes. However, this closing down of directions for interpretive work may be inherent to the discourse analytic process, with its weighting towards the interests of the researcher, and it may thus constitute a limit on possible accounts of over-determination produced within the field.

Ultimately, this contrast might be understood as the difference between a process of free association in which the discursive elements are produced by a subject in relation to, but other than, the analyst; and a process whereby discursive associations are collated by the analyst in response to a particular question that emerges prior to the investigation. Although the body of the analyst acts as a constraint in the production of the artefact of free association within the clinical relation, the analyst is necessarily, I think, a more conscious and directive presence in the selection of data within a research project. This might, though, be an idealization of psycho-analytic practice. Inevitably, the specific instantiation of an 'evenly hover-ing attentiveness' will vary from case to case; it will vary from session to session within the process of an analysis; and it will vary across the differ-ent stages of a research project. Research settings might, from this perspec-tive, produce new ways of thinking about the technical production of free association and the meanings of 'evenly hovering attentiveness'.

The debates over technique and the method of free association that rage in the field of psychoanalysis are not evident in the field of discourse theory. While Freud's accounts often intertwine theoretical and technical considerations, there tends to be far less elaboration of the relation between theory and technique in currently published work within the field of discourse theory (Critchley and Marchart, 2004; Howarth *et al.*, 2000, Howarth, 2000b). David Howarth suggests that discourse theory uses a variety of qualitative methodologies to generate and collect empirical data (Howarth, 2000b, p. 140). These include the use of published and unpub-lished documents, and also participant observation and in-depth inter-views. He suggests that 'discourse analysts have to be sensitive to the theoretical postulates governing their research practice' (ibid., p. 140), but does not elaborate the technical implications of this relation between 'theory' and 'method'. Perhaps it is because of the range of methods it incorporates that the field is unified more through its theoretical vocabulary than its articulation of a specialized set of techniques.

It is certainly possible to argue that the lack of a specified methodology can make it difficult to distinguish analyses drawing on Laclau and Mouffe's discourse theory from other forms of ethnographically informed discourse analysis. I have argued that a Lacanian conception of the unconscious is implicit in Laclau and Mouffe's conception of discourse, and this psychoanalytic element distinguishes their approach from other discursive methodologies. Glynos and Stavrakakis (2004) have gone further, arguing for a fuller incorporation of Lacanian notions of fantasy and *jouissance* into discursive methodologies drawing on Laclau's work. Perhaps the theoretical vocabulary should be understood more as an orientation to analysis than as a limitation on methods of generating data. Laclau and Mouffe's conceptualization of discourse might be said to open up, rather than to close down, methodological possibilities for political analysis. It might also be said to open up, rather than to close down, understandings of what might constitute a psychoanalytic, or a psychoanalytically informed methodology.

Finally, it may be useful to reiterate the similarities in the position of affect and psychical force within the contrasting methodologies. It is possible to distinguish, in both Freud and in the work of the discourse theorists, two psychical or affective constructions. The first is the affective intensity associated with the dream thought. In Freud's analysis of the May-Beetle Dream this is the explicitly articulated feelings of disgust or desire that are displaced in the dream content. Howarth's study has a parallel to this in the account of the way Coloured and Indian identities could not be accommodated under the signifier of 'blackness', which suggests that the political effect of a discourse is dependent on its potential to displace affective attachments. So while sexual desire is displaced in the manifest content of the May-Beetle Dream, the discourse of the BCM was not able to displace the affect associated with Indian or Coloured cultural identities. Howarth's account suggests that in order for a discourse to become hegemonic it must have the potential to displace or invert these instantiations of affect. The second psychical construction is the force or desire that drives the mechanisms of the dreamwork within both instances. While the affective intensity associated with the dream thought is empirically elaborated (the dreamer reports her affective responses; Coloured activists report the loss they feel at the prospect of being subsumed within a generalized 'black' identity) the psychical force or desire that drives the flow of meanings and intensities through the chain of linguistic associations is a more speculative construction.[6] We come to understand this force only through the condensations and displacements that punctuate the signifying chain.

Freud argued that in order to understand dreams we need to foreground the symbolic relations, the networks of signification, within which the dream elements are situated. This initial conceptualization of a complex web of signification that overdetermines psychical symptoms is crystallized in Lacan's articulation of the Symbolic Order that captures, constrains and enables social activity. For both there is an additional psychical force that energizes the churning flow of meaning across the signifying elements of the symbolic system. For Freud, at some points, this force can sometimes be understood as a 'psychical agency in the mind', but in Lacan, the psychologistic distinction between internal and external that this suggests is broken down in his conceptualization of the unconscious as brought into being in the act of symbolization.

Lacan's rearticulation of Freud's interpretation of symbolic relations within the dreamwork provides a conceptual tool for expanding the application of Freudian theory to explore social and political relations through the analysis of a wide range of discursive material. The nodal point or 'master signifier', the 'battery of signifiers' that are already there (Lacan, 2007, p. 13), the psychical force and a divided subjectivity are all present *within* a Lacanian conception of discourse: discourse holds these elements in a tense and unstable relation to each other. So language, which Lacan describes as the material support for discourse (1957, p. 163), can be understood as necessarily instantiating the kinds of unconscious symbolic relations that from a traditional psychoanalytic perspective are brought into view through the process of free association, in jokes, or in slips of the tongue. This makes it possible to explore the relations between dispersed instances of data as constitutive of a complex web that condenses meanings and displaces psychical intensities across chains of signifiers. This shift in methodology also facilitates a de-individualization in the conceptualization of psychic processes, foregrounding the discursive field as the site of symbolic relations and psychical intensities.

3 Textures of resistance
'Discourse' and 'psyche' and 'the compulsion to repeat'

Introduction: the opposition between 'discourse' and 'psyche'

I want to begin with Derrida's nostalgic reflection on the notion of 'resistance'. The chapter as a whole focuses more on the conceptualization of resistance in the work of Freud, Foucault, Butler and also Lacan, but Derrida's delicate and reflexive account in *Resistances of Psychoanalysis* (1998) has helped me to develop an understanding of these other theorists. He begins with an account of his own attachment to an idea of resistance, saying that for him 'the word "resistance" does not play just any role'. He talks about his love for the word and associates this affection with the specific meanings the word connotes in French, which, he suggests, cannot be translated:

> This word, which resonated in my desire and my imagination as the most beautiful word in the politics and history of this country, this word loaded with all the pathos of my nostalgia, as if, at any cost, I would like not to have missed blowing up trains, tanks and headquarters between 1940 and 1945 – why and how did it come to attract, like a magnet, so many other meanings, virtues, semantic or disseminal chances? I am going to tell you which ones even if I cannot discern the secret of my inconsolable nostalgia – which thus remains to be analyzed or which resists analysis, a little like the navel of a dream.
>
> (Derrida, 1998, p. 2)

Derrida evokes an attachment to an emancipatory notion of resistance as an organized campaign of action aimed at the intentional overthrow of a political regime. Yet, as he suggests, the term 'resistance' holds many other meanings. He draws our attention to the impossibility of interpreting his nostalgic associations, suggesting that his account might itself be interpreted as a form of resistance. The sense of nostalgia for a lost moment of agentic, organized resistance is articulated in relation to post-structuralist and psychoanalytic thought, where resistance takes on a meaning closer to that given within the physical sciences: 'the opposition offered by one body to the pressure or movement of another' (O.E.D, 1983). This evokes a sense of the material oppositional force that arises when differentiated physical bodies come together, rather than an intentional or agentic resistance to political regimes or ideologies. Derrida's reflection brings together these different senses, placing the excessive, 'inconsolable' aspect of his attachment as an unfathomable centre or origin for his fascination with the term.

The conceptualization of resistance within the work of Michel Foucault might perhaps better be understood within the paradigm of the physical sciences, rather than within a paradigm of intentionality. For Foucault resistance is a force within discourse, rather than a force within the subject. This force appears within the material structure of discourse and acts in opposition to the regimes of power that constitute the objects of discourse. For Foucault, then, resistance is politicized, in that it constitutes possibilities for the resignification of hegemonic discourses, but is de-politicized in so far as he negates the role of an intentional, agentic subject. Psychoanalytic conceptions of resistance within clinical practice can also be interpreted as constituting the individual as passive object, rather than active subject of resistance. However, where for Foucault resistance is a discursive force that acts in opposition to dominant discursive structures, within psychoanalysis resistance is a psychical or unconscious force, and what is resisted is therapeutic knowledge offered in the process of analysis. So there is a similarity in that both frameworks constitute resistance as a refusal of knowledge; but there is also a sense of a concept with very different textures: for Foucault resistance is constituted in the materiality of discourse; in psychoanalytic frameworks, resistance is constituted in the material of the psyche.

The alternatives of 'discourse' versus 'psyche' can appear as an intractable theoretical, methodological and political opposition. The reduction of everything to discourse can appear as a denial of significant forces that need to be differentiated from totalizing structures of discursivity, while the insistence on the psyche can appear to relegate resistance to an inaccessible, individualized unconscious, ignoring other spaces from which changes in knowledge or discursive structures might emerge.

The argument of this chapter is not intended to privilege either 'discourse' or 'psyche' as site of resistance, but rather to foreground resonances between the two conceptual frameworks.[1] There is, within both frameworks, a notion of repetition inscribed within an instance of resistance. In Foucauldian approaches this is the parodic, subversive repetition of the categories of the hegemonic discourse; while within psychoanalysis the reiteration of unconscious patterns constitutes the subject's resistance to knowledge of the self. By foregrounding resonances between these two theorizations of resistance as repetition, I hope also to put into question the clarity of the distinction between the two frameworks. I am arguing for the productivity of thinking hard about the meaning of the repetitions that seem to emerge in the analysis of data. We might think of instances of repetition as having distinct textures, and we might think of notions of 'discourse' or 'psyche' as ways of beginning to think about these differing textures.

Another way of putting this might be through the notion of play or playfulness. There is, I would like to think, something playful in my argument that there is no difference, or little difference, in the conceptualization of resistance in Freud and Foucault. I am not trying to be overly respectful to their oeuvres. Rather, I am trying to think through the implications of their contrasting conceptualizations for empirical analysis – and I want to see where we get to if we decide that there is no significant difference between them; if we construct a perspective from which the repetitions attributed significance within psychoanalysis cannot be distinguished from the repetitions to which significance is attributed in Foucauldian discourse analysis. The methodological questions that might follow for empirical researchers within the social sciences are, first, how might we recognize an instance of repetition/resistance, and, second, what is the productivity of conceptualizing such an instance as either 'discourse' or 'psyche'?

In order to do this the first half of the chapter sets out in some detail first Freud's and then Foucault's conceptualizations of resistance. In these first sections I try to explain both the position of repetition within each, and the way the two theorists make a connection between instances of repetition and a notion of either 'psyche' or 'discourse'. I also draw on the work of Judith Butler, who has explored similar territory, suggesting that Foucault's account of discursive repetition leaves questions that might be answered through the conceptualization of a psychical aspect of power. The first half of the chapter closes with an account of an empirical study that engages with both discursive and psychical interpretations of resistance. Alex Moore's (2004, 2006) research into teachers' responses to policy initiatives is used to explore the different textures of resistance that emerge in the analysis of empirical data.

The second half of the chapter advocates a more reflexive use of notions of resistance within research. I suggest that the persistent attachments, the 'discursive' or 'psychical' repetitions that we might interpret within our data, are also evident within the process of analysis. Lacan suggests that 'there is only one resistance, the resistance of the analyst' (1991, p. 228). This formulation repositions resistance, shifting away from a concern with the site of resistance within the psyche to an understanding of resistance within the practice of analysis, and thus of the relation between resistance and interpretation. For Lacan, the interpretation of resistance reveals as much about the discursive positioning of the analyst as it does about the subject. This reflexive inversion is not only instructive for psychoanalysts interpreting within the clinic, but also for researchers in their interpretive work with empirical data. The final section of the chapter explores Lacan's reflexive suggestion, and closes with an account of Alice Pitt's (1998) analysis of the resistances within her research practice. Pitt's analysis reveals how her interpretation of her participants' resistance was constituted through her own reiterations of political and disciplinary affiliations.

It seems to me important for us to play with conceptualizations of resistance and repetition, 'discourse' and 'psyche'; and equally important for us to reflect continually on the resistances that emerge within our own practice.

Freud's conceptualization of resistance and/as the compulsion to repeat

In chapter 3 of *Beyond the Pleasure Principle* (1920) Freud begins discussing resistance and ends talking about the compulsion to repeat. Freud begins by describing how the aims of psychoanalysis have developed as the effects of interpretation within therapeutic practice failed to conform to his initial expectations. He suggests that initially there was no expectation that the patient might put up a resistance to the physician's interpretation, and it was only through practice that he began to recognize what came to be understood as resistance:

> Twenty-five years of intense work have had as their result that the immediate aims of psychoanalytic technique are quite other to-day than they were at the outset. At first the analyzing physician could do no more than discover the unconscious material that was concealed from the patient, put it together and, at the right moment, communicate it to him. Psychoanalysis was then first and foremost an art of interpreting. Since this did not solve the therapeutic problem, a further aim quickly came in view: to oblige the patient to confirm the analyst's construction from his own memory. In that endeavour the chief emphasis lay upon the patient's resistances: the art consisted now in uncovering these as quickly as possible, in pointing them out to the patient and inducing him by human influence ... to abandon his resistances.
>
> (p. 288)

Freud makes some complex moves in this caricature of early psychoanalytic practice. As Freud presents it, the work of the analyst initially focused on interpreting the patient's associations in order to 'discover the unconscious material that was concealed from the patient'. This constructs a gap between the interpretation and the patient: a gap that was thought to be overcome at a conscious level by the analyst communicating their discoveries in order to effect a cure. However, Freud suggests, when this approach proved unsuccessful, the patient was brought in to the process of analysis, and asked 'to confirm the analyst's construction from his own memory'. A distinction is introduced between the patient's memory and the resistance, and the memory becomes a site of the repressed 'unconscious material'. The resistance is thus constituted as that which obstructs the patient's memory. So we have, initially: the concealed material as interpreted by the analyst; the patient's memory that is necessary to confirm the analyst's interpretation; and the resistance, which blocks the patient's memory. The analyst's task is still to interpret the unconscious material but also to inter-pret the resistances,[2] and to 'point them out' to the patient, who, once aware of their resistance, will be able to 'abandon' it.

This initial development in the conceptualization of resistance, however, seems simply to push the difficulty in bringing about a cure back one stage: instead of persuading the patient of the nature of the repressed material, it was now necessary to persuade the patient of the nature of their resist-ances. Freud tells us that this method was no more successful than the initial approach in helping the patient to recognize the repressed material (ibid., p. 288). However, Freud's observations lead him to speculate further and to formulate a second aspect of resistance:

> The patient cannot remember the whole of what is repressed in him, and what he cannot remember may be precisely the essential part of it. Thus he acquires no sense of conviction of the correctness of the con-struction that has been communicated to him. He is obliged to *repeat* the repressed material as a contemporary experience instead of, as the physician would prefer to see, remembering it as something belonging to the past.
>
> (p. 288)

Freud reports that when the patient is not persuaded by the analyst's inter-pretation, rather than remembering the repressed material, the patient 'repeats' it. He goes on to explain that the repetition is 'invariably acted out in the sphere of the transference, of the patient's relation to the physician' (p. 289). This repetition within the clinical relationship constitutes a second mode of resistance, less explicit, perhaps, than the denials and avoidances that can also signal a patient's resistance to progress within analysis.

In the clinical setting, Freud suggests, the enactment of repetitions is facilitated by the relation with the physician in the ongoing treatment which will have 'loosened the repression' that may block the expression of the compulsion to repeat (p. 290). This constitutes a distinction between the act of repetition within analytic relationship and the compulsion to repeat. The compulsion to repeat is theorized as ever present, awaiting the appropriate conditions in which to find a means of expression. These con-ditions might arise – or, invariably will arise – throughout the patient's life. Freud notes that this kind of repetition is not confined to the neurotic, suggesting a range of instances where repetitive and unpleasurable patterns can be observed in people's relationships. On the basis of this he concludes: 'Enough is left unexplained to justify the hypothesis of a compulsion to repeat – something that seems more primitive, more elementary, more instinctual than the pleasure principle, which it overrides' (p. 294).

With the theorization of a compulsion to repeat unpleasurable relationships, the analytic context can be reconceptualised as a safe, controlled environment in which the compulsion to repeat can be both enacted and, eventually, recognized and transformed. Freud says:

> The physician cannot as a rule spare his patient this phase of the treatment. He must get him to re-experience some portion of his forgotten life, but must see to it, on the other hand, that the patient retains some degree of aloofness, which will enable him, in spite of everything, to recognize that what appears to be reality is in fact only a reflection of a forgotten past.
>
> (p. 289)

Importantly, then, the compulsion to repeat constitutes the resistance, or a resistance, to knowledge and to change. The analyst, in Freud's account, brings about a repetition that parodies or subverts the repetitions the patient has been locked into throughout their life. This parodic repetition introduces an ambiguity into the object of resistance: what was initially conceptualized as resistance to the analyst's interpretation might also be understood, within the clinical context, as a resistance, or a potential resistance to the unconscious compulsion to repeat.

An underlying question within Freud's theorization of resistance is the relation between the ego and the unconscious and the role of each in the production of resistance. Initially he equates the unconscious with the repressed and suggests that the unconscious 'offers no resistance whatever to the efforts of the treatment'. He identifies resistance with the ego, which he suggests contains 'the higher strata and systems of the mind' (p. 289). However, his recognition of the difficulty of overcoming resistance through conscious engagement at the level of the ego and of the re-emergence of resistance within the transference leads him to rethink the relation between the ego and the unconscious. He acknowledges that while all of the repressed is unconscious, the unconscious is not limited to the repressed. He suggests, perhaps somewhat warily, that aspects of the 'coherent' ego must also be unconscious, saying: 'A part of the ego too – and Heaven knows how important a part – may be *Ucs.*, undoubtedly is *Ucs*' (1923, p. 18).

In *Beyond the Pleasure Principle* he maintains a distinction between resistance, which he associates with the ego, and the compulsion to repeat, which, he says, 'must be ascribed to the unconscious repressed' (p. 290). Later on, however, in the addenda to 'Inhibitions, Symptoms and Anxiety' (1926), he concedes that the compulsion to repeat might itself be described as a resistance:

It must be that after the ego-resistance has been removed, the power of
the compulsion to repeat – the attraction exerted by the unconscious
prototypes upon the repressed instinctual process – has still to be overcome. There is nothing to be said against describing this factor as the
resistance of the unconscious.

(pp. 159–160, italics in original)

It seems that there is something significant at stake for Freud in the attribution of resistance to the ego alone; an attachment that has to be given
up to make room for the possibility that resistance might be situated in
the unconscious. One object of this attachment, Freud suggests, is the
meaning and precision of his conceptual schema. He seems to regret the
loss of the clarity of his concept, noting: 'The characteristic of being
unconscious begins to lose significance for us. It becomes a quality which
can have many meanings' (1923, p. 18). However, it may be that the
placement of resistance beyond the coherent ego, and beyond the conscious agency of the subject requires Freud to overcome his attachment to
other ideas or ideologies. The theorization of the compulsion to repeat as
a 'resistance of the unconscious' that is both beyond the ego and more
than the repressed, attributes an agency to the unconscious that challenges the autonomy or agency of the ego. Can the rational, coherent ego
control the unconscious compulsion to repeat? This question raises the
problem of agency and puts into question the possibility of reasoning
with resistance: it is a question that is equally relevant in both the clinical
context and in more political or sociological conceptualizations of
resistance.

I want to note two significant strands in Freud's articulation of the relation between resistance and the compulsion to repeat. The first of these is
the conceptualization of repetition as potentially able to subvert that which
it repeats. There are, I think, traces of this idea in a Foucauldian conception of resistance. The second significant strand is the conceptualization of
the compulsion to repeat as a force distinct from an instance of repetition.
Derrida has suggested that the compulsion to repeat offers the possibility
of unifying the disparate conceptual and methodological categorizations of
resistance,[3] describing it as 'the thread of the irreducible resistance' (1998,
pp. 22–23). However, he also suggests that this most abstracted notion of
resistance 'has no meaning'. He reflects:

The paradox that interests me here is that this repetition compulsion,
as hyperbolic paradigm of the series, as absolute resistance, risks
destroying the meaning of the series to which it is supposed to assure
meaning (this is an effect of formal logic, in a certain way, as I noted a
moment ago) but still more ironically, it defines no doubt a resistance
that *has no meaning* – and that, moreover, is not a resistance.

(ibid., p. 23)

The idea of the repetition compulsion as 'hyperbolic paradigm' recalls, for me, the inaccessible excess connoted in Derrida's account of his nostalgic attachment to the word 'resistance' (ibid., p. 2). In the same paper, Derrida refers to Freud's discussion of the 'navel' of a dream: 'a tangle of dream thoughts which cannot be unraveled', 'the spot where it reaches down into the unknown' (Freud, 1953, cited in Derrida, 1998, p. 14). The methodological question that Derrida raises, as I understand it, is whether this navel is simply a resistance, which might be overcome – and he cites Freud's claim that having overcome various resistances in the meantime, he can now interpret his early dreams more effectively than he could when he first wrote about them (ibid., p. 16) – or whether this navel constitutes an irreducible limit to analysis. Derrida's reflections on the repetition compulsion a few pages later raise similar questions: is the repetition compulsion available to interpretation; or is it a remainder, an irreducible trace that is beyond the interpretive process (and thus not a resistance)? Indeed, the cycle of reiterations of the same question within Derrida's account might itself be interpreted as an instantiation of the same compulsion that he is trying to understand.

Resonances and discontinuities between Foucault's conception of resistance and Freud's compulsion to repeat

Freud's account of resistance, then, develops a range of images of competing forces: the ego pitted against the interpretations of the analyst (resistance of the ego); the unconscious also pitted against change or progress within the analysis (the compulsion to repeat, or the resistance of the unconscious); and the ego, having once given up its resistances, pitted against the unconscious compulsion to repeat. Similar images are conjured in interpretations of Foucault's conceptualization of resistance: subject, body and psyche are theorized as forces constituted both within and against (or destroyed by) discourse. Ongoing discussions over how to interpret Foucault's accounts can be understood in terms of these images, or as series of questions: How does Foucault conceptualize the body? How does Foucault conceptualize the subject? Are the body and the subject wholly inscribed through discourse? Is resistance sited in a body or psyche that exceeds discourse? Or is resistance a reiterated category within discourse that shifts the relations within which it is constituted? Foucault's writing, of course, leaves room for multiple interpretations of his ideas in relation to these questions.

Theorizing the subject of resistance in/to discourse

It is difficult to begin to understand the conceptualization of resistance in Foucault's work without some sense of his account of the subject and of the production of the subject in discourse. At the end of the first chapter of

Discipline and Punish (1977) Foucault states emphatically that there is no 'real man' who is displaced by the effects of power; instead man is 'already in himself the effect of a subjection much more profound than himself' (p. 30). In general it appears that for Foucault this effect, 'man' or the subject, is produced within discourse, without reference to a bodily or psychical excess beyond discursive power relations. From this perspective, resistance appears to lack a subject, and is constituted instead in repetitions that re-signify the terms of subjectivating discourse. However, slippages or ambiguities in Foucault's account provide grounds for interpretations that foreground continuities with Freud's conceptualization of resistance and the compulsion to repeat as extra-discursive psychical phenomena. These readings explore the possibility of a pre- or a non- discursive origin of resistance that occupies a similar conceptual space to Freud's compulsion to repeat, the resistance of the unconscious. However, it is important to distinguish interpretations suggesting that Foucault reinstates a naturalized body or individualized subject from more sophisticated interpretations that explore Foucault's nominalist use of language as a place-holder for an a-rational, uncategorizable force that Spivak describes as a 'subindividual preontic substance'[4] (Spivak, 1993, p. 32; see also Hoy, 2004; Butler, 1997).

In Foucault's analysis of the shifting relation between the body and the subject there is a tension between a sense of a totalizing discursive construction and a more essentializing language that might appear to reinstate both body and subject as a universal or pre-discursive force. One of the main arguments of *Discipline and Punish* is that within the modern state, body and subject are no longer unified as the object of punishment. The classic opening of the study contrasts the bodily punishment of a regicide in 1757 – '*the flesh will be torn from his breasts, arms, thighs and calves with red-hot pincers...*' (p. 3) – with the rehabilitative rules of a 'house of young prisoners' eighty years later – '*At twenty minutes to eleven, at the drum role, the prisoners form into ranks and proceed in divisions to the school...*' (p. 6). Foucault argues that this change in penal practice constitutes a change in the meaning of both subject and the body:

> But the punishment-body is not the same as it was in the torture during public executions. The body now serves as an instrument or intermediary: if one intervenes upon it to imprison it or to make it work, it is in order to deprive the individual of a liberty that is regarded both as a right and a property. The body, according to this penality, is caught up in a system of constraints and privations, obligations and prohibitions. Physical pain, the pain of the body itself, is no longer the constituent element of the penalty.
>
> (p. 11)

Where once there had been no distinction between subject and body, so that punishment of the disobedient subject was identified with punishment of the body, in modernity the body is produced as 'an instrument or inter-mediary' through which to act on the individual, now constituted as a dis-embodied 'soul'. This argument suggests the body is produced as a meaningful entity in relation to a state or penal system. A system where the individual is engaged directly through the flesh produces a different body to a system in which the body is constituted through regulative practices that disassociate the individual from their material being. However, when Foucault says 'the body now serves as an instrument', 'the body ... is caught up in a system of constraints', or when he talks about 'the pain of the body itself', 'the body', in the position of grammatical subject, is con-jured as a universal essence that prefigures its instantiation within a discur-sive regime. The linguistic slippage into a discourse that appears to naturalize the body while articulating an argument against the naturalized body creates a tension in Foucault's argument.

A less ambiguous kind of essentializing trace is suggested in Foucault's account of power and its relation to the subject. He describes power as the effect of the strategic positions of the 'dominant class', not something that is possessed, but something that is manifested within or through those who are dominated:

> In short this power is exercised rather than possessed; it is not the 'privilege', acquired or preserved, of the dominant class, but the overall effect of its strategic positions – an effect that is manifested and some-times extended by the position of those who are dominated. Further-more, this power is not exercised simply as an obligation or a prohibition on those who 'do not have it'; it invests them, is transmit-ted by them and through them; it exerts pressure upon them, just as they themselves, in their struggle against it, resist the grip it has on them.
>
> (pp. 26–27)

In this extract Foucault constructs and then subverts an image of the subject as wholly constituted through the effects of power. Power, he says 'invests' those who are dominated, and 'is transmitted by them and through them'. This produces an image of the subject as a medium for rela-tions of power. At the same time he constructs an image of the subject, or the position of the subject, as exerting a resistant force. First he suggests that power can be extended 'by the position of those who are dominated'. It seems clear here that the paradigm is still one within which possibilities are determined by relations of power: the 'position' of the dominated can 'extend' but not create the effects of power. The second image of a resist-ant force is more ambiguous: Foucault suggests that those who are domi-nated 'struggle against' power and 'resist the grip it has on them'. Where does this resistance come from? This might be read as reinstating an auton-omous subject free of the relations of power and discourse. It is possible to interpret a contradiction here, a failure to live up to the constructivist implications of his analysis.

Alternatively, as Spivak has suggested, we might interpret these 'slip-pages' in Foucault's account as a self-conscious acceptance of the impossibility of escaping the terms given within language. Spivak reminds us of Foucault's assertion of the 'need to be nominalistic' (Foucault, 1979, p. 93), i.e. the need to use words in a way that is not indicative of a corresponding object or reality, and she goes on to explore the impossibility of maintaining a pure nominalist position within an ideology of language that presumes that a name must have an empirical referent (Spivak, 1993, p. 27). Thus, she suggests, even an explicitly nominalist use of words is always 'cracked and barred' by two senses: a 'narrow' sense of an implied empirical referent; and a 'general' sense that connotes a realm or a substance that is not reducible to the word (p. 28)[5]. From this perspective, Spivak suggests, Foucault's use of substantives that appear to contradict his repudiation of a naturalized body, subject, or power might be seen as a deliberate catachresis, a paradoxical application of a word 'to a thing that it does not properly denote' (O.E.D, 1983).

The slightly crude opposition between constructivism and essentialism displaces the detail and specificity of Foucault's account of the subject and the body as 'directly involved in a political field' (Foucault, 1977, p. 26). This suggests that whatever the essence of the body, it is always brought into being through the specific practices of a particular regime. Foucault enumerates the processes through which the political field shapes the body:

> power relations have an immediate hold upon it; they invest it, mark it, train it, torture it, force it to carry out tasks, to perform ceremonies, to emit signs. This political investment of the body is bound up, in accordance with complex reciprocal relations, with its economic use; it is largely as a force of production that the body is invested with relations of power and domination; but, on the other hand, its constitution as labour power is possible only if it is caught up in a system of subjection ... the body becomes a useful force only if it is both a productive body and a subjected body.
>
> (pp. 25–26)

The account suggests both the ritualized shaping of the body in 'tasks', 'ceremonies', and the emission of 'signs', but also the economic and political shaping of the body, as, simultaneously, a productive unit and subjected 'labour power'. Foucault depicts the body as a complex element of a system through which it is both subjugated and invested with its own productive power. Judith Butler calls this the 'double valence of subordinating and producing', whereby subjection, she says, 'signifies the process of becoming subordinated by power as well as the process of becoming a subject' (1997, p. 2).

The account of the subject as product of a double movement of subordinating and bringing into being leaves us with an uncertain conception of resistance. Is the subject only able to resist as an extension of discursive power relations? And if this is the case, do we need to theorize a psyche or body that is beyond discourse? Or can we account for this extension/subversion/resistance to discourse within discourse itself?

Resistance in the domain of discourse or the domain of the psyche

Foucault's account might be said to attribute epistemological priority to discourse, in the sense that his account opens a space in which the forces of body, power and resistance are only intelligible as exercised in the material of discourse. Thus, discourse is the instrument through which we might come to understand the exercise of power, but its discontinuous elements can disrupt as well as express relations of power. In his explicit theorization of resistance in the first volume of *The History of Sexuality* (1979) Foucault foregrounds multiplicity, irregularity and discontinuity. Instances of resistance, he suggests, do not share a form or an origin, they do not emerge with any regularity or in a consistent relation to subjects, groups of subjects, bodies or practices:

> there is no single locus of great Refusal, no soul of revolt, source of all rebellions, or pure law of the revolutionary. Instead there is a plurality of resistances, each of them a special case: resistances that are possible, necessary, improbable; others that are spontaneous, savage, solitary, concerted, rampant, or violent; still others that are quick to compromise, interested or sacrificial; by definition they can only exist in the strategic field of power relations. But this does not mean that they are only a reaction or rebound, forming with respect to the basic domination an underside that is in the end always passive, doomed to perpetual defeat. Resistances do not derive from a few heterogeneous principles; but neither are they a lure or a promise that is of necessity betrayed. They are the odd term in relations of power; they are inscribed in the latter as an irreducible opposite. Hence they too are distributed in irregular fashion: the points, knots, or focuses of resistance are spread over time and space at varying densities, at times mobilizing groups or individuals in a definitive way, inflaming certain points of the body, certain moments in life, certain types of behaviour.
>
> (ibid., p. 96)

Foucault's objection to the idea of a 'single locus of great Refusal' might be interpreted as a direct reference to the psychoanalytic conception of the unconscious as the site of resistance. Against this notion Foucault posits a multiplicity of instantiations of resistance that, despite being inscribed within relations of power, are nevertheless not 'doomed to perpetual defeat'. Just as strategies of power can only be perceived within discourse, so, Foucault suggests, multiple resistances emerge as oppositional forces *within* the determining parameters of power-knowledge. It seems that resistance can be constituted in this way precisely because of the discontinuities that characterize discourse. Foucault says:

> we must conceive discourse as a series of discontinuous segments whose tactical function is neither uniform or stable.... We must make allowance for the complex and unstable process whereby discourse can be both an instrument and an effect of power, but also a hindrance, a stumbling block, a point of resistance and a starting point for an opposing strategy. Discourse transmits and produces power; it reinforces it, but also undermines and exposes it, renders it fragile and makes it possible to thwart it.
>
> (pp. 100–101)

This formulation positions resistance within discourse. Discourse 'transmits and produces power' but also 'undermines and exposes it' and 'renders it fragile'. Resistance, then, can appear in multiple forms, it is constituted within the discontinuous segments of discourse, and its effects can be seen 'at varying densities', sometimes 'mobilizing groups or individuals in a definitive way', sometimes 'inflaming certain points of the body, certain moments in life, certain types of behaviour'. The political difficulty is to know whether or how it might be possible to influence or control this irregular and unpredictable resistance in any particular moment of domination. The difficulty in relation to empirical research is to say what might count as an instance of resistance, or, further, what might count as an instance where the gaps in discourse have allowed power to be thwarted.

Foucault does not, then, provide a definition of the form resistance might take or of how it might be recognized.[6] He does, however, provide multiple examples of discursive moves that might be interpreted as resistance to articulations of power relations instantiated in discourse. These examples can be interpreted as instances of repetition of segments of discourse that are constituted as centres of power-knowledge. Foucault argues, for example, that the body of the child comes under surveillance: 'surrounded in his cradle, his bed or his room by an entire watch-crew of parents, nurses, servants, educators and doctors, all attentive to the least manifestations of his sex' (p. 98). The definition of expressions of childhood sexuality as a 'vice' is initially articulated in the regulation of the behaviour of the child. However, Foucault suggests, this initial articulation of the nexus of concern around the child's body 'was subjected to constant modifications':

> Whereas to begin with the child's sexuality had been problematized within the relationship established between doctor and parents (in the

form of advice, or recommendations to keep the child under observation, or warnings of future dangers), ultimately it was in the relationship of the psychiatrist to the child that the sexuality of adults themselves was called into question.

(p. 99)

This modification in the discursive articulation of child sexuality as a centre of power-knowledge constitutes a radical shift, from child to adult as the site of aberrant sexuality. Resistance is instantiated in a repetition that maintains an insistence on the problematic of childhood sexuality, while modifying subject-object relations *within* this problematic.

A more explicitly politicized instance of resistance as discursive repetition is traced in the history of the category of 'homosexual'. Foucault argues that homosexuality was brought into being when it emerged within the discourse of psychology and medicine (p. 43). Constituted as a psychological or medical category, homosexuality became a form of sexuality, associated with 'a kind of interior androgyny', replacing the practice of sodomy, which had no ramifications for the sexual identity of the subject. However, this discursive segment can also undermine the power-knowledge nexus that brought it into being, and, Foucault argues, 'homosexuality began to speak on its own behalf':

There is no question that the appearance in nineteenth century psychiatry, jurisprudence, and literature of a whole series of discourses on the species and subspecies of homosexuality, inversion, pederasty, and 'psychic hermaphrodism' made possible a strong advance of social controls into this area of 'perversity'; but it also made possible the formation of a 'reverse' discourse: homosexuality began to speak in its own behalf, to demand that its legitimacy or 'naturality' be acknowledged, often in the same vocabulary, using the same categories by which it was medically disqualified.

(p. 101)

As Judith Butler notes (1997, p. 93), this repetition of the subordinating term does not subvert heterosexual norms: it does not call up the 'different economy of bodies and pleasures' that Foucault speculated might one day replace the 'austere monarchy of sex' described in his study (Foucault, 1979, p. 159). But neither is it merely an instrument of that austere regime. The effects of moments of resistance are unpredictable, and the interpretation of these moments as either 'efficacious insurrection' or 'painful resubordination' is likely to be unstable or inconclusive (Butler, 1993, p. 137; see also Hoy, 2004, p. 83). The repetitions of discourse that constitute the 'odd term' in relations of power may produce modifications within those relations, or they may simply be accommodated or co-opted within the existing regime.

In *Discipline and Punish* Foucault offers a similar range of interpretations of resistance. He argues that the category of 'delinquency', produced in the margins of the prison system, provided opportunities for resistance to the avowed juridico-legal regime. The organization of delinquency under the surveillance of the police enables the control, subjugation and also the exploitation of 'those who are liable to transgress the law' (1979, p. 272). Police supervision or surveillance of brothels, arms trafficking, drug trafficking or the sale of alcohol are instances whereby the control of delinquency helps to produce profits that filter through to the dominant classes (ibid., pp. 278–280; see also Hoy, 2004, p. 84). Thus categories produced through the penal system support the illicit activities that it claims to deplore, with the potential to disrupt the fragile balance of power within the disciplinary regime. A more intentional instance of resistance within the same discourse is the accusations of delinquency deployed by workers' newspapers against the bourgeoisie (Foucault, 1979, p. 288). Again, this is a discursive repetition that might perhaps shift the strong association of moral degeneracy with the poor, but that at the same time constitutes a risky reiteration of a subordinating category.

In each of these instances there is a repetition of a category inscribed within an existing disciplinary or discursive regime. The irreducible insistence of existing discursive elements within moments of resistance has resonances with the repetitions of the transference in psychoanalysis. In both cases the transposition of existing terms into a new context opens up possibilities for the resignification of subjugating categories. However, while Freud situates the compulsion to repeat in the realm of the psyche, for Foucault potentially subversive repetitions emerge wholly in the discursive domain. The prioritization of the discursive, or, we might say, the reduction of resistance to the discursive, raises serious political and methodological questions.

Here, again, Spivak's (1993) interpretation of Foucault's nominalism might suggest that his account of resistance as positioned within discourse maintains two senses that connote substances beyond discourse: an individualizing, intentional aspect that inheres in the linguistic heritage and that cannot be completely shed; and a subindividual, preontic substance that can only be connoted, but not directly named or referenced as such. This Derridean interpretation points towards an inaccessible, uninterpretable aspect in Foucault's conceptualization of resistance that might be aligned with Derrida's own discussion of the Freudian concept.

Judith Butler makes the link to psychoanalysis more explicit. In *The Psychic Life of Power* (1997) Butler asks the question: Why do we turn to meet the hail of discourse? Why do we repeat discursive categories? And, importantly, echoing Freud's disconcertion at the failure of the pleasure principle, why do we seem to be attached to our own subordination? She seeks the answer to these questions in psychoanalysis and in the concept of the unconscious. She distinguishes the subject from the psyche, suggesting that the psyche is defined by its inclusion of the unconscious. It is this psy-chical aspect that she argues is missing or suppressed[7] within Foucault's account of the subject.

The unconscious, Butler suggests, can be understood as 'whatever resists the normative demands by which subjects are instituted' (ibid., p. 86). This constitutes the unconscious as a remainder that resists, but that is also therefore defined by the discourses that bring the individual into being as a social subject. Butler suggests we can explain unconscious attachments to subjection in relation to this double valence of the unconscious: the primary unconscious attachment, she suggests, is a narcissistic attachment to the possibility of existence as a social subject. This complicates an account of the unconscious as that which resists normative demands, and instead, Butler speculates, suggests an unconscious that cannot be consti-tuted outside of power, 'something like the unconscious of power itself':

> Called by an injurious name, I come into social being, and because I have a certain inevitable attachment to my existence, because a certain narcissism takes hold of any term that confers existence, I am led to embrace the terms that injure me because they constitute me socially [...] As a further paradox, then, only by occupying – being occupied by – that injurious term can I resist and oppose it, recasting the power that constitutes me as the power I oppose. In this way, a certain place for psychoanalysis is secured in that any mobilization against subjec-tion will take subjection as its resource, and that attachment to an injurious interpellation will, by way of a necessarily alienated narcis-sism, become the condition under which resignifying that interpella-tion becomes possible. This will not be an unconscious outside of power, but rather something like the unconscious of power itself, in its traumatic and productive iterability.
>
> (p. 104)

It is, Butler argues, our attachment to the terms of our subordination, the ambiguous repetitions at the heart of resistance, that suggest the need for psychoanalytic perspectives to elaborate Foucault's account of power, dis-course and the subject. Her theorization of the unconscious of power as the mobilization of the terms of discourse against the discursive context in which they are produced, draws attention to the unconscious as a mode of attachment to being that is open to destabilization, as opposed to interpre-tations that foreground the unconscious as an inaccessible navel that is beyond interpretation.

From the perspective of empirical methodology, what is important is that that repetition is always in some way inscribed into resistance. For Foucault this repetition can, perhaps, be positioned within the complex relation between power and the discontinuous elements of discourse, but it might also be explained through a theorization of an unconscious that is tied to the production of the subject, as Butler has suggested, an unconscious that is somehow woven into the effects of power. Both of these accounts focus methodological attention on moments of repetition within discourse, in contrast to theorizations that look beyond discourse to that aspect of resistance that can only be glimpsed as an unknowable, inaccessible force.

Interpreting discursive and psychical repetition in an empirical study

Alex Moore's delicate analysis of teachers' responses to new policy initiatives (2004, 2006) explores the contrasting methodological implications of a more Foucaultian/sociological understanding of repetition within discourse and the psychoanalytic compulsion to repeat. Drawing on two interview-based projects investigating teachers' professional identities, Moore begins by tracing teachers' positioning within the contemporary discursive context and then shifts his analysis to some of the more personal, or idiosyncratic traces in participants' accounts. The first mode of analysis focuses on the discursive texture of reiterated categories; the second raises questions about a more psychical force or texture that might help to explain the persistence of these discursive repetitions. He suggests a need for both modes of analysis in order to develop more complex and reflexive understandings of professional practice, and he opens a space in which to theorize a relation between these contrasting interpretations or textures of resistance.

In the first stage of his analysis, Moore explores teachers' identities in relation to the opposition between 'traditional' and 'progressive' approaches to education. Moore's analysis suggests that identifications with 'traditional' or 'progressive' approaches have been superseded by a more pragmatic discourse within which the earlier dichotomizing positions are perceived as unhelpfully politicized, and as having had a negative impact on children's learning (2004, p. 127). This new pragmatic discourse is aligned, Moore suggests, with 'wider social and political agendas': shifts demanding greater accountability, instantiated in more centralized regulation of curricula and assessment and in the devolution of budgetary responsibility to individual schools. Moore refers to 'a recent avalanche of mandated educational reform which challenged or threatened much received wisdom and through which teachers had to navigate a path in such a way as to remain sufficiently comfortable with their own pedagogic practice' (ibid., p. 127). Teachers' foregrounding of pragmatism as a rationale for their professional practice can thus be understood as one means by which Moore's participants were able to constitute a relatively comfortable identity within a prevailing discursive context of effectiveness and accountability.

Within this dominant discourse of pragmatism Moore traces three modes of subjection within, or resistance to, the avalanche of new initiatives and policies. Responses by teachers who appeared to be most aligned with the new educational context articulated what Moore refers to as 'ideological pragmatism'. For practitioners positioned within this mode, Moore suggests, pragmatism had become a new orthodoxy, and the supposed depoliticization of education instantiated in approaches requiring objective measurement, standards and 'looking at the evidence' was understood to help in the identification of 'what works best for the kids' (Moore, 2004, p. 137). In a second category of responses, while not articulating a commitment to the broader ideology of contemporary educational policy, teachers avowed pragmatism in terms of an openness to adopt whatever approach worked best within their practice. This position was instantiated in what Moore calls a 'principled' adoption of specific approaches to classroom practice or policy initiatives. Teachers articulating a principled pragmatism suggested, for example, that a combination of traditional and progressive techniques that they had adopted, they said, on pragmatic grounds, might be considered as generally good educational practice (ibid., p. 135). The third mode constituted a position that seemed to be least closely identified with the prevailing educational orthodoxy. This mode, labelled 'contingent pragmatism', was instantiated in responses where participants justified their acceptance of new approaches in relation to a particular set of circumstances: the innovation was justified because of the particular pressures within the school just now, or because of the school's location, or the particularities of its intake. Moore suggests that teachers making these kinds of statements 'often feel constrained or resigned to be pragmatic, adopting pragmatism as a kind of coping strategy' (p. 132). Examples included teachers who had argued against the introduction of a new policy – setting by ability, for example, targets and the 'performance culture' – but, having lost the argument, found ways to justify the new system. Moore describes this as 'the temporary suspension of previously held values and philosophical or pedagogical orientations' (p. 132).

It is notable that all three modes involve some level of re-articulation of the dominant discourse of effectiveness and accountability. The effects of these repetitions are unpredictable: both principled and contingent pragmatisms leave potential spaces for modification of the monolithic discourse of governmentally imposed educational reforms; ideological pragmatism too, in its excessive adherence to the rationales of educational policy within the field of educational practice, constitutes a form of drag that might, potentially, reveal the constructed nature of the orthodoxy that it avows (c.f. Butler, 1990).

While not strictly Foucauldian, this first stage of Moore's analysis is consistent with Foucault's account of resistance as constituted within discourse. However, Moore is not satisfied that this account can fully explain the lack of more organized, politicized resistance, or capture the complexity of desire, transference and the compulsion to repeat in the positioning of individuals within the dominant discourse (Moore, 2006). His interview

data provides him with the means to explore these aspects of his participants' positioning – and his analysis of this data provides a focusing point
for some methodological questions in relation to the theorization of resistance and repetition. His exploration of these ideas in his analysis of two
cases suggests several possible ways of conceptualizing repetition in relation to discourse, the psyche and the compulsion to repeat.

The first case Moore discusses is that of Bill, an assistant principal in his
mid-fifties who had been teaching for nearly thirty years. Moore presents
Bill's account as an example of 'contingent pragmatism', illustrative of his
continuing ambivalence towards recent changes within his school, which
include a move away from mixed ability teaching and the introduction of a
compulsory school uniform. Bill had opposed these changes, but in the
interview he suggested that he had come to see that 'probably, overall,
[introducing uniform] was the right thing to do' (2006, p. 496). Within the
interview Bill spent some time justifying the school's decision, and in his
account there are traces of the dominant educational discourse: he suggests
the uniform was necessary to enhance the school's 'competitiveness', he
says that 'parents like it', that 'our intake has gone up' and that he thinks
the introduction of the uniform 'might lead to an improvement in exam
results'. Moore suggests that this 'elaborate defence' is indicative of his
'continuing lack of comfort with his personal shift of view' (p. 496). The
question Moore raises is why, given his discomfort with these policies,
does Bill come to the point of not just accepting, but defending them? In
order to explain this Moore explores what he suggests may be more psychical aspects of Bill's account.

In addition to the rationales he was now able to give for the new policies, Bill had explained his concurrence in relation to the open or democratic nature of the process by which the decision was agreed: 'I suppose
it's like the mixed ability thing: I'm willing to go along with whatever we
agree democratically' (p. 496). Moore suggests that this is indicative of the
way Bill described himself at other points in the interview:

> Bill sends out a clear message in reflecting on his initially reluctant
> support for school uniform and ability setting, that he did not want to
> rock the institutional boat: a position reflected elsewhere and repeat-
> edly throughout his interview, through references to himself as 'a
> pretty reasonable bloke', as 'liking to get on with everybody regardless
> of their educational views', as being 'a middle of the road sort of
> socialist', and (indeed) as 'not liking to rock the boat'.
>
> (p. 497).

Moore interprets Bill's repeated references to himself as a 'reasonable
bloke' who 'gets on with everybody' as a direct expression of desire, and
suggests that Bill's reassertions of his 'reasonable bloke' identity within the
interview, as well as his ambivalent acceptance of the new policies, might

be understood in terms of the Freudian compulsion to repeat. He suggests that when Bill is subjugated within a pragmatic educational discourse what has triumphed is not the dominant educational ideology, but a sense of compulsion that should be understood as more psychical than discursive. Moore concludes:

> To apply our *initial* (essentially sociological) analysis to an understanding of Bill's response, we might say that here is an example of the victory of a dominant over a non-dominant ideology … Without in any way wishing to undermine such an analysis, our second analytical pass suggests that we are also seeing a triumph of desire … over ideology…
>
> (p. 497)

For Moore, there is a contrast between discursive repetition of the dominant ideology and the psychical repetition of desire. I wonder, though, whether these two aspects of Bill's account might not be more similar in their construction than this interpretation suggests. Moore interprets Bill's account of himself as 'not liking to rock the boat' as a direct articulation of desire: 'the desire for popularity, for acceptance, for personal and institutional equilibrium' (p. 497). An alternative interpretation might suggest that Bill is in fact performing a particular kind of masculinity, and that his insistence on his 'middle of the road' identity is compelled by the requirement to produce a coherent gender identity within prevailing discourses of compulsory heterosexuality.[8] This reading would reintroduce Freud's distinction between the act of repetition and the compulsion to repeat, and also raises methodological questions about the availability of the repetition compulsion to interpretation. We can observe Bill's repeated assertions of his reasonableness; we cannot observe what compels this reiterated identity. Or, in a more theoretical language: we can trace the discursive instantiations of reiterated desire, but we cannot, perhaps, gain access to desire itself.

If we interpret Bill's bloke-ish account of himself as constitutive of a particular discourse of masculinity, and if we theorize a psychical or unconscious compulsion to explain the attachment to this subordinating (in this instance) identity, then we can construct a similar reading of his reiteration of the terms of the dominant discourse within education. Bill's iteration, despite his ambivalence, of commitment to 'competitiveness', 'what parents want' and 'improvement in exam results' as significant considerations in pedagogic decisions might require the theorization of a psychical aspect to discourse that constitutes the compulsion to repeat. When we ask the question 'why is he attached to the terms of his own subordination?' we might, perhaps, find the answer in a psychical space beyond discourse, in the peril of non-identity, or in something like Judith Butler's unconscious of power.

From a political perspective, the direction of resistance in this instance is very slippery. Bill's ambivalence suggests traces of his commitment to a more progressive educational ideology, which might potentially modify the new orthodoxy of pragmatism, but the desire to produce an identity coherent within hegemonic gendered and educational regimes appears to stifle more politically effective articulations of resistance.

The repetition explored in the second case Moore discusses has a texture that might fit less easily within a Foucauldian paradigm of discursivity. Graeme taught at the same school as Bill, and his account of the recent changes was similarly ambivalent. Moore interprets Graeme, like Bill, as illustrative of a position of contingent pragmatism, articulating justifications for policies that he did not originally support (p. 499). However, this position was not a stable one for Graeme and, after 25 years as a teacher, he was seriously considering leaving the profession. Moore reports Graeme's disillusionment, brought about by 'increased bureaucracy', 'the insistence of a results and performance culture', and by 'changes in teacher-parent and teacher-student relationships'. These changes had forced Graeme into a professional identity that he was no longer comfortable with: 'I have become less progressive: I have become reactionary, I find ... I have become less liberal ... in my thoughts about education. As a teacher, I have become more abrasive' (Graeme, quoted in Moore, 2004, p. 134). This shift in his professional identity is clearly difficult and painful for Graeme. Moore asks the question: 'What was it about Graeme that had made him so desperate, so unwilling to continue to do as he was told, when others in his school of a similar ideological disposition had been willing to carry on?' (2006, p. 499).

To answer this question, Moore turns to a section of the interview where Graeme was explaining what had brought him into teaching. He talked about hating his own education, 'such an appalling school experience', and described how he 'did no "O" levels, started the sixth form and couldn't stand it any longer and dropped out'. He said that this experience 'led me to think perhaps I would like to make it better for others' (2006, p. 499). For Moore, resonances between this account and Graeme's current position are suggestive of Freud's conceptualization of transference and repetition. He suggests that 'what is at stake for Graeme is not simply a threatened ideological/educational stance, but a threatened *re-enactment*': 'we can suggest that Graeme's genuinely felt aspirations for his students connect very strongly – and semi-consciously – to the brutality of his own schooling and a need to expiate that brutality' (2006, p. 500). When Graeme finds himself teaching in a context that replicates some of the brutality of his own schooling, the response he considers, leaving the profession, is a repetition of his earlier response: dropping out of the sixth form when he 'couldn't stand it any longer'.

The repetition suggested in Graeme's account is much more like the psychoanalytic 'return of the past' (ibid., p. 497) within the transference than the previous instances of discursively textured repetitions. However, it is not wholly separable from the discursive regime of education. The transference appears in the encounter between a repetitious life story and a dominant discourse that replicates elements of this story. Nevertheless, in leaving the profession, Graeme might be said to bring about an efficacious break with the pragmatic position he has been forced to occupy. There is, perhaps, limited potential for his action to bring about a modification of the dominant discourse, but his refusal of the identity it has subjected him to constitutes a space within which such modifications might, in theory, begin to emerge. As with the other cases explored in Moore's analysis of the discourse of pragmatism in teachers' accounts of their practice, it is possible to understand Graeme's response to the new educational regime as resistance; although resistance within this analysis has unpredictable, unstable and inconclusive effects.

Graeme's resistance is also, of course, constituted within the context of Moore's research. The interview provided a site in which Graeme was able to articulate some of the complexities of his response to contemporary policy initiatives, and Moore's analysis rearticulates Graeme's experience within the signifying practices of educational research literature. Moore ends his discussion of Graeme by calling for a more reflexive environment, in which Graeme's concerns might have been recognized and supported in order to develop a more effective resistance to the prevailing educational discourses of pragmatism and accountability (2006, p. 502). In Moore's writing, then, we might begin to trace the effects of Graeme's resistance across the different textures of the social terrain.

Putting into question the discursive/psychical opposition: textures of repetitious iterations

Moore's account of teachers' responses to new policy initiatives puts flesh into the theorization of resistance and, I have suggested, might help to put into question the distinction between instantiations of repetition within discursive and psychical realms. Any repetitious iteration of the terms of the dominant discourse begs the question: What compels the repetition? A psychical or unconscious compulsion to repeat can therefore be theorized as inherent to discourse. Inversely, repetitions within personal life stories that might appear as idiosyncratic or 'beyond discourse' can be reinterpreted within a more discursive frame. I have suggested that Bill's account of himself as a 'reasonable bloke' might be read through the discursive requirement to produce a coherent gendered/classed/professional identity, and I have also indicated how the fragility reiterated within Graeme's personal history is constructed in the encounter with abrasive educational regimes. This suggests that the psychical can never be constituted in the absence of the discursive. Nevertheless, instances of resistance do not all have the same texture: we can distinguish between monolithic repetitions that leave little space for discursive modification and iterations that construct complex spaces between the discontinuous elements of discourse; and we can begin to trace the effects of these reiterative moments as potential disruptions to hegemonic regimes.[9]

It is also useful to consider the role of the analyst in the production of notions of discursivity and/or psyche. In his original analysis, Moore foregrounded the more conscious aspects of his participants' accounts. So in the first case study he restricted his claims to Bill's conscious articulations of his desire, rather than theorizing the unconscious, inaccessible forces that might drive these articulations. Similarly, in the second case study, Moore noted the way the brutality of the educational regime re-evokes Graeme's conscious or semi-conscious desire to protect himself/his students. He was less explicit in his interpretation of the unconscious repetition instantiated in Graeme's flight from the brutal situation. Moore explains this orientation towards the more consciously articulated aspects of his participants' accounts in relation to his nervousness about invoking the unconscious.[10] In moving towards a more psychoanalytically informed or psychosocial mode of analysis, Moore is both breaking with more familiar, sociological approaches, and also stepping into a field that, he feels, tightly polices the use of its conceptual vocabulary. There are elements here of resistances within the interpretive process, associated both with the analyst and with the disciplinary field(s) in which they are located.

Reflexivity and the analysis of resistance within the interpretive process

Theorizing resistance within the interpretive process

In *Seminar II* (1991) Lacan foregrounds resistance as an effect constituted in the process of interpretation. He does not ignore the elaboration of instances of resistance as 'frictions' within the psyche: the oppositions between ego and unconscious; or, in more Lacanian terms, between imaginary and symbolic,[11] which, he says, 'constitute obstacles to what Freud calls the flow of unconscious thoughts' (ibid., p. 127). However, he suggests that the generalized understanding of resistance as 'everything which stands in the way of interpretation' implies that resistance is not a psychological process, since it 'only acquires value in relation to work':

> You must admit that this generalization of the theme of resistance allows one to think that he [Freud] doesn't include it in a psychological process. Resistance only acquires value in relation to work. It isn't at all considered from the point of view of the subject's psychic properties.
>
> (p. 127)

What Lacan calls the 'generalization of the theme of resistance' might be understood in several ways. It might suggest the way the interpretation of resistance is given over to the analyst, who might constitute what they please as that which 'stands in the way of interpretation'. Or it might connote the generalized meanings an experience takes on when narrated by the analysand in the context of their analysis. This is the meaning suggested in Freud's footnote – also cited by Lacan – when he discusses the way in which an apparently external event such as war or natural death might be interpreted as a resistance. Freud points out, 'even if the interrupting event is a real one and independent of the patient, it often depends on him how great an interruption it causes' (1958, p. 662), suggesting the way an event can be generalized, by the patient, into something with the power to impede their analysis. The notion of generalized resistance also has connotations of the compulsion to repeat, which Derrida understands as that which unifies the multiple categorizations of resistance, but also as that which is beyond interpretation. Each of these readings constitutes resistance as specific to the analytic process. Lacan says: 'resistance is not thought of as being internal to the subject, on a psychological level, but uniquely in relation to the work of interpretation' (1991, p. 127). He goes on to explain in more concrete terms how analysts construct the resistance in their rush to interpret.

In *The Interpretation of Dreams* Freud suggests the impossibility of fully elucidating the structure of dreams. He warns that in the attempt to do this 'every path will end in darkness' (1958, p. 654). In *Seminar II* Lacan berates psychoanalysts for failing to accept this impossibility, for wanting Freud to answer their questions for them, and for taking his teachings as a set of techniques they can apply in their own practice (see also Ragland-Sullivan, 1986, p. 119). His account of analysts' practice echoes the caricature Freud constructed in *Beyond the Pleasure Principle*:

> When Freud maintains that sexual desire is the heart of human desire, all those who follow him believe it, believe it so strongly that they manage to persuade themselves that it is all very simple, and that all that's left to do is to turn it into a science, the science of sexual desire, a constant force. All it takes is to remove the obstacles, and it will work all by itself. All it takes is to tell the patient – you don't realize it, but the object is here. That at first sight is what an interpretation seems to be like.
>
> (Lacan, 1991, p. 227)

Like Freud, Lacan points out that the assumption that 'all it takes is to remove the obstacles, and it will work by itself' does not produce the desired acceptance of the analyst's interpretations. It is at this point, he says, that analysts rush to interpret the subject as resistant. However,

Lacan says, the attempt to follow Freud's teachings in this way only blocks the process of interpretation. He mocks analysts' imitative approach, asking 'Why do we say that? Because Freud also said it.' This suggests that when we say the subject is resisting, the resistance is in fact the resistance of the analyst:

> it is said that the subject resists. Why do we say that? Because Freud also said it. But we haven't understood what *resisting* means any more than we have understood *sexual desire*. We think we should press on. And that is when the analyst himself succumbs to the lure. I showed you what the insistence on the side of the suffering patient means. Well then, the analyst places himself at the same level, he insists in his own way, an obviously far more stupid way, since it is conscious.
>
> (ibid., pp. 227–228)

What does it mean for the analyst to 'press on', to 'insist in his own way'? It means, I think, that the analyst is reiterating the discourse of 'psychoanalysis', believing it can produce an interpretation, rather than waiting for an interpretation to be offered by the analysand. 'In this perspective which I'm opening up for you', Lacan says, 'it's you who provoke resistance ... it only resists because that's where you're pushing' (p. 228). Lacan argues that what analysts interpret as resistance is in fact only inertia. The subject does not resist, but the analyst, confronted with inertia, interprets resistance, and tries to push the subject beyond this imagined resistance. It is only when the subject is pushed by the analyst that resistance emerges within the analysis. Thus the resistance is the product of the analyst's interpretation rather than an internal psychological phenomenon: 'There is only one resistance, the resistance of the analyst' (p. 228).

In this account of resistance Lacan points out the impossibility of the analyst knowing in advance the desire of the subject. He says: 'what's important is to teach the subject to name, to articulate, to bring this desire into existence ... If desire doesn't dare to speak its name, it's because the subject hasn't yet caused this name to come forth' (p. 228). Thus, for Lacan, the imposition, by the analyst, of pre-existing notions of desire within the analysis constitutes an act of resistance, rather than an act of interpretation. It is only when the analyst is able to bring the subject to the point of naming their own desire, bringing forth 'a new presence in the world', that what he calls 'the action of interpretation' can be conceived (pp. 228–229).

Once again, the notion of resistance slides away in this account. What appears as a resistance of the analysand, or the subject, is revealed as the resistance of the analyst, or of psychoanalytic discourse. In *The Four Fundamental Concepts of Psycho-Analysis* (1979) Lacan clarifies that 'the first resistance' is that of discourse: 'We must distinguish between the resistance of the subject and that first resistance of discourse, when the discourse proceeds towards the condensation around the nucleus' (p. 68). In this formulation it seems that resistance for Lacan, very much as for Foucault, lies in the repetition, condensation or fixing, of the terms of an established discourse – although, there is still a difference between the two in the way in which they understand the positioning of the 'nucleus' or 'nexus' of repetition. For Lacan, it must be 'designated as belonging to the real' (p. 68), whereas for Foucault it is understood as a discursive expression of a strategy of power.

Another difference is that Lacan directs his analysis of resistance at his own practice, producing a reflexive understanding of resistance within the interpretive process. The questions underlying Lacan's account of resistance as the resistance of the analyst may be: Why are the analysts so attached to their subjugation to Freud's ideas? What is so scary, perhaps, about not knowing their patients' desire? What psychical or discursive force makes them rush to interpret? In what way does psychoanalytic discourse act as a guarantee of their identity?

Analysing researcher resistance within the interpretive process

This kind of reflexive question has been raised within qualitative research, especially, perhaps, within approaches labelled as 'post-structural', 'feminist' or 'neo-Marxist'. Patti Lather (1991) positions her exploration of students' resistances within feminist classrooms as an attempt to go beyond a perspective that views students' refusal of 'liberatory' knowledge as false consciousness. She says: 'I want to explore what these resistances have to teach us about our own impositional tendencies' (p. 76). Alice Pitt (1998) suggests her study of students on a women's studies course had a similar starting point; but she goes further than Lather in applying a psychoanalytic perspective to explore how her 'impositional tendencies' might be understood as an unconscious reiteration of a coherent identity within a particular mode of feminist politics. Her reflexive analysis of her own practice can thus be understood in terms of Lacan's injunction to be wary of imposing pre-existing frameworks in the place of more difficult acts of interpretation.

Pitt suggests that there are 'two moments' or 'two potential spaces' constituted within a piece of research. In the first, which she suggests may be similar to the psychoanalytic encounter, learning is constituted in the gap between the participant's account and the researcher's 'interpretive retelling' of the participant's story. In the second, the gap for learning is in the space between the researcher's account and the academic or political field:

> One location is the space between the researcher and the participant. Here the researcher's interpretive work occurs in the immediacy of the encounter and returns to the participant for further consideration.

A second location lies in the space between the researcher's interpretive retelling and a community that shares an interest in the dilemmas
under consideration.

(1998, p. 542)

This account of the two locations of interpretation might be interpreted as
both over- and under-playing consistencies between research and psychoanalytic practice. The distinction between the psychoanalytic focus on the
desire of the subject, and the research focus, which must, I think, always be
understood in relation to the desire of the researcher, confuses the objective
of interpretive work within the research encounter. However, Lacan's
account of the resistance of the analyst reveals that the 'second location', in
a community beyond the immediate clinical encounter, is as important to
the psychoanalytic relation as it is in the field of research. Pitt's account of
her positioning within both feminist politics and the field of critical education studies has clear resonances with Lacan's account of psychoanalysts'
positioning in relation to Freud and the psychoanalytic community.

Pitt suggests that her engagement with her data should be understood
in the context of the theorization of resistance within critical education
studies. She outlines the shifting or multi-directionality of the concept
within this field, which incorporates an emancipatory notion of resistance as 'the refusal of official discourse', but also a recognition of the
need to theorize the ways in which students appear to resist emancipatory knowledge. In her study of students on a Women's Studies course
Pitt set out to re-theorize students' resistance to knowledge of their patriarchal oppression. She says: 'I began my original research with a question
of how a psychoanalytic conceptualization of resistance ... might enrich
our understandings of what was at stake in students' refusals of feminist
knowledge' (p. 536). However, her analysis of her interpretive process
suggests that she found it difficult to shed some of the assumptions
embedded within the more sociological perspectives of her field. Thus,
her exploration of student resistance is transposed into an analysis of her
own resistances within the research process.

The participants in Pitt's study each kept a journal which recorded their
impressions of the Women's Studies course they were following, and also
'their ideas about how the course was affecting their perspectives on what
it means to be a woman and a feminist' (p. 545). Pitt's analysis of her own
resistance draws on entries from the journal of a student, Tanis, whose
responses she had initially felt were not relevant to her study. The student's
writing described what Pitt calls 'an adventure of self-discovery'. She
quotes sections of the journal:

Taking women's studies courses is a revelation of my true self. It helps
me understand why I feel the things I do, explains those feelings, and
as a result, I feel whole, special, at peace with myself.

There is a gentleness to courses of this nature. Being taught by
women who naturally teach by talking, calmly, peacefully, is so exciting. It makes me want to know more and more. Like a child listening
to an adventure story. For discovering yourself is a real adventure.

(Tanis' journal, quoted in Pitt, p. 545)

Pitt suggests that Tanis' account is consistent with 'the epistemological
framework of academic feminism'. She describes this framework as 'a way
of knowing that centres on women's experiences' and says that it constitutes feminist knowledge as 'a politics of collective and individual action of
resistance against oppression' (p. 545). From this perspective, Tanis'
account might not appear as an instance of resistance to the imposed
knowledge of the curriculum. In her initial analysis of the data, Pitt says,
she felt that she would 'learn more about the subject positions offered
within "Women's Studies" from students who refused to occupy them'
(p. 546). However she goes on to raise the possibility that Tanis' repetition
of the authoritative discourse of academic feminism might also be understood as resistance to feelings of uncertainty, doubt and loss associated
with significant decisions from her own history.

Another extract from Tanis' journal describes her upbringing as pro-
scribed by traditional gendered expectations, and the anger she felt at the
recognition of inequality when she followed the expected path of marriage
and motherhood. In her account, she merges her own experience with that
of her sisters:

My parents never had any expectations of us, except to be obedient
perhaps. All of us four girls, to escape our meager home life, married
by the ages 18 and 19. We all became wives and mothers, and paid
workers. Surprisingly, we managed to juggle all of that, but what
really made us unhappy, angry, and sometimes severely depressed was
that we couldn't have any kind of equality in our own homes; we
couldn't even be who we really were but rather only what suited our
husbands, and what suited all of them was that we be under their
control.

(Tanis' journal, quoted in Pitt, pp. 547–548)

Pitt points out Tanis' use of the past tense in this extract, and the unifying 'we', and she suggests that these linguistic features may indicate a
tension in the account. Tanis was in fact the only one of her sisters to
have left her husband. Pitt suggests that the account might thus cover
over the pain that this rupture with the sisters' shared trajectory might
have constituted for Tanis: leaving her husband might have left Tanis
with 'a certain kind of loneliness and alienation from her sisters' (p. 548).
Pitt argues that the Women's Studies course provides Tanis with a feminist discourse through which she can reconstruct her decisions as part of a

coherent narrative in which feminist knowledge has transformed her life and has the potential to transform the lives of her sisters. Her identification with the course and her idealization of the 'exciting' experience of being taught by 'women who naturally teach by talking calmly, peacefully' (p. 545), provides her, Pitt argues, with the sense of omnipotence conferred by authoritative knowledge. Thus Tanis' account helps Pitt to explore the notion of feminist knowledge as resistant, and to unpick how her own identification with this knowledge might have influenced her analysis of her data.

Pitt suggests that since feminist knowledge is necessarily oppositional to dominant accounts, feminist politics has required a certain resistance to doubt: 'When resistance masquerades as omnipotence, what is at stake is the refusal to admit the limits of one's real power. Elizabeth Grosz ... suggests that just such resistance may be necessary for and integral to feminist subjectivity' (p. 549). She concludes that her initial interpretation of Tanis's account as irrelevant to her analysis of resistance within Women's Studies may be related to the threat that this might have posed to her own political identity and attachment to feminist knowledge:

> By dismissing Tanis's story as having relevance for my study, I was able to hold onto my own contradictory belief that feminist discourse was a system of representation and that it was capable of telling the truth about my life. This was the traumatic perception I could not tolerate.
>
> (p. 550)

The inability to acknowledge the intolerable traumatic perception constitutes a disavowal of the fallibility of feminist knowledge, which leads Pitt to dismiss data that she later considers to be significant. Where Lacan accuses analysts of rushing to interpret, here we see Pitt preemptively refusing to interpret what she sees. Her investments in both the feminist knowledge instantiated in the course and in critical educationalist assumptions that student resistance is constituted in a refusal of curricula knowledge situate Pitt within multiple chains of signifiers that overdetermine her initial position; her reiteration of these ideas constitutes her own resistance within the interpretive process. Her introduction of a more psychoanalytic perspective enables her to look again at this process and to unpick some of the constitutive elements of her resistance; but it also constitutes a real threat to her identity, an acknowledgement that her feminist knowledge, like any other knowledge, is not impermeable to tensions, contradictions and doubt. Just as, according to Lacan, psychoanalysts transform Freud's teachings into technique, so Pitt's account of the interpretive process within her research reveals the teachings of sociology and feminism transformed into powerful, omniscient dogma that stifle the interpretive process.

In relation to Pitt's account we might also ask how best to understand the disavowed traumatic perception that explains or drives her resistant reading of her data. Can notions of psyche, discourse, or an unconscious of power help us to locate Pitt's resistance? Is there an unspeakable trace of desire irreducibly beyond our interpretive powers? Or is it brought within the realms of the articulable through Pitt's own reflexive analysis? And in what ways does our cleaving to these ontological frameworks itself constitute a repetitive insistence that allows us to maintain a sense of an identity within the field, but that impedes the interpretive process?

Conclusion: resistances within resistances

The Lacanian perspective, shifting resistance into the analytical process, enables us to turn the question of resistance back onto the theoreticians discussed within the chapter. Why is Freud initially so attached to the notion of resistance residing within the ego? Why does Foucault deny any attachment to psychoanalysis, to a conception of the psyche, or, indeed, to fixed methodological principles (see Derrida, 1998)? Why does Lacan reiterate his Freudian lineage? What kinds of fragile identities are resisted and reiterated within these theoretical positions?

While I have argued that a notion of repetition constitutes a significant continuity between Freud and Foucault's theorizations of resistance, it is clear that the contrasting analytical affordances and political connotations of 'psyche' and 'discourse' will continue to disperse positions within and across fields of empirical enquiry. Methodologically, these different positions might produce different approaches: Foucauldian discourse analysis orients the researcher towards re-articulations of political, cultural or professional categories; while Freudian or psychoanalytic interpretations tend to foreground the idiosyncratic appearance of repetitions as they emerge within individual life histories. I have suggested that we should examine to what extent these apparent differences in the materiality of resistance within our data might signify the attachments of the researcher, rather than the nature of the resistance, so that our interpretative orientations might not preclude the exploration of the specific psychical/discursive texture of an instance of resistance.

It is, finally, perhaps worth drawing attention to the ambiguous status of the analyst/researcher in the process of interpretation. Within psychoanalytic theories, the analyst is, to varying degrees, attributed a privileged status of conscious engagement that might, or should, enable them to control, in some way, the effectivity of the resistances they encounter within their practice. For Foucault, in *The History of Sexuality* and *Discipline and Punish*, the status of the analyst does not seem to be distinguished from that of any other subject, as product of totalizing discursive structures. While he recognizes that it is the 'strategic codification of ... points of resistance that makes a revolution possible', he shies away from an attempt to theorize a subject of this strategy, suggesting instead that strategy must be understood as 'immanent in force relationships' (1979, pp. 96–97). Both the privileging of the analyst and the refusal to do so are in different ways troubling: the reflexive analytical stance recommended by Lacan, and an appropriate respect for that which is beyond interpretation suggest, perhaps, some ways of moving between these positions of dangerous authority and paralysed subjection.

4 Signifying chains in academic practice

The appearance and disappearance of affect, politics and methodology

Introduction

The previous chapter raised a series of questions about the resistances that emerge within analysis, suggesting the way the repetition of methodological categories might be interpreted as discursive repetitions or psychical attachments that constitute a limit to the interpretive process. Throughout the book I have been arguing both for the impossibility of escaping existing conceptual vocabularies, but also for the possibility of using these concepts playfully and of maintaining a sense of that which cannot be captured within the terms of our interpretations. Nevertheless, it is very difficult, I think, to avoid moments, or epochs, of submission to authoritative methodological frameworks. In this chapter I am exploring my own articulation of a Lacanian conceptualization of repression, disavowal and foreclosure and I am trying to note the ways in which my attachment to this framework constitutes, perhaps, a resistance within my analysis.

The chapter is based on my own analysis of data produced in an ongoing study investigating knowledge practices within higher education. The aim of the study is to produce an account of subjective/psychical relations within institutionalized, academic knowledge practices. In order to achieve this, the methodology draws explicitly on psychoanalytic approaches. The participants – eight academics working within the humanities and social sciences – have agreed to take part in up to eight interviews over a period of up to two years. Prior to each interview participants are asked to select a text that in some way represents their disciplinary interests. In the interviews participants reflect on their choice of text, their experience of reading/writing the text, and their thoughts and feelings about it. My interventions within the interviews are intended to elicit additional meanings or associations. I also share initial interpretations with the participant during the interviews. These interventions are intended to draw participants' attention to ways in which they may be idealizing, denigrating, objectifying or identifying with aspects of their practice, and to provide opportunities for them to elaborate, correct or refine these interpretations. In practice, in the early stages of the project it didn't feel as if there was as much time as I had hoped to discuss and refine interpretations within my meetings with participants. Because of this, I built an additional stage into the research process. Between the fifth and the sixth interviews I am writing case studies of individual participants. With their agreement, I send the case study to the participant and this becomes the prompt for discussion in interview six. This chapter is based on three of these case studies, and also draws on these participants' responses to reading my interpretations of the texts produced in our meetings.

There are several strands to the argument developed within the chapter. The analysis explores the appearance and disappearance of signifiers of affect, politics and disciplinary methodologies within participants' accounts of their practice and suggests that these signifiers can be troubling or difficult to position in the articulation of an academic identity. This is the main strand of my argument in relation to the data. However, I am also exploring the possibility of understanding these appearances and disappearances through a psychoanalytic conception of repression, disavowal and foreclosure. My starting point is a Lacanian conceptualization of these psychical processes, but the aim is to elaborate the specific mechanisms through which these modes of negation are enacted in the context of academic practice, and this necessarily detaches Lacan's ideas from their clinical association with the diagnosis of neurosis, perversion and psychosis. Because of this, there is a question about the productivity of this analysis of methodological practice – if it is not a clinical diagnosis, what is it? My aim is to trace hidden or unknown dimensions of knowledge in order to unsettle conceptions of methodology that ignore or discount suppressed aspects of scientific and social scientific practice. Lacan's conceptualization of the psychical processes through which signifiers are kept out of a signifying chain offers a tool by which to explore the network of suppressed and articulated discourses that constitute legitimized academic knowledge. However, my analysis rearticulates these concepts: the focus of my analysis is a social practice rather than an individual subject; and the objects of the processes of repression, disavowal and foreclosure are not the same as in the clinical psychoanalytic categories. In addition, the clarity of the distinction between repression and foreclosure is not always easy to trace in the data produced within my project. So, in addition to developing an argument about psychical relations to signifiers of affect, politics and methodology within academic practice, I am also exploring the recontextualization of psychoanalytic terms, and I am trying to note where my attachment to these terms constitutes a point of resistance within my analysis.

The substantive argument developed in my analysis of the interview data is that signifiers of affect, politics and methodology seem to have significant effects in relation to the subject of legitimized disciplinary knowledge; they seem to constitute specifically charged aspects of identity in the context of academic research practice. What I mean is: it is possible to trace the way signifiers related to all three – affect, politics and methodology – are either repressed or disavowed, or, alternatively, used as a reference to regulate and legitimize practice.

Affect, closely associated with notions of subjectivity, has always had a problematic relation to scientific and social scientific conceptions of knowledge. Affective responses are not generally incorporated into the articulated procedures of research, and affective responses that emerge in the wider context or hinterland of the research process are also usually ignored or considered problematic or illegitimate. It is perhaps not surprising, therefore, that where conceptions of affect have been brought into explicit formulations of methodological procedures – as in some schools of psychoanalysis and literary studies – the position of this signifier is frequently contested or unstable. In a similar way political affiliations, although not as transient and necessarily subjective as experiences of affect, have often been associated with notions of ideology and prejudice that are in opposition to ideals of objectivity within the research process. Although many disciplinary fields within the humanities and social sciences position themselves as explicitly politicized formations of knowledge, there is still some uncertainty about the position of politics within academic practice. Research is frequently positioned as an objective source of evidence that informs the political process, and research that announces its political affiliations may be seen as in some way tainted or suspect. Signifiers of political attachment, like signifiers of affect, can be troubling objects in the context of academic practice and research. In contrast to affect and politics, methodology might be considered a defining feature of scientific and social scientific practice. Indeed, it might be possible to suggest that methodology acts as first signifier within any disciplinary field, the guarantor of the discourse. Nevertheless, or perhaps as a direct corollary of this privileged position, signifiers of disciplinary methodologies seemed to be troubling, in similar ways to affect and politics, in the interview accounts produced in the context of the study. What happens when the signifier that guarantees disciplinary identity is seen to be lacking? What happens when signifiers that put disciplinary identities into question reappear within academic practice? What psychical processes push and position signifiers within or outside discourse? These are the questions that emerged in my initial analysis of the interview data produced in my study. They are also relevant questions to pose in relation to my own engagement and my interpretation of data within the project.

The next section outlines in a little more detail the conceptual structures of repression, disavowal and foreclosure, which I have used as a starting point for my analysis of relations to signifiers within my research data. The remainder of the chapter presents three case studies of participants in my project, academics working in departments of cultural studies, literature and politics.

Repression, disavowal and foreclosure: psychical relations in the field of discursivity

Lacan's account of the contrasting mechanisms of repression, disavowal and foreclosure as the libidinal relations associated with, respectively, neurosis, perversion and psychosis, is a development of Freud's conceptualization of contrasting libidinal types. Freud suggests that we can 'perceive' libido 'concentrating upon objects, becoming fixed upon them or abandoning them, moving from one object to another and... directing the subject's sexual activity' (1905, p. 217). He distinguishes between this 'observable' object-libido and the ego- or narcissistic-libido, 'the great reservoir from which the object-cathexes are sent out and into which they are withdrawn once more'. He speculates that this narcissistic energy within the ego is 'the original state of things, realized in earliest childhood, and ... merely covered over by the later extrusions of libido' (ibid., p. 218). However, he suggests that further research into the libidinal cathexis of the ego is beyond the psychoanalytic methodology:

> We are then faced by the difficulty that our method of research, psycho-analysis, for the moment affords us assured information only on the transformations that take place in the object-libido, but is unable to make any immediate distinction between the ego-libido and other forms of energy operating in the ego.
>
> (p. 218)

He concludes that 'for the present ... no further development of the libido theory is possible, except upon speculative lines'.

Lacan articulates a speculative theorization of libido. For Lacan, libido is an objectification of a desire that cannot be named within the symbolic order of discourse. He says 'libido allows one to speak of desire', where 'desire is a relation of being to lack ... the lack of being properly speaking' (1991, pp. 221, 223). Libido, then, expresses, in an objectified form, the lack of the subject: it directs energy to produce objects that conceal the lack of the speaking subject (p. 223). So, the analysis of libidinal relations can help us to understand how particular objects or signifiers are constituted as nodal points that organize the formation of identities within a specified discourse.

A Lacanian conceptualization of repression, disavowal and foreclosure cannot be separated from an understanding of the symbolic order and the signifying chains of articulated discourse. Lacan's account of discourse as constituted in chains of signifiers that articulate symbolic relations between linguistic elements thus provides a framework for the analysis presented in this chapter. The symbolic order is the universe of signifiers with no fixed relation to a particular discourse or signified (Evans, 1996, p. 203). A signifying chain, in contrast, constructs a relation to a field of signifieds, but it is never a closed system, a signifying chain always maintains the potential to evoke or articulate relations to other elements of the symbolic order. Lacan describes this openness, saying: 'There is in effect no signifying chain that does not have, as if attached to the punctuation of each of its units, a whole articulation of relevant contexts suspended 'vertically', as it were, from that point' (1957, p. 170). Here Lacan implies two modes or dimensions of relations between signifiers. There are the links within the signifying chain, understood as linear or metonymic relations within a discourse; and there are the 'punctuations' associated to each signifier that constitute a potential symbolic relation to other signifiers, outside the articulated signifying chain. These other signifiers are in a 'vertical' or metaphorical relation to the chain of signifiers: they are in the position of an unconscious or repressed aspect of discourse (see Evans, 1996, p. 188). So, for example, where the discourse of 'methodology' constitutes metonymic links between signifiers such as 'validity', 'sampling', 'interpretation', 'epistemology' and the like; relations to other signifiers that do not appear to fit within the discourse of methodology, perhaps 'power' or 'politics', for example, may punctuate these signifiers, and enact an unconscious symbolic relation to conscious articulations of methodology. These suspended elements that punctuate the units of discourse are where discourse says something other than what it appears to say.

In general repression refers to the psychical process of expelling a thought or an experience from consciousness into the unconscious. The process of repression is associated with neurosis, and the expelled element relates to an unwanted or unacknowledged instinct or desire. Since what is repressed relates to an instinct or desire, the process of repression involves a dual action of attraction and repulsion, desire and the alienation of desire. However, it is important to note that for both Freud and Lacan what is repressed is not the affective experience or instinct, but its 'ideational representation' (Laplanche and Pontalis, 1973, p. 393; see also Evans, 1996). In more Lacanian terms we might say the object of repression is not an instinct or an affect, but the signifier that represents an instinct or affect within the symbolic order. There is thus an important distinction between the instinct and its representation in language or signifiers.

For Lacan, the subject's relation to language constitutes the primary repression, which can be distinguished from secondary repressions that act on specific signifiers within language. Dylan Evans explains how for Lacan the primary repression is understood as taking place in the moment that the subject enters into language:

> Primal repression is the alienation of desire when need is articulated in demand. It is also the unconscious signifying chain. Primary repression is repression of the first signifier. 'From the moment he speaks, from

that precise moment and not before, I understand that there is repression' (S20, 53). Lacan does not see primary repression as a specific psychical act, localizable in time, but as a structural feature of language itself – namely, its necessary incompleteness, the impossibility of ever saying 'the truth about truth'.

(p. 165)

The quotation in the third sentence of this extract is from *Encore* (Lacan, 1998, p. 53) and in the passage Evans cites Lacan emphasizes the way the terms 'primary' and 'secondary' create a misleading illusion of a temporal ordering. Rather than a position in time, 'primary' repression indicates the subject's relation to language, and the repression of the necessity of the break between the signifier and that which it is taken to represent. The repression of the first signifier thus constitutes the expulsion from consciousness of the signifier *as* signifier. The entry into *any* discourse might be conceptualized as a primal repression in which the subject finds a way of articulating desire that simultaneously involves the repression of the inadequacy of that articulation.

Secondary repression involves the expulsion of a signifier from the linear, metonymic axis of the signifying chain into the unconscious, metaphorical dimension. However, in this action the signifier is not destroyed, but remains present as one of the unconscious punctuations in a 'vertical' relation to the discourse. Ellie Ragland-Sullivan suggests: 'The supplanted signifier ... falls from the level of consciousness to the level of unconsciousness, where it acts as a kind of latent unconscious signifier grafted onto an unconscious chain of associations' (1986, p. 234). Because it remains in the signifying system, the repressed is always available to return, and indeed, in a sense it only exists in its return, in the form of jokes, dreams, slips of the tongue, etc. The repressed, therefore, is a signifier of an unwanted or unacknowledged desire; repression does not get rid of either the desire or the signifier, and so both are likely to re-emerge as a symptom within discourse.

Where repression relates to an instinct or desire, disavowal relates to a 'traumatic perception' that is both acknowledged and also denied. Freud initially developed the concept to account for fetishism, in which one specific object becomes the focus of sexual desire, a prerequisite of sexual arousal. The traumatic perception in relation to which the concept was originally formulated is the female lack of a penis: Freud suggests that children 'disavow the fact and believe that they do see a penis all the same' (Freud, cited in Evans, 1996, p. 43). At the same time, the perception cannot be completely denied, as, Freud says, it is not possible for 'the ego's detachment from reality to be carried through completely' (Freud, cited in Evans, p. 43). Nevertheless, the denial is symbolically represented by the fetishist in the construction of an alternative object of desire, to replace the penis that is missing from the female. As Laplanche and Pontalis (1973) point out, in this account it is difficult to pin down the object of denial, and the play of absence and presence represented by the lack of a penis:

> If the disavowal of castration is the prototype – and perhaps even the origin – of other kinds of disavowal of reality, we are forced to ask what Freud understands by the 'reality' of castration or by the perception of this reality. If it is the woman's 'lack of a penis' that is disavowed, then it becomes difficult to talk in terms of perception or of reality, for an absence is not perceived as such, and it only becomes real in so far as it is related to a conceivable presence. If, on the other hand, it is castration itself which is repudiated, then the object of disavowal would not be a perception – castration never being perceived as such – but rather a theory designed to account for the facts – a 'sexual theory of children'.
>
> (p. 120)

Is the object of 'traumatic perception' the idea of castration, which cannot be perceived? Or is the object of 'traumatic perception' an absence that the fetishist needs to turn into a presence? Lacan's account offers a possible resolution to these question.

Lacan's reconceptualization of the notion of disavowal abstracts the concept from the perception of the absence of the penis in women. Evans suggests 'whereas Freud relates disavowal to the perception of the absence of the penis in women, Lacan relates it to the realization of the absence of the Phallus in the Other' (1996, p. 44). This 'realization of the absence of the Phallus in the Other' is equivalent to the realization of the inadequacy of language, or the impossibility of desire. Evans, again, explains this relation between disavowal and lack:

> The traumatic perception is, in Lacan's account, the realization that the cause of desire is always a lack. It is this realization that disavowal concerns; disavowal is the failure to accept that lack causes desire, the belief that desire is caused by a presence (e.g. the fetish).
>
> (p. 44)

Disavowal, from this perspective, relates to the difficulty in accepting lack as a cause of desire. It evokes the desire for complete fulfillment and the refusal to accept weakness in an object of desire. In relation to signifiers of 'methodology', then, an act of disavowal might signify a refusal to accept the flaws inherent in any methodological procedure, the impossibility of attaining secure knowledge. Alternatively, disavowal might also, perhaps, constitute a kind of liberation from the strictures of attachment to rigid disciplinary methodological frameworks.

There appears to be a relatively clear distinction between the two conceptual structures discussed so far. While repression involves the exclusion of the signifier of the subject's desire, disavowal involves the denial of lack as a cause of desire. In repression, the signifier of desire is expelled from discourse. In disavowal, an alternative object is constructed to take the place of the absent the cause of desire. However, the interpretation of these structures in relation to empirical data may be more problematic, and the distinction between psychical processes is not always clear. It seems to me particularly difficult to articulate an empirical distinction between instances of repression and instances of foreclosure.

Laplanche and Pontalis suggest two distinctions between repression and foreclosure. They cite Freud's account of psychosis where he suggests that 'the ego rejects the incompatible idea together with its affect and behaves as if the idea had never occurred to the ego at all' (1973, p. 166). This differs quite clearly from repression, where it is the signifier alone that is rejected, not the affect associated with the signifier. The second distinction concerns the position of the repudiated signifier. They suggest that the act of foreclosure constitutes the Real, that which is beyond symbolization. Whereas in repression, the signifier remains within the symbolic domain, foreclosure, they say 'consists in not symbolizing what ought to be symbolized ... it is a "symbolic abolition"' (p. 168). The repressed object remains within the symbolic domain; the foreclosed object is abolished from the symbolic domain. A final contrast that follows from this relates to the reappearance of the object of the two processes: in repression the expelled signifier re-emerges from the unconscious chain of symbolic associations in the form of dreams, jokes, slips of the tongue or neurotic symptoms; in contrast, the foreclosed object reappears in the Real in the form of hallucination or delusion. While these distinctions make sense theoretically, I am not sure how sustainable they may be in exploring the productivity of these concepts in the analysis of empirical research data.

There are several methodological difficulties inherent in the interpretation of a distinction between repression and foreclosure. It is not necessarily clear, for example, how we might distinguish between the reappearance of an object in the Symbolic and the reappearance of an object in the Real. Most importantly, though, the contrast between the two mechanisms is defined in relation to the presence or absence of affect. So in using this distinction we would need to find a way to substantiate claims about the affect related to signifiers within empirical research data. We might rely on participants' reports of their affective experience; or we might find alternative evidence of affect in discontinuities and disjunctures within the research data (see for example Sagan, 2008). An alternative approach would be to use the notion of projective identification to draw on the affective responses of the researcher; however, from a Lacanian perspective, this is highly problematic, as affective identifications between analyst/researcher and patient/participant are always to be discounted as constituted in the imaginary domain. My approach to this varied in the analysis of the case studies from my project. Where a participant talks explicitly about affective responses, I felt able to use these reports as a basis for interpreting the presence of affect. In other instances, where a participant denies affective experiences or retracts signifiers of affect, I have struggled to find a way to support my initial interpretation of this retraction as the repression of knowledge of a presence, as opposed to the reporting of an absence. Exploring this troubling interpretation with colleagues, I toyed with alternatives to a strict Lacanian position, and I wondered about the conscious and unconscious limits to my own methodological position.

There is also a question remaining about the object of foreclosure: what exactly is it that is repudiated? Evans gives an account of the development of Lacan's thinking in relation to this question:

> In 1954, when Lacan first turns to the Freudian concept of Verwerfung [foreclosure] in his search for a specific mechanism for psychosis, it is not clear exactly what is repudiated: it can be castration that is repudiated, or speech itself, or 'the genital plane'. Lacan finds a solution to the problem at the end of 1957, when he proposes the idea that it is the Name-of-the-Father (a fundamental signifier) that is the object of foreclosure. ... When the Name-of-the-Father is foreclosed for a particular subject, it leaves a hole in the symbolic order which can never be filled; the subject can then be said to have a psychotic structure, even if he shows none of the classical signs of psychosis.
>
> (Evans, 1996, p. 65)

Two important points are clarified here. First, the object of the foreclosure in cases of psychosis is the Name-of-the-Father. The Name-of-the-Father constitutes a fundamental signifier in the constitution of the subject as subject of the symbolic order. To this extent, the refusal of the Name-of-the-Father is equivalent to the refusal of speech, or the refusal of submission to the law/language, the refusal of castration. Thus foreclosure involves the repudiation of a position as a subject within discourse. The second important point is the strong association between Lacan's articulation of the concept of foreclosure and the category of psychosis. If we want to broaden the concept, to free it from its diagnostic associations, it may be possible to reinterpret the notion of the fundamental signifier. The fundamental signifier can be interpreted as the entry point to a particular discourse, rather than to 'discourse' or 'language' as such: it is the law that must be accepted in order to constitute a recognizable identity within a particular political, professional or cultural community.

Judith Butler's account of the foreclosure of homosexual attachment, discussed in Chapter 1, both accepts and subverts Lacan's account of foreclosure, implicitly positing homophobia as a form of psychosis. When, for a particular subject, both the signifier and the experience of homosexual attachment are expelled into the realm of the unsignifiable, the subject is left with no way of articulating what is a constitutive element of their heterosexuality. Their same sex emotions return as a terrifying, delusional experience that provokes an attack on normal homosexuality. Here the fundamental signifier is same sex attachment; and Butler's account of the repudiation of this signifier produces an understanding of heternormative discourse as a form of cultural psychosis.

Butler's account demonstrates the importance of drawing a distinction between structure and object in the psychical processes of repression, disavowal and foreclosure. It is important consider the implications of the fact that that the *objects* of these psychical processes are not the same in the clinical context as they are in my research into academic practice. My analysis takes psychoanalytic conceptual structures as productive tools for analysis, but detaches them from the specific objects related to the clinical categories of psychoanalytic discourse. So, for example, the methodology of the clinic prioritizes an individual subject and in this context notions of castration and the Name-of-the-Father are understood as metaphors for an originary instantiation of the subject in infancy and the relation to such an object is indicative of a clinical diagnosis. In contrast my study foregrounds the practices associated with institutionalized academic knowledge and the relation to a fundamental signifier is understood as one iteration of the subject's multiple social bonds within discourse. To be more precise, I am trying to shift the focus towards the multiplicity of relations to signifiers within a specified discursive field, in this instance the field of academic research, and away from an analysis of individual subjects.

The following sections present data from the study in the form of case studies of individual participants. My analysis suggests that it is possible to interpret multiple libidinal relations within each of my participants' accounts of their practice. The outcome is an interpretation of the way signifiers of affect, politics and methodology constitute objects of repression or disavowal, or, alternatively, how these signifiers come to act as points of identification within academic practice. The first case presented here, Andy,[1] a lecturer in cultural studies, was the first case study that I wrote. As I was writing it, I was also reading references to the concept of the libidinal economy (Hook, 2008a), and this had a significant influence on my analysis. Conceptualizations of the libidinal relations of repression and disavowal seemed extremely relevant and productive in my interpretation of Andy's account of his practice. In particular, his disavowal of traditional disciplinary affiliations, his construction of idiosyncratic methodological principles within his research, and his repression of his political commitments in his professional academic practice. In my analysis of the following cases, Carol, a lecturer in literary studies and Jeff, a lecturer in Politics, I was aware that I was trying to sustain the framework I had developed in my analysis of Andy's interviews. In Carol's case it was possible to trace a relation between her strong identification with historicist methodology and her repression of her affective responses in her interpretations of literary texts. In contrast, Jeff articulated an ambiguous relation to methodological frameworks, repressing some aspects of his practice, which he found difficult to articulate in the terms of mainstream political science methodology. At times Jeff's relation to methodology could be described as a form of disavowal, in which he identified the demand for methodology with the institutional bureaucracy of funding bodies and sought alternative modes of legitimacy in consultancy and media work and in management roles within his university. However, while the concepts of repression and disavowal seemed productive as a way of reading my interview data, to some extent, I think, it is possible that this framework, and in particular the notion of repression, reinforced resistances already present in my interpretation of my data. These resistances emerged most explicitly in relation to Jeff's interviews, and are explored in some detail in the third case study presented below.

Case Study 1: disavowal of disciplinary identifications and the repression of politics within academic practice

Andy's current post is in a Cultural Studies department, but he has degrees in philosophy, literature, and art and design. He has a broad range of interests that relate in various ways to the contrasting disciplines he has studied. At the moment his main research interest is uses of new media, but he still attends conferences and writes papers that develop his other areas of expertise. Andy has also previously been active in the animal liberation movement, and although he does not currently write in this field, he is aware of work in the emerging field of Animal Studies and sometimes wonders whether it might be possible to make closer links between his academic research and his political activism. In his account of his work, three slightly idiosyncratic elements emerged as key features of his methodology: writing, tangents and structure. These signifiers seemed to fill a place left empty by Andy's disavowal of approaches to research within the various fields in which he had studied and worked.

In talking about his work, Andy often seemed to focus on the material process of writing and developing ideas. In the first interview he explained:

> I don't like to see a distinction between the process and the content, in that – I keep using the word discipline, I don't know, maybe it's because I keep reading Foucault, but I enjoy the discipline of writing as much as the content of it – it's not quite true – but there's almost a sense in which I don't mind what I'm writing, really, I enjoy the writing of it. So I enjoy talking about gadgets and Foucault and all the rest of it, but I also enjoy writing, arranging words in sentences sort of writing.
>
> (Int. 1, p. 3)

Andy attempts to blur the opposition between 'process' and 'content' in order to foreground two aspects of his practice: first, his enjoyment of the materiality of writing, 'arranging words in sentences'; but he also says 'there's almost a sense in which I don't mind what I'm writing', which suggests a disinterestedness towards the substantive content of his research. Signifiers of 'process' or 'writing' seem to contain several meanings for Andy: the concrete act of putting together stylistically elegant sentences; but also the possibility of shifting or displacing the more substantive focus or topic of his research.

Andy also described his research practice in terms of 'following tangents', which he described as central to the creative process. He said 'it's often the weird tangential things that become most interesting and end up being central' (Int. 1). He described, for example, spending time 'looking things up in the O.E.D', and said that he tried not to worry about whether or not the outcome of these lengthy detours would result in a significant piece of writing. Like the focus on the materiality of writing, the idea of following tangents displaces the notion of a stable, substantive object of research. This account seems to construct Andy's practice as distinct from more conventional articulations of methodology within a specified disciplinary field.

Another characteristic of Andy's research and writing that emerged during the interviews was what he described in relation to one piece of work as 'the fantastically anal way I structured the project' (Int. 5). The structure, based on a line from a poem, had been the starting point for this project, and Andy had then carried out the research and written up the project to fit his self-imposed structure. This had involved ensuring that the piece included 101 examples of gadgets, each of which had to be analysed according to a specified organizing principle. He suggested a positive aspect of this approach was that it forces you to think very hard, facilitating new ideas. However, he acknowledged that the approach also has its limitations:

> It may well be that one part of the structure just was never appropriate, but you're forced to think through it anyway. So you might end up having to write stuff that isn't really of any great value, I suppose. That would be the danger of imposing literary structures, for instance. So there are some examples in the project that I'm not that keen on. I love idea of the poem as a structure, but I've got 101 gadgets, you know, the structure requires that there are 101. Lots of those gadgets work really well, I mean, they do exactly what they're supposed to do … Lots of them don't, I mean, lots of them I'm really struggling to try and force a feeble argument that a particular gadget is actually doing anything in the text apart from just being there to make up my 101. I haven't worked out what the proportions are. So that would be the sort of down side to the structure, I suppose. … But I hold by both positions. I do think it facilitates. I like a good structure.
>
> (Int. 5, p. 12)

Although the gadget project seemed to be the epitome of Andy's use of formalistic structures to generate his research, other pieces of his own work that he discussed in the interviews were all written, to a greater or lesser extent, to fit a preconceived structure. He also imposed an order onto his participation in the project, introducing a way to structure his choice of texts for each interview.

Alongside the foregrounding of writing, tangents and structure as central aspects of his methodology, Andy seemed to disavow identifications with traditional disciplinary identities. In his account of the fields he has been associated with through study, teaching and research, the nearest he came to articulating a positive identification is when he referred to being 'interested in ideas', 'philosophy in its broadest sense' (Int. 1). At other times there was a far more explicit distancing from fixed fields or disciplinary positions: 'I don't feel like I do belong in any one field or discipline' (Int. 1); 'That detailed textual English studies approach can be really uncomfortable' (Int. 1); 'Traditional philosophy fails to engage in the lived experience of ethics ...' (Int. 1, Int. 4); 'Lots of awful things have happened in cultural studies...' (Int. 1). Describing some of the work emerging in the field of Animal Studies he said: 'It's quite uncomfortable to hear people talk about the importance of their work... a close reading of some painting in which there are some animals...' (Int. 1, Int. 4). At other points in the interviews Andy talked enthusiastically about certain philosophers and theorists whose work he admired and enjoyed, but he never presented himself as a disciple of any one theorist or methodological approach.

The kind of tentative argument I'm constructing here is that Andy's strong affirmation of his enjoyment of writing, his commitment to pursuing tangents, his 'heartfelt belief in the importance of reading the O.E.D entries' (Int. 1), and his need to impose slightly artificial literary or conceptual structures onto his research, fill the gap left by his disavowal of any disciplinary affiliation. Andy's enjoyment of style and his strict use of self-imposed structures – as opposed to the structures imposed through identification with a disciplinary methodology – to direct his thinking and creativity could be said to constitute a fetishistic practice in relation to academic discourse. This alternative methodological presence suggests that we might look for a traumatic absence in the disciplines that he disavows. In Andy's case it is possible to suggest that, rather than the failure to produce satisfying knowledge, it may be an ethical or political lack that makes him turn away from institutionalized disciplinary positions. However, the idiosyncratic methodological apparatus that he constructs does not seem to constitute a more satisfactory fulfillment of his political desires, which seem to be repressed in relation to his current academic practice.

When I sent Andy the case study based on his first five interviews, we agreed that he would annotate the text with his comments before we met to discuss his response to my interpretations:[2] the version he sent back had sixty-one comments on my twenty-one page case study. The comments were mostly positive – e.g. 'definitely…', 'true…', 'this is interesting' – and he sometimes elaborated points, adding information that he thought might be helpful. In addition, several comments engaged with the methodology underpinning my interpretations. In the interview he commented that as he'd been reading the case study he had started to get more interested in my methodology than in specific interpretations of his own practice (Int. 6). One instance of this was his response to the section where I presented an initial version of my interpretation of his disavowal of disciplinary affiliations:

> Comment 33: This is very interesting. It's not how I've thought of this previously (in terms of disavowal or displacement), but it certainly doesn't sound 'wrong' either. But I'd be really interested to discuss with you this question: 'by what criteria could we judge whether this interpretation is true or accurate or productive or useful?' Having observed that I embrace certain modes of writing, and disavow certain affiliations, how does one get from one to the other? This sounds like I'm resistant to, or rejecting your interpretation, which I'm not (or at least, I don't think so). It is a methodological question I'd be very keen to discuss. I'm wondering if this is the difference between Foucault and Freud here: Foucault observes disjunctions; Freud connects them. Perhaps that's too crass.

This comment raises several interesting methodological questions. The more explicit issue relates to my introduction of something like the unconscious to construct a link between Andy's account of his writing/methodology and his disavowal of disciplinary affiliations. The distinction he raises between the Foucaultian impulse to foreground disjuncture and the psychoanalytic use of the unconscious to formulate conjunctions is important to note, in order to keep a check on the voluntaristic aspect of speculative interpretive moves that may have serious ethical implications. Another possible line of interpretation of this extract would be to consider Andy's response to the case study as an aspect of his practice repeated in the context of the project: his concern not to give the impression that he is rejecting my interpretation has resonances of the discomfort he feels giving negative feedback, which he talked about on several occasions during the interviews. For the moment I just want to note both of these issues, as kind of punctuations in the more linear argument I am trying to construct about the relationship between Andy's methodological avowals and disavowals, and his political commitments, which he tries to keep separate from his academic work, but which slipped back in to our discussions within the interviews.

The text Andy selected as the prompt for the first interview explicitly engages with the nature of Animal Studies as a field, and, implicitly raises issues that might be related to an activist position. However, as suggested above, in the interview Andy distanced himself from the field, and didn't initially talk about any potential relation between the paper on Animal Studies and animal activism. Eventually, just over half an hour into the interview, I asked a question exploring Andy's interest in the paper:

CL: You said that you don't actually work in Animal Studies, but you've chosen this text, you are interested in something, in writing about animals in some way. What's you're?

A: My personal, well, my background, I was an activist before I was an academic, I suppose that's true. I've had a strong political commitment to animal issues for a long time, and when I was doing my masters I thought about following this through, in my dissertation, but then I got more interested in gadgets, the computer stuff. My masters dissertation was about cyborgs, hybridity, these kinds of challenges to humanism, and that led into the PhD...

(Int. 1, 34: 55)

My intervention prompts Andy's first reference to activism. However, he seems quite hesitant in giving this account of himself: the statement 'I was an activist before I was an academic' is qualified by 'I suppose that's true', and he quickly moves on to talk about the central focus of his research. This hesitation can be interpreted in several ways. It is possible that Andy's hesitancy in talking explicitly about his activism was to do with his assumptions about the interview, and about what counts, or what I would count, as academic practice. When I raised the issue of activism again near the end of the first interview he asked: 'are you interested in hearing about the activism?' as if there was a possibility that it wasn't relevant to my study. His hesitancy might also be related to his scepticism about the political impact of academic work and the contrast between direct action, 'tramping around the countryside, sabotaging fox hunts and things like that, saving lives, or being vegan and not eating animals', and the kind of textual analysis that might be presented/accepted as political within the confines of the academy (Int. 1). Alternatively, his hesitancy might relate to a slightly negative image of the activist that he sometimes articulated: at the end of the first interview Andy expressed a concern that he might be described as 'this guy they met today who's obsessed by animals' (Int. 1), and he suggested that it would be uncomfortable to say too much about his ethics in case he started to sound like 'the arsy vegan' (Int. 4). In interview 6, he explained this, describing the discomfort of social situations where he has been 'outed' as a vegan and expected to defend his principles. This constitutes an element of his personal discursive trajectory that contributes to his repudiation of signifiers of his politics in the context of his academic work. These contrasting interpretations suggest that there are multiple discursive strands that overdetermine the repression of passionate, political signifiers in Andy's account of his academic practice.

The instances Andy described where his politics reappeared in some form within his academic practice suggested an ambivalence in relation to the way academic culture might act as a constraint on political activity. These instances constituted a sense of an exclusionary structure that regulated Andy's practice and set a limit on the possibility of introducing politics into his work; but also a sense of his own complicity or relief in the exclusion of a potentially difficult aspect of his identity.

In the second interview Andy talked about a text that challenges the concept of 'species' that he used in his teaching on a third year cultural studies module. He said the text made him nervous in several ways, partly to do with the difficulties students had with it, but also to do with the sense that in using the text he might be inappropriately introducing or imposing aspects of his politics. He felt uncertain about introducing a text about animals in his role as a cultural studies lecturer, and he also felt concerned about imposing ideas related to his animal activism within his teaching. He explained his ambivalence by referring to his sense that he was breaking two unspoken codes: the canon of cultural studies and the ideology of liberal humanist university teaching.

It might be possible to say that Andy invoked these two regulatory codes, the canon of cultural studies and liberal humanist pedagogy, as an oppressive structure that he was able to resist (for example in his use of the 'species' text), also as a mechanism that he used to police his own introduction of animal activism into his work. There is evidence of this self-policing in his articulation of the tension within his practice between the activist who wants to persuade students to adopt a particular political position and the liberal humanist pedagogue who wants to help students to think for themselves:

> And I suppose, there's a part of me, as an activist, that feels guilty about pushing the liberal, humanist agenda, as a tutor, it's repressed, because there's a job to do, and I don't get to control, to a large extent, the content of my courses. Yeah, that would be a tension or a worry, from an activist's perspective. But, similarly, to the extent that I adopt a professional, liberal, humanist perspective, I worry that, by including a text that criticizes the concept of species, I'm browbeating my students and trying to turn them vegan or something, so, there's a tension from both sides. I'm not suggesting that I adopt one or the other subject position. They're maintained in tension.
>
> (Int. 2)

Although Andy explicitly acknowledged a sense of two subject positions held in tension, it is the activist aspect that appeared, as he said, to be repressed in his professional teaching role. He constructed a caricature of his use of the species text as 'browbeating my students and trying to turn them vegan'. The worry this image evokes polices his practice and, perhaps, stopped him from introducing ideas directly related to his activism into his teaching and research.

While in practice Andy seemed to regulate his teaching from the liberal humanist position, he said that intellectually he was suspicious of this idea, but at the same time he said he was 'committed to it professionally', and he suggested that it was 'something one is encouraged to adopt' (Int. 2). When I questioned the source of this humanist regulation of Andy's teaching, he agreed that it was self-imposed, but again constructed a caricature of a more activist alternative:

CL: And you're constructing, again, this sense of a looming disciplinary eye over your teaching, and I'm wondering again, whether –
A: Well, again, there's absolutely no – there isn't – that's all me. Well, it's not all me, because I know that if I started forcing students to become vegans and failing them if they didn't agree with my position then, eventually, that would come to light and I would be chastized and whatever else, so, it's not entirely me. But, yeah, I've not had any input at all. I suppose it's an internalized structure of oppression.

(Int. 2)

Andy's vacillations articulate a tension within his position. There is a sense that he is constructing activism as something potentially dangerous that should be avoided, at least within his teaching. His slightly idealized account of an ideology of liberal humanism in higher education pedagogy,[3] and earlier in the interview of the strict cultural studies canon, constitutes an image of powerful institutional structures, capable of displacing a practice that might be more informed by the activist part of his identity. His caricature of activist pedagogy as 'forcing students to become vegans and failing them if they didn't agree with my position' seems to negate the possibility of an alternative to the liberal humanist approach.

As I said, in general, in the first five interviews Andy seemed to avoid elaborating his position in relation to animal politics. However, in interview 4, when he was talking about research in the field of Animal Studies that claims to be 'politically engaged', Andy articulated his own position in relation to some of these authors. He compared himself to people within Animal Studies who are vegetarian, saying 'I'm vegan, so I'm more politically motivated'. He also referred to some projects and practices within Animal Studies – projects that engage with farming, for example, or the construction of artworks that exploit animals – as 'sort of like dabbling in the Ku Klux Klan if you're interested in post-colonial issues'. At these points he seemed to be expressing a visceral response, saying 'I find it quite disturbing and problematic' and 'that's how it feels anyway'. At these moments, an aspect of Andy's identity that is usually repressed in the context of both the interview and his academic practice seemed to leak out.

This leakage of activist sentiments is especially significant, perhaps, in relation to the efforts Andy makes to keep animal issues outside his practice, while, at the same time, constructing a position – through his flirtatious dalliances with animals studies – that leaves open the possibility of developing a more explicit animal focus in his own work. There is a similar duality in his construction of an injunction against introducing animal liberation politics into his teaching, which appears to be a mechanism by which he can police his own practice, rather than something explicitly imposed by the institution in which he is working. Andy's ethical and political interests suggest a possible academic identity that he represses, but that cannot be kept completely at bay. This repression can also, perhaps, be related to his disavowal of disciplinary identifications and his idiosyncratic account of his own methodology, neither of which is able to express or satisfy Andy's political desires.

Case Study 2: the articulation and repression of contrasting methodological signifiers within literary studies

Carol works on the borders between gender studies, cultural studies and literary studies, but identifies most strongly with the field of medieval studies. She is a specialist in medieval texts and much of her work has explored texts written by female mystics. She works in a Literature department and described her research as literary history. The methodological criteria that she prioritizes in judging her own work, and also that of others, are the ideas associated with historicism, which she describes as being about 'how texts come from their historical material circumstances' (Int. 2). She also identified her work with broader trends in post modern literary criticism associated with the 'the death of the author' and the idea that 'texts are written within signifying systems' (Int. 4). In contrast, her account tended to problematize claims to know through affective or religious experiences, which conflict with materialist historicist methodological principles. Nevertheless, her adherence to historicist principles was not excessively purist. She often appeared to be exploring the limits of historicist approaches in an attempt to formulate a path somewhere between an overly rigid understanding of historicism and an acceptance of notions of a direct connection to the past.

For our fourth meeting the text Carol selected was Marguerite Porete's *The Mirror of Simple Souls*. Carol explained that Porete was a female mystic and that the book was a radical account of her perception of union with God. Eventually the book was condemned as heretical, Porete was ordered to stop distributing it, and was later condemned to death and burnt as a heretic. Carol commented that she felt this biographical knowledge was important to her in reading the text. However, she also saw the use of this knowledge as problematic, because historicist trends in literary studies have problematized the position of the author in relation to the meaning of the text. She reflected:

I do think of this text in biographical terms, as well, in ways which are maybe not completely legitimate as literary criticism. Well, it's a commonplace in post-modern literary criticism that the biography of the author only gets you so far, that texts are written within signifying systems, that even if – what the author thought they meant by it does not give you the full meaning of the text by any means.

(Int. 4, 17:00)

Here Carol specifies the 'commonplace' of historicism that 'texts are written within signifying systems'. However the extract also suggests the power of this methodological injunction to make her question her own approach. She explains that the traditional notion of the author as in control of the meaning of the text is not seen as 'legitimate' within post-modern literary criticism. The 'commonplace', 'postmodern' position suggests that the author's biography will not necessarily provide clues to the meaning of a text. What I thought was interesting here was the way this very specific demarcation of the limits of the role of the author seems to make Carol doubt the legitimacy of allowing biographical information to influence her thinking about a text in any way. Her hesitation about the legitimacy of her reading suggests that the injunction against reifying the position of the author has the power to, briefly, destabilize her own practice. Carol's hesitation punctuates her interpretation with some complicated methodological questions: Does knowledge of Marguerite Porete's martyrdom distort or support her interpretation of the text? Is it possible to infer textual significance from biographical knowledge? Is this legitimate or illegitimate as a mode of literary criticism? Carol's hesitation suggests both her strong identification with the commonplaces of historicism, but also, potentially, ways in which her practice might either elaborate or call into question the meaning of these commonplaces.

Tensions in the articulation of a historicist position were also evoked later in the same interview. Talking about the fact that Porete is now recognized for her text, which was published anonymously in the period after her death, Carol commented: 'And now she is remembered, which I daresay is not what she was interested in, I don't think she would have been that bothered about whether we remembered who she was …' (Int. 4, 28: 46). This comment seemed to me to conjure an image of Porete as a person – someone who wouldn't be bothered about being remembered – rather than as a textual construct. When I asked about this, Carol suggested that her casual reference to what Porete might have thought or felt is based on the textual evidence, not on an ability to envisage her directly: 'I'm trying to follow through the logic of what she writes', 'I don't feel I can see inside her', 'the textual relationship is more direct' (Int. 4, 29: 35, 30: 17). I commented that this felt like a retraction from her original comment, in which she had seemed to briefly reconstruct Porete. In her response she talked about the difficulty of ever claiming to know another person, and suggested ways in which she might maintain a position that is more 'methodologically purist':

> And nevertheless we cannot reconstruct. Indeed. And I think this is unarguable. And you cannot, it's hard enough constructing the experience with people one is personally acquainted with, let alone dead ones. Let alone dead ones that belonged to an alien belief system, etcetera. But, yes, if I want to be methodologically purist about this, I would say that the text is generating an author figure, but acknowledging that this is not only the text, it is not purely the text, it is the text combined with para text, your information, like we know that Marguerite Porete was burnt at the stake.
>
> (Int. 4, 31: 13, also Int. 2, 48: 24)

What interests me here is the tussle between an everyday discourse within which we readily (re)construct images of people who we cannot know in the detail that we imagine – as Carol says in relation to Porete 'I don't feel I can see inside her' – and a more rigidly principled methodological discourse. What does it mean to move between these discourses? In what sense is there an excess in the everyday construction that is not accounted for within the methodological practice of historicist textual analysis? I also wonder if it might be possible to interpret Carol's conditional identification with methodological purism – 'if I wanted to be methodologically purist about this' – as a distancing move that might leave open the possibility of a less purist exchange between the two discourses. She comments elsewhere: 'historicism is not a full answer to most of the questions' (Int. 2, 48: 24).

Within Carol's account of the field of medieval studies, the methodological practices that seem to trouble historicist criteria are those that use notions of affect, as opposed to language or textuality, to interpret historical texts. Carol described this body of work as 'post-historicist' and suggested that authors taking this approach were less cautious than historicist researchers in talking about a direct relation to the past. In the interviews Carol also talked about her own affective responses to texts, but she discounted the possibility of incorporating these into her academic analysis. It seemed as if there was no language in which she could account for the affective experience of reading in methodological terms: signifiers of affect seemed to be repressed within her methodological practice.

In her second interview, Carol explained why she didn't feel able to develop interpretations of affect within her work:

> I don't personally find the idea of being touched by the past, as I was saying, I don't find it really an imitable model to work in, because I

don't know how to question it, how to put it to the test, because that's surely what one always does with writing, you write something, does this add up? Does this make sense? Is this consistent? And if you're saying something like, 'well, I'm feeling a connection here' you can't ask any questions of that, you know, it's a feeling. Maybe I felt it, maybe didn't, but I can't see what you can do with that apart from register it.

(Int. 2, 49: 26)

Her account here focuses on the methodological problem of how to test out interpretations based on an affective response: 'I don't know how to question it, how to put it to the test'. She seems to be suggesting that the historicist methodology of exploring textual, signifying systems provides you with a more solid, testable, basis than affective responses. She points to the difficulty of interrogating the nature of an affective connection, and notes the extreme intangibility of such responses: 'it's a feeling, maybe I felt it, maybe I didn't'. This extract seems to position Carol's practice within a methodological discourse about the validity of different kinds of data, marking out a distinction between a signifier, which has a materiality that is available for checking, and an affect, which disappears and cannot be checked. However, in a later interview she made a similar point in a way that connotes a more personal aspect to her practice in relation to the use of affect within literary analysis.

In our third interview Carol talked about *The Book of Margery Kempe*, partly, she said, because it is a text that tends to provoke strong affective responses. She described the difficulty of getting students to maintain a distinction between the author and the character of Margery Kempe within the text, and she also talked about her own affective responses to sections of the text. She described one section that she found 'excruciating', 'terribly embarrassing', when Margery Kempe is first involved in a flirtation, but is then turned down when she tries to take things further. I asked Carol whether this affective response might come into her interpretation of the text in any way:

CL: So then, what's happening when you're reading Margery Kempe and you come to this excruciating incident about the exchange with the man – what's happening? What do you do with that? Or does that get put to the side in your analysis?

CAROL: It's a good question. I mean. I never have written about the excess bit. I've written about the explicable bit, not the excess emotion. So yes, I have put it to one side. And there is, because I'm not sure of what interest it would be to anyone to say 'well, I find this excruciating', you know, why should anyone care about my response, unless I can find a way of making that into a dialogue…

(Int. 3, 21: 35)

In this instance, what I find interesting is that Carol does not raise meth-odological concerns about the nature of affect, or whether the affect might have a direct connection to the past. Instead she articulates an assumption about what might interest other people, saying: 'I have to put it to one side ... because I'm not sure of what interest it would be to anyone ... why should anyone care about my response?'. The concern that her affective response won't be of interest to others is consistent with Carol's under-standing of the nature of academic work as a 'dialogue' with other ideas in the field, which she talked about at other points in the interviews. However, it might also be interpreted as something more personal, an expectation that her feelings or ideas won't be of interest to others. This adds another layer of complexity to her methodological arguments about the use of affect within academic analyses of texts. The methodological discourse within which these arguments are located is inflected with a more individualized subjective/psychical relation to the expression of affect.

It seems, then, that experiences and conceptualizations of affect in some way trouble Carol's historicist methodological position. However, in the interviews she was also critical of the way Christian devotional writers have interpreted texts written by the medieval mystic Julian of Norwich. She said that her first response to these authors had been quite hostile. In the interview she described their work as 'stupid stuff', 'historically illiter-ate', and she said 'they need the idea of the medieval but not anything like knowledge of it' (Int. 2, 42: 11). She contrasted her own approach to more religious readings saying emphatically: 'I don't believe it. I do not believe that God inspired Julian of Norwich, I believe she wrote from the cultural materials available to her' (Int. 2, 43: 23). It is also worth noting that she was politically suspicious of the religious interpretations suggesting that they might be using history to 'say something about the present that is questionable' (Int. 2, 46: 03). Her response to these texts appeared more categorical than her response to post-historicist uses of affect and notions of a direct connection to history, so the two modes of interpretation seem to be excluded from her methodological discourse in slightly different ways. It might be possible to suggest that while signifiers of affect are repressed in relation to her academic identity, in contrast, the very experi-ence of religious belief appears to be pre-emptively foreclosed as an aspect of Carol's subjectivity.

The complex methodological and political nature of Carol's response to both affective and religious methodologies was rearticulated a little later in the interview. She described the way that it is possible to align religious and post-modern approaches to textual analyses:

> I did write a couple of paragraphs about this, and it hasn't been pub-lished yet, but it's about the way in which the – I would say the post-modern response to medieval women authors is on the face of it, not that much different to devotional authors' interpretations of Julian of

Norwich, that one perceives her as a living presence. And, therefore, maybe the post-modernist, post-historicism is not as radical as it thinks.

(Int. 2, 47: 36)

The analysis Carol outlines here constructs an analogy between methodologies that might normally be considered to be in opposition. She suggests a methodological similarity in the notion of a direct affective response to history and a notion of God speaking across time through religious texts. The conclusion of this argument, though, is political rather than methodological: 'therefore', she suggests, 'post-historicism is not as radical as it thinks'. This might be seen as quite an aggressive move, puncturing the political pretensions of the post-modernist stance, and I wonder what this analysis might be said to achieve. In methodological terms, the post-historicist willingness to play with notions of affect is more troubling to Carol than the religious position, because it incorporates aspects of her own responses to texts that are not legitimate within historicist analyses. The Christian model which suggests that the meaning of religious texts comes directly from God is less troubling, because it bears no relation to her own practice. In a way, it might be possible to speculate that by bringing these two approaches together, Carol is strengthening the boundary she has marked out between her own work and the more troubling aspects of post-historicism.

Finally it is worth noting that when she read the case study, Carol said that she had 'no complaints about the representation' (Int. 6, p. 1). In so far as she had a negative response to my account of the interviews, it was because she felt that she had been too categorical in some of the things that she had said:

> It made me feel, okay, I'm overstating it here, I should leave more room, I should be more open to the possibilities here, whether it's allowing more space for what other people are doing, or allowing more space for how my practice might change.

(Int. 6, pp. 13–14)

She seemed to be shifting between a position of methodological openness, and a tendency to retract, or bounce back to a safer position where she wouldn't have to engage with new approaches. She speculated:

> There is affect going on all the time, but that's not necessarily, or not usually what I'm trying to convey. On the whole it's my job to *deal* (emphasized) with the affect as part of the process ... Maybe I'm so worried about affect because I think it would be a good idea to try doing more with it. It doesn't really fit with anything I'm wanting to do at the moment.

(Int. 6, pp. 9–10)

In this extract the recognition of the presence and interpretive potential of affect seems to be checked or negated by Carol's current interests and by her more persistent methodological attachments. The articulated desire to be open to other methodologies, both in her own work and in other people's interpretations, thus seems to be held at bay.

Case Study 3: the articulation of methodological signifiers within institutional discourse

Jeff studied and gained his first two academic posts in Area Studies depart-ments. He is a specialist in Area (think of somewhere like, perhaps the Middle East, China, Eastern Europe, India or Japan), and he sees it as part of his role to keep up to date with Area's news and culture. He also acts as a consultant on the politics of Area for both governmental and non-governmental organizations. His current post is in a Politics department and during the course of the research he was appointed to a senior man-agement role within his university.

There seemed to be several distinct aspects to Jeff's methodological posi-tion: an explicitly articulated methodological discourse of social scientific method as borrowing from the natural sciences; a less explicitly articulated 'discourse approach' that he describes as 'taking seriously what is being said by politicians, the media and citizens in Area' (Int. 4); and a more implicit, embedded or thick understanding of the culture and politics of Area, which seems to be closely associated with his 'discourse approach'. His relation to each of these was characterized by a certain ambivalence. He articulated positive associations in relation to scientific method, sug-gesting that 'it sounds pejorative to say that Area Studies has less of the scientific method than Political Science' (Int. 5), but also noted what he called 'the central contradiction' of social science: 'it takes the scientific method and applies it to people, and people don't behave in a scientific way' (Int. 1). Despite this acknowledgement of the limitations of the approach in relation to social science, these comments taken together seem to construct scientific method as a sort of unattainable ideal, or, perhaps, as a set of criteria that can or should be used in order to evaluate research.

Jeff's slightly ambivalent relation to scientific method was also evident in his account of a funded project he had recently finished on democracy and the policy process in Area. He described the conceptual framework he had adopted in this study as:

> the nearest I've ever got, in my own work, to the social science idea that you use the scientific method. You have a series of tests in this model, put the politics in one end and run it through the test. And we try, throughout the book, to not make too many judgements about whether it was a good policy or not...
>
> (Int. 4, p. 4)

One of the things that attracted him to this particular analytical framework seemed to be the way it replicated some aspects of scientific method and the way it seemed to offer the potential for developing a 'non-judgemental analysis' (Int. 4). The framework itself, however, seemed to be disposable: he went on to describe it as 'a mechanical academic model'; and rather than a commitment to this particular analytical tool, he talked about its pragmatic value, saying 'you don't get a grant unless you have a decent academic framework' (Int. 4). In some ways Jeff seems to see methodology as a relatively subsidiary, pragmatic aspect of his work. In another interview he commented, for example, that he enjoyed writing review articles because 'you don't have to think of a methodology' (Int. 5). So while signifiers of scientific method sometimes appear as an abstract ideal or first signifier of methodological discourse, they also appear as an element of the institutional discourse of funding bodies and the criteria for obtaining a grant. Jeff's pragmatic relation to his methodological framework relegates signifiers of methodology to a position within this institutional discourse. We might see this move as a form of disavowal in which the limitation or lack in social scientific methodology is both acknowledged and rejected.

Jeff's approach to discourse analysis, the second aspect of methodology he talked about in the interviews, seemed to be bound up with his embodied engagement with the region which constitutes a part of his identity as an academic. He frequently talked about his ongoing and time consuming material engagement with the culture and politics of Area. There also seemed to be a relation between his approach to discourse analysis and his sense that both academic interpretations and policy responses to Area are often ideological or stereotyped, failing to look closely enough at 'what people actually say' or 'what is actually going on' in Area (Int. 3). In contrast, he suggested, his approach to analysing discourse offered a better interpretation of the political situation in the region. He frequently expressed the idea that 'the discourse gets me back to my point about taking seriously what they say' (Int. 4).

Jeff thus defined his approach in opposition to alternative methodologies that he positioned as lacking. In interview 3, talking about a paper he was writing on political leaders in Area, he contrasted his approach with another article which he described as 'very sort of broad brush'. I think I was trying to get a little more sense of the contrast he was making between the two approaches when I asked him to talk about the empirical basis of his article. In his response, he reiterated his sense that interpretations of Area frequently seem to dismiss what the citizens of Area are actually saying or thinking:

CL: Say a bit about the empirical basis of this article.
JEFF: Well, it's what people – it's speeches, it's opinion polls, it's policy decisions. Again, merging the policy and the academic – I was speaking at a fairly high level policy thing a couple of weeks ago, and my

whole, I could sum up everything I said – we've got to take what the people in Area say, and that's empirical, you know. You look at what they say and you don't just dismiss it as 'well, they would say that anyway'. Even if they would say that anyway, it shapes their policy, it shapes their thinking. If you can't understand what people are think- ing, you can't engage with them unless you take seriously what they say. Which I know it sounds obvious, but it doesn't always happen in policy terms…

(Int. 3, p. 12)

As he points out, this account merges his policy/consultancy work with his academic research. It also indicates the way his interpretation draws on a wide range of data: 'speeches', 'opinion polls', 'policy decisions'. He sug- gests that it is through looking at this data that you might begin to 'under- stand what people are thinking' – something that he implies other approaches do not achieve. In addition to looking at specific documents, however, at other times he referred to his more embedded, expert know- ledge as an important factor informing his interpretation of these specific instances of data:

For good or ill, when I look at Area, as you know, I've looked at Area for 25 years, from all sorts of angles, and I know the politics, and I know the social structure and the culture, and I've lived there and I know the literature, and I know what they have on TV and, you know, you bring all of that.

(Int. 5)

If you're an expert in a country, you're far more aware of what the discourse is, you know, that's my sort of bread and butter, ongoing scholarship, if you like, is having an awareness of what the Area leadership is saying.

(Int. 4)

These accounts taken together suggest the way Jeff's approach to analysis combines an ongoing, day to day engagement with Area's culture and pol- itics with the analysis of specific documents, and how taken together these constitute a sense of expertise and understanding that is contrasted with interpretations based on assumptions or generalizations.

It might be possible to say that Jeff's 'thick'[4] material engagement with Area constitutes his expertise and academic identity, and that this also con- stitutes his response to interpretations that he described as 'knee jerk nega- tivity' or 'simplistic' (e.g. Int. 5). To an extent he identified with Area, and this identification appears in his dislike of stereotyped or ideological inter- pretations of the region. He explained 'one thing I'm often doing is to say 'it's not as different as you make out. It's not some weird other land'

(Int. 4). He thus constitutes himself as a sympathetic mediator/analyst, in the face of interpretations that may be inclined to foreground the negative.

I have been discussing the material engagement of time that is a major aspect of Jeff's methodology for studying Area and that also constitutes a basis for his approach to discourse analysis. I am particularly interested in the way that this was both present and absent in his account of his research practice. It was present because he talked about it at several points during the interviews, but it was absent because he didn't seem to attribute it the status of methodology. There was a sense in which this aspect of his work wasn't acknowledged, or he felt that it wasn't acknowledged, as being of institutional or intellectual value. When he talked about the more material aspect of his work, he talked very much in terms of time, and he made comparisons with other fields that don't seem to require the same kind of constant engagement and reading:

> I have a theory about academic work rates... what you never look at, because it's unspoken, is, does your specialism require more work than somebody else's? And mine certainly does. I think anybody whose specialism is a contemporary country, I just have to keep up with Area. And you know, that's a constant ... it's two hours a day you'd have to spend, reading the papers, and I don't have the time to do that. But, because I'm an expert on Area, the media phone you up, you've got to know everything. What's my specialism? Area. In some other disciplines, it's not so relentless, well, occasionally there might be an important book you've got to catch up on, but those of us who – well, while I'm bigging myself up – not only do I study something that has to be looked at every day but I do it in another language, so I have to have that expertise as well, and it's a long way away and hard to get to. So I'm not as hard done by as some people, but I'm slightly more hard done by than somebody whose specialism is contemporary USA or British politics. But, all of us together have to do more work than somebody whose specialism doesn't change so much. Are you feeling sorry for me?
>
> (Int 2, pp. 11–12)

Although Jeff says at one point that he may be boasting about the difficulty of his field – 'bigging myself up' – there is also a clear sense of being 'hard done by' in terms of institutional recognition of the time required to research his particular specialism. This might also be understood in relation to the lack of explicit, legitimized, methodological/intellectual status attributed to the kind of detailed ongoing observational work that he is describing: the 'two hours a day you'd have to spend reading Arean papers' (Int. 2). As he suggested at other points in the interviews, this aspect of his research doesn't seem to count academically, which is why you need conceptual frameworks: 'you can't just say what's happening, because that's not academic analysis, you know, nobody would publish a book, you certainly wouldn't get a grant' (Int. 4).

Jeff's account suggests that the time consuming requirement to keep up to date with current events in Area is inherent to the field of study. I wonder, though, to what extent it is right to generalize this aspect of his methodology to others in the field; or whether it might not be specific to his own practice. Although at several points in the interviews he portrayed media and consultancy/policy work as an external demand on his time – he said: 'something will happen in Area and I'll get twenty calls in one day' (Int. 3) – his relationship with both of these fields seemed ambivalent, something that he enjoyed but that he also found difficult and time-consuming. He said, 'I still love engaging with the media ...' but continued: 'why do I say yes? ... the media as a forum is very difficult...' (Int. 3). Indeed, even in relation to his academic publications, he often talked about responses and recognition he had received from outside the academy, rather than modes of recognition that are institutionalized within the university. He seemed to shift between a sense that the continual need to keep up was a demanding imposition inherent to his field of study and a sense that this was something he chose to do to facilitate his engagement with the media and policy world, which were valued aspects of his practice and sources of external validation. In so far as it might be possible to argue that Jeff disavowed methodology, he might be said to construct his external roles in the media and policy worlds as alternative sources of potential satisfaction.

There is a complicated set of relations between signifiers at play in this account. Signifiers of scientific method are recognized, but in a sense disavowed when Jeff justifies his use of academic frameworks in relation to institutionalized funding processes. He cites discourse analysis as his methodological approach, but this seems to be heavily dependent on his lived experience of Area, and he doesn't seem to have a way of incorporating this embodied relation to his field into his methodological discourse.[5] Instead, his account of this aspect of his work falls or is repressed into a discourse of institutional injustice in relation to differing workloads. There is thus a space in the place of methodology, the guarantor of academic identity. Opportunities for media and consultancy work and for recognition outside the world of higher education seem to offer an alternative guarantee of professional identity. However, from the perspective of the academy, signifiers of the media and policy world are often seen to be lacking: so, from the elitist intellectual position of Jeff's highly rated, research intensive university department, his enjoyment of these external activities might be read as a perverse or fetishistic form of satisfaction.

Another notable aspect of the interviews was the way that Jeff tended to avoid or deny the possibility that he might have an emotional investment in his work. Talking about his relation to Area in interview 5 he said, 'I actually self conceptualize as somebody who could take it or leave it'. This conceptualization of himself as someone who isn't emotionally attached seemed to apply to his work more generally, not just to his relation to Area. Jeff went on to explain this idea a bit more fully, suggesting that he sees, or tries to see his work as just a job, something that he would be happy to give up if he didn't need the income. There were several moments in the interviews where he asserted his detachment, or quite vehemently rejected any suggestion I might make that he might be emotionally invested in any aspect of his work. So, for example, if he said he was worried, and I asked him to explain his worry, he would retract, repeating on several occasions: 'I don't lose any sleep over it' (Int. 1, Int. 4, Int. 5). Or when he said he was jealous of a colleague's work, and I repeated this back to him, he denied feeling the negative emotion that he understood the word to imply (Int. 2). Clearly, this could be interpreted in relation to my resistance as interviewer: I pushed interpretations too far, or too fast, imposing my own framework onto my participant. However, I also wonder if his strong rejection of the idea that he might feel any emotion in relation to his work might perhaps relate to notions of objectivity associated with scientific method; and this might also partially account for his dislike of ideological or politically motivated research within his field. Or, alternatively, it might be precisely the intensity of the personal investment necessarily involved in any intellectual work that requires him to construct a sense of distance or detachment.

At several points it seemed to me that Jeff denied emotional responses, or retracted signifiers of emotional attachment when he was grappling with issues that directly related to aspects of his work to which he had committed significant time and thought: publication of a book that represented Area in a way he disagreed with, institutional pressure to publish, reading research in his field that achieved a breadth of perspective and insight that he felt his own work did not achieve. When I picked up on an emotional connotation in his account of these instances, he would deny or retract. He explained: 'It's not, I'm not an unemotional person, it's just that I don't want to get emotional about things like books about Area' (Int. 1). Similarly, in response to reading the case study I sent him, where I presented a fuller interpretation of some of these instances, Jeff reiterated his denial of any significant affective responses in relation to his work, feeling that in some cases I had 'massively over-interpreted' what he had said. He said:

> I genuinely don't lose sleep over any of these things. But it's interesting because, you know, I sit down and have these conversations with you because you're asking me questions, but, you know, 90 per cent of this stuff, I genuinely don't think about between our conversations, but of course, that's all you have on me, what's on this tape. So if I say 'oh yeah, I worry about this,' I don't for a minute mean to suggest, you

know, it enters my mind on a regular basis, but if somebody brings it
up, I'll say, yeah, 'I quite like that, I don't like that.'

(Int. 6)

This response to my interpretations raises some interesting ethical and
methodological questions that there is not space to fully develop in this
chapter. My initial interpretation was that Jeff does have affective
responses to things that occur in relation to his work, but that the articulation of these responses in signifiers of affect is repressed in order for him to
maintain his conceptualization of himself as not emotionally invested in his
work. This would suggest that it might be quite irritating for him to
encounter these signifiers in my account of the interviews. However, taken
at face value, Jeff's account suggests that it is not only signifiers of affect,
but the experience of affect itself that is effectively excluded from his academic practice. This interpretation suggests a structure of exclusion that is
closer to foreclosure than to repression. Empirically, I can't substantiate
my assumption about Jeff's affective responses. It seems plausible to
suggest that, for the moment at least, my interpretation subsists at the level
of Imaginary identification, rather than at the level of the Symbolic, i.e. my
interpretation of Jeff's affect might have more to do with my own affective
engagement in my work, and my current anxieties about writing my first
book, than it has to do with my participant's relationship to his practice.

Where both Andy and Carol appeared in most cases to accept my interpretations, or to be willing to play with them, Jeff's response feels more
resistant: but it is not clear to me how this might be interpreted any
further. In a meeting with colleagues to discuss these preliminary interpretations[6] several other possible lines of interpretation were suggested. Olivia
Sagan suggested that the concept of projective identification might provide
a tool for exploring my interpretations of affect in my interviews with Jeff.
She advised that instead of focusing on my perception of his feelings in the
interviews I might reflect on my own affective responses and consider
whether they might provide useful evidence of what had occurred. In interview 6 I had felt fearful, of Jeff's response; guilty, for misinterpreting him;
misunderstood, when he made wrong assumptions about my interests; and
frustrated that he was not more open to reflecting on my interpretations.
Within a psychoanalytic framework that foregrounds the experience of
projective identification it would be legitimate to explore the possiblity that
these are all affective responses that my participant might be having, either
in relation to his work, or in relation to the interview itself, and so I might
be carrying the feelings for my participant. However, these feelings might
also relate to my own anxieties about the research process, and so, for me,
it is impossible to separate out 'my stuff' from 'his stuff'. For me it still
feels illegitimate, or further, perhaps, it feels dangerous and arrogant to use
my emotions as evidence of my participant's affect. The process of reflecting on these emotions in the meeting with colleagues made me more, not

less, persuaded of the problems inherent in my initial interpretations of my participant's affect. Nevertheless, it still is legitimate to ask the question: how is the participant using the interview, in the psychoanalytic sense, to deposit feelings or to repeat psychical processes.

In the same meeting with colleagues, Alex Moore suggested that it might be worth asking what other possible meanings might be contained within Jeff's articulation and retraction of signifiers of affect. Perhaps rather than focusing on the literal meaning of these signifiers – the emotion associated with the vocabulary of affect – it might be more productive to explore the meaning of the retraction. It might be possible, for example, to trace a chain of repetitious associations between Jeff's rejection of my interpretations within the interviews and his account of his responses to ideas and interpretations within his field of research. If this line of inquiry were to prove productive, it might be possible to draw on notions of transference to account for my interaction with Jeff within the interviews.

It is possible to distinguish three moments of resistance evident within my interpretations here. First, I clung to my initial interpretation of Jeff's feelings, finding it difficult to accept the extent of the doubt surrounding this interpretation. Second, it might be argued that this initial interpretation was also limited by my analysis of the previous case studies, my interest in exploring the concepts of repression, disavowal and foreclosure and my desire to produce a neat, linear argument. And finally, I am aware of my continuing resistance to seriously exploring the validity of using my own affective responses as a basis for interpretation[7]. These resistances pull in different directions, so that initially I refuse to give up my more intuitive interpretation, but then, having put this interpretation into doubt, I am unwilling to explore methodologies that might retrieve and justify my intuition. I feel extremely uncomfortable at the possibility of relaxing my understanding of affect as unavailable to knowledge. This would involve shifting long-standing theoretical commitments and destabilizing a relatively secure epistemological retreat that prioritizes language over affect as the object of interpretation. I'm also wary of falling into the evangelical piety of the born again: 'Yes, I used to be absolutist about language and affect, but now I can see the weaknesses of that position...' I don't want to claim that it is in some way more mature or subtle to allow the possibility of affect as a solid basis for interpretation... And I don't think this is true. I still think that claiming knowledge of another person's affect is an extremely insecure and potentially dangerous interpretive strategy.

Conclusion: reflexivity, repression and disavowal

The analysis presented in the three case studies suggests a variety of mechanisms through which instances of repression and disavowal are articulated within academic practice. Both methodological and institutional discourses act as depositories for repressed signifiers, disavowed objects of desire, and as the location of prohibitions against affective and political affiliations. In Andy's account, institutionalized discourses of curriculum and pedagogy are identified with a prohibition that de-legitimizes signifiers of politics that re-emerge within Andy's academic practice. This allows him to suppress his own collusion in the repression of politics within his practice. Carol's account constitutes oppositional methodological discourses, historicism versus post-historicism, and repressed signifiers of affect are simultaneously ejected from her own methodology and attributed to the discourse that she disavows. In contrast, in Jeff's account of his practice, signifiers of ongoing and experiential engagement with the object of study, Area, are deposited in an institutional discourse of workload, and remain unarticulated as an element of his methodology. The play of signifiers in these instances of repression is inflected with more personal elements: Carol's suggestion that her affective responses may not be of interest and Andy's concern not to appear as 'the arsy vegan' are elements of discursive strands constituted in individualized histories, which intersect with regulative discourses of methodology and institution to overdetermine the repression of highly charged signifiers of affect, politics and methodology.

Instances of disavowal are also constituted through multiple discursive mechanisms. Jeff's articulation of signifiers of methodology as a part of the bureaucracy of institutionalized discourses of grants and funding can be interpreted as a disavowal of methodology as the guarantor of knowledge and status. For Jeff, consultancy and media work constitute an alternative object of identification. Andy's explicit disavowal of traditional disciplinary discourses leaves an absence that is filled with his idiosyncratic methodological foregrounding of language, tangents and structure. The normative connotations of perversion and fetishism are largely dissipated in these instances although traces may still remain in the regulative authority of the established discourses to distribute professional status and symbolic power.

It seems that signifiers of affect, politics and methodology are pushed into or expelled from disciplinary and institutional discourses in the production of diverse academic identities. All appear equally vulnerable, held in place through psychical relations of repression, disavowal and foreclosure. It is worth noting that while methodology might appear to have a relatively secure position within discourses of legitimate knowledge, this position is increasingly fragile. Jeff's identification of the demand for methodology with the bureaucracy of funding bodies may be indicative of a more general repositioning of the authority to guarantee knowledge, as government and the market increase their grip on higher education and research. It might be argued that the multiple psychical relations to signifiers of affect, politics and methodology constitute a powerful, shifting, unconscious force within the field of academic practice.

Finally, the chapter also constitutes an attempt to introduce a reflexive awareness of points of resistance within the process of research. There are clear resonances between my own interpretive practice and the psychical relations to affect and methodology that I have explored in the case studies of my participants' practice. Carol's repression of signifiers of affect is closely replicated in my own repression of affect within my methodology, and in my suppression of the interpretive potential of psychoanalytic approaches that foreground notions of projective identification. Andy's imposition of predetermined structures in the production of his research resonates with my exploration of the concepts of repression, disavowal and foreclosure. However, he foregrounds the productivity of this approach, while I am hesitant about the way, in my work, the pre-given structure might act as a resistance within the interpretive process. For Andy, the structure seems to constitute a mechanism that liberates the analysis precisely by forcing productivity from unlikely lines of analysis. For me the structure feels like a reiteration of my obedience to authoritative frameworks that may impede my engagement with my data. Nevertheless, the structure also opens up the possibility of playing with the concepts, trying to shift their meaning, to tie them into the context of my research. I have also noted a tension between the desire to produce a coherent, linear argument and the desire to punctuate the narrative with alternative possible readings and observations of my own resistances. I don't want to completely undo my analysis, but I want to create some sense of openness, of the possibility for interruptions, and of the incompleteness of the interpretive process.

5   From psychic defences to social defences

Recontextualizing strategies and Klein's theory of ego development

Introduction: psychical aspects of recontextualization

I am beginning with a deviation to reflect briefly on the relation between sociology and psychoanalysis, before moving on to outline the more central focus of this chapter. Pierre Bourdieu and Basil Bernstein were both major sociologists working from the 1960s to the beginning of the twenty first-century. Both were interested in the relation between class and knowledge and their work in this area was central to the development of the field that became known as the new sociology of knowledge (Young, 1971). In addition, the work of both men suggests that they were influenced by the psychoanalytic theories that dominated in their respective countries at the time they were writing: for Bourdieu, in France, Lacanian ideas; for Bernstein, in the UK, the ideas of Melanie Klein. And finally, neither appears to have fully acknowledged the relation to psychoanalysis within their work. The similarity in the use and suppression of psychoanalytic ideas in the work of these two sociological theorists provides a basis for speculation on the relation between the two fields, sociology and psychoanalysis. It raises the possibility that the field of sociology did not find it easy to accommodate the insights of psychoanalysis. This constitutes, I think, an important context for a consideration of moments in their individual writings where psychoanalytic sources are either rejected or ignored.

George Steinmetz (2006) has argued that Bourdieu's relation to psychoanalysis can be understood in terms of the Freudian concept of (de)negation, in which a repressed idea is admitted to consciousness, but is not fully recognized or accepted by the subject (p. 445). He explains:

> In some writings, especially the earlier ones, Bourdieu rejects psychoanalysis out-right. In *Outline of a Theory of Practice*, for example, psychoanalysis is reduced to a biological reductionism, completely ignoring Freud's shift from the theory of childhood abuse in the early *Studies in Hysteria* to the theory of sexual fantasy that he developed in the course of his self-analysis. But his treatment of Freudian psychoanalysis more often takes the form of admitting Freudian terminology

and even some psychoanalytic arguments into his texts while surrounding these passages with rhetorical devices that seem to condemn
psychoanalysis.

(ibid., pp. 445–446)

While he says it is not his aim to psychoanalyse Bourdieu, Steinmetz speculates on possible reasons for this refusal to acknowledge the influence of
psychoanalytic or, more specifically, Lacanian ideas on his work. He suggests, for example that 'Lacan's combination of "nobility," externality to
the academic field, and his disregard for rational scientific discourse were
obviously distasteful to Bourdieu' (p. 459). However, Steinmetz proposes
that a 'deeper' reason can be found in Bourdieu's statements asserting a
distinction between sociology and psychoanalysis: '*Sociology does not
claim to substitute its mode of explanation for that of psychoanalysis*; it is
concerned only to construct differently certain givens that psychoanalysis
also takes as its object' (Bourdieu, cited in Steinmetz, pp. 446 and 459,
Steinmetz's emphasis). Steinmetz argues that 'while expressing a desire for
differentiation from psychoanalysis, [Bourdieu] does not actually explain
what the difference would be' (p. 446):

> If Bourdieu had explored this relationship in more depth he might
> have seen that they were not alternatives, but that psychoanalysis filled
> some of the lacunae in his own theoretical approach. His sociology did
> not so much construct the same object in a different manner as to con-
> struct it inadequately.
>
> (p. 459)

There are two strands to Steinmetz's argument. Firstly there is an exploration of psychical relations within Bourdieu's articulation of his theory;
and second there is an attempt to demonstrate how Lacanian psychoanalytic theory might enhance the central concepts of this theory. Steinmetz's
paper goes on to offer an account of the relation between Bourdieu's conceptualization of 'symbolic capital' and 'habitus' and Lacan's symbolic and
imaginary orders, suggesting that the Lacanian theoretical framework can
solve some of the problems associated with Bourdieu's ideas.

This chapter is imitative of both aspects of Steinmetz's approach. I am
exploring ways in which Basil Bernstein both uses and suppresses ideas
associated with Melanie Klein's theorization of the psychic defences, and I
am also attempting to reconstruct these aspects of Bernstein's work, elaborating his use of Kleinian terminology to show how a further engagement
with psychoanalytic ideas might enhance his conceptualization of processes
of recontextualization. It should be noted that the notion of recontextualization appears twice within my argument: I am looking at the way Bernstein recontextualizes psychoanalytic ideas in his conceptualization of
processes of recontextualization. However, his is not the only example I

am drawing on to explore the recontextualization of Kleinian ideas. The chapter also looks at two studies emerging from the Tavistock Institute of Human Relations, a therapeutically oriented consultancy that integrates psychoanalytic approaches into the social scientific study of organizations: Elliott Jaques' (1951) consultancy/research into industrial relations in a factory and Isabel Menzies Lyth's study of a nursing service in a large teaching hospital (1959). Where Bourdieu and Bernstein suppress the relation to psychoanalysis, the Tavistock studies explicitly advertise their psychoanalytic origins.

I am using my exploration of contrasting recontextualizations of Kleinian ideas to develop existing conceptual frameworks within the sociology of knowledge, and I will use the remainder of this introduction to briefly sketch out some of the antecedents of my analysis.

Paul Dowling's theory of constructive description, or 'social activity method' (Dowling, 2009) foregrounds the ongoing process of construction of any social formation. Dowling's approach conceptualizes any instantiation of knowledge as a part of an ongoing social engagement, an enactment that forms social alliances or oppositions. He defines these social engagements as strategies and his work has developed several analytic schemas for describing the strategies deployed in the recontextualization of disciplinary knowledge. One example is the 'domains of action schema' which distinguishes between articulation of content (signified) and expression (signifier) in the formulation of knowledge. In his analysis of the recontextualization of mathematics in school textbooks Dowling (1998) argued that both content and expression can be either highly specialized (strongly institutionalized) or less specialized (weakly institutionalized). The analysis thus developed an account of four possible recontextualizing strategies. The language of academic mathematics is usually articulated in a highly specialized mode of expression that signifies highly specialized meanings, or content. Dowling describes instances of such specialized content and expression as strategies within the esoteric domain. Mathematics textbooks, in contrast to academic mathematics, tend to recontextualize mathematical knowledge in two possible ways. The first of these maintains the specialized content, but expresses this content in a more accessible, less specialized language; Dowling calls this the expressive domain. The other strategy is to deploy the specialized language of academic mathematics, but to transform or simplify the content to which the language refers: the descriptive domain. The final possibility is to use neither the specialized content, nor the specialized vocabulary, to establish something that may be called mathematics within a school context but that appears to have no relation to what is called mathematics by mathematicians: this type of action constitutes what Dowling calls the public domain.

The question is: In what way are the terms of one discourse repeated and transformed in a new setting? This question is significant in relation to the further question: In what way does the repetition and transformation of the terms of a discourse constitute social alliances and oppositions? Dowling's analysis suggests ways in which the recontextualizing strategies articulated in school textbooks aimed at contrasting groups of students might contribute to the socially differentiated distribution of educational opportunities.

This approach to the analysis of social activity might be productive in exploring the relation between any two discourses. Steinmetz's analysis of Bourdieu's relation to psychoanalysis might be rearticulated in the terms of Dowling's language. According to Steinmetz, Bourdieu sometimes uses the specialized language of psychoanalysis, without taking on the full implications or meanings associated with these terms, while at other times his own language expresses, without acknowledgement, specialized meanings associated with Lacanian psychoanalysis. Steinmetz's account thus suggests that, in relation to psychoanalytic discourse, Bourdieu's work constitutes activity within Dowling's expressive and descriptive domains. However, in describing this activity in terms of (de)negation or disavowal, Steinmetz's analysis also suggests psychical aspects to Bourdieu's relation to psychoanalysis that are not accounted for within Dowling's schema.

In order to introduce an explicitly psychical relation into the analysis of recontextualizing strategies, we might think of texts as instances of either articulation or substitution of signifiers and signifieds. As discussed in Chapters 2 and 4, the concepts of articulation and substitution describe the relation between the symbolic order and discourse (Lacan, 1957; Laclau and Mouffe, 2001). The free floating signifiers of the symbolic order are ordered and articulated within discourse, but can also be excluded through psychical mechanisms of substitution, such as the disavowal that Steinmetz traces in Bourdieu's relation to Lacan. The articulation of a signifier within a specified discourse constitutes an identification (in Dowling's terms, perhaps, an alliance) between that discourse and other discourses in which the signifier is also situated. In contrast, when one signifier is substituted for another an oppositional relation is established with the discourse into which the expelled signifier is deposited. Steinmetz suggests that at times Bourdieu explicitly rejects psychoanalysis, accusing Freud of biological reductionism, thus constituting an opposition between sociology and the negative associations of biologism that are deposited onto the discourse of psychoanalysis. In addition, Steinmetz's analysis suggests that the articulation or substitution of signifiers of personal or disciplinary origins (mentioning or failing to mention Lacan, for example) may be of relevance to the analysis of recontextualizing strategies within disciplinary knowledge practices.

This understanding of processes of discursive articulation and substitution provides an initial frame for the exploration of contrasting uses of Melanie Klein's theoretical language presented in this chapter. The account developed in the chapter draws attention to the way contrasting pieces of research either articulate or substitute different aspects of Klein's theory of ego development, and also notes where the same pieces of work articulate or substitute a relation to 'Klein', the author, as a significant influence or origin. The analysis constructs a trajectory from Jacques' work, which repeats Klein's conceptual framework in more or less its original form, to Lyth's work, which extends and elaborates Klein's theory in recognition of the 'emotional world of the organisation' (Armstrong, 2005), and finally to an exploration of Bernstein's work, which deploys Kleinian vocabulary in a way that has the potential to radically subvert the association between notions of the psyche and notions of the individual.

Two aspects of Melanie Klein's theory: the development of the infant ego and the psychic defence mechanisms

In order to explore contrasting articulations of Klein's work it will be useful to distinguish two aspects of her theory: first, there is a speculative, inferential story about the development of the infant in the earliest stages of ego formation; and second there is a set of concepts that define possible relations between a subject and the objects that, in Kleinian terms, constitute the internal world of the subject. The speculative story narrates the infant's construction of an internal world of good and bad objects, and their development from a sense of being persecuted by dangerous part objects to a sense of whole objects that are ambivalent and vulnerable in nature. The different stages[1] in the story are characterized by different kinds of defences in the infant's construction of psychical objects: violent defences in the paranoid stage and more conciliatory defences as the infant perceives the wholeness of, and develops a more ambivalent relation towards, their objects. It is through their changing relation to these objects, mediated by the presence of the mother, that the infant begins to develop a more stable sense of their own identity. The second aspect of Klein's theory is her specification of different forms in which the psychic defences might appear. The concepts of splitting, projection and introjection are elaborated in Klein's articulation of principles that distinguish different possible instantiations of these relations between subject and object. I will explain both these aspects of Klein's theory in more detail in the following sections.

Within Klein's own work there is a relation between the interpretation of specified forms of defences within the behaviour of individual patients and her diagnosis of their current psychical position; and the generalized narrative of ego development is understood to be an inference based on the experience of these defences in clinical psychoanalytic work. This chapter explores the extent to which these kinds of inferences from the observation of specific psychical defences to psychologizing accounts of ego development are rearticulated or substituted in research carried out in non-clinical settings.

Klein's narrative of the development of the ego, the paranoid schizoid and the depressive positions

The first aspect of Klein's theory, then, is her narrative of the development of the ego. This narrative constructs an account of human infancy that prioritizes an intensely affective primary encounter with both internal drives and the external world. Klein's narration of this encounter suggests that experiences of the drives and the external world are internalized, gradually building up a parallel world of inner objects. However, this inner world is, in Klein's words, 'inaccessible to the child's accurate observation and judgment', and 'phantastic' – the product of unconscious fantasy – giving rise to an overwhelming sense of doubt and anxiety (1940, p. 149). This anxiety, for Klein, is related to the death drive, the infant's own destructive impulses, and also to the painful experience of bodily needs and functions, all of which are felt as persecuting and attributed to 'objects' over which the infant has no control:

> I hold that anxiety arises from the operation of the death instinct within the organism, is felt as fear of annihilation (death) and takes the form of fear of persecution. The fear of the destructive impulse seems to attach itself at once to an object – or rather it is experienced as the fear of an uncontrollable overpowering object. Other important sources of anxiety are the trauma of birth (separation anxiety) and frustration of bodily needs; and these experiences too are from the beginning felt as being caused by objects.
>
> (1946, p. 179)

This extract suggests the transformation of the direct experience of an internal drive, the 'destructive impulse', into an inner object that the infant experiences as 'uncontrollable and overpowering'. Similarly, the infant's experience of the external frustration of bodily needs is transformed into an inner object that is the cause of its distress. The conceptualization of 'inner objects' provides a powerful metaphor for the infant's initial, unstable relation to the sensations that arise in response to its experience of both inner drives and external world. In these early stages of development, external objects are only partially represented internally, as they are only experienced in so far as they relate to an immediate bodily need and are thus satisfying or frustrating, good or bad. The concepts of 'inner object', 'part object' and, later on, 'whole object' are integral to Klein's account of infant development.

According to Klein, then, at this early stage the infant does not have a sense of itself as differentiated from the external world. This inability to separate leads to a sense of overwhelming persecution, as the infant feels itself subject to attack from internal bodily sensations and from frustrating part objects that fail to gratify bodily needs. This sense of persecution gives rise to great anxiety and fear of annihilation. According to Klein, the infant defends against this anxiety by attempting to control the attacking objects, which s/he does by the interrelated processes of splitting, projection and introjection (1946, p. 182): in phantasy, the infant splits off the good and bad parts of the object, and is thus able to control them, through processes of denial, idealization, projection and introjection, thus gaining some relief from the persecutory anxiety. However, the relief is incomplete, as the defences in this stage are largely destructive. Klein summarizes: 'In paranoia the characteristic defences are chiefly aimed at annihilating the 'persecutors', while anxiety on the ego's account occupies a prominent place in the picture' (1935, p. 118).

Klein emphasizes the unconscious, phantasmatic nature of these processes, and also their psychical effects:

> It is in phantasy that the infant splits the object and the self, but the effect of this phantasy is a very real one, because it leads to feelings and relations (and later on, thought processes) being in fact cut off from one another.
>
> (1946, p. 181)

This is what Klein terms the paranoid schizoid position. According to Klein, this is the dominant position of the infant in the very early development of the ego: the unconscious defences bring relief from the overwhelming sensation of destruction, but they also weaken the ego and impede integration and stability.

In the normal development of the infant, according to Klein, the dominance of the paranoid schizoid position is followed by dominance of the depressive position, within which the infant begins to recognize whole objects that contain both good and bad aspects. At this stage the infant begins to learn to tolerate ambivalence, but this brings with it a new array of difficult feelings. Klein argues:

> in my view, already during the sucking period, when it comes to know its mother as a whole person and when it progresses from the introjection of part objects to the introjection of the whole object, the infant experiences some of the feelings of guilt and remorse, some of the pain which results from the conflict between love and uncontrollable hatred, some of the anxieties of the impending death of the loved internalized and external objects...
>
> (1935, p. 142)

Whereas in the paranoid schizoid position, the infant is only concerned with its own survival, in the depressive position it comes to recognize other objects as also vulnerable, and experiences guilt related to its own feelings of hatred and its destructive attacks on these objects, both internally and in the external world. While paranoid fears are reduced in the depressive position, feelings of guilt, remorse and responsibility for loved objects come to the fore. Klein clarifies:

> I am aware how difficult it is to draw a sharp line between the anxiety contents and feelings of the paranoiac and those of the depressive, since they are so closely linked up with each other. But they can be distinguished one from the other if, as a criterion of differentiation, one considers whether the persecution anxiety is mainly related to the preservation of the ego – in which case it is paranoiac – or to the preservation of the good internalized objects with whom the ego is identified as a whole. In the latter case – which is the case of the depressive – the anxiety and feelings of suffering are of a much more complex nature.
>
> (ibid., p. 124)

For Klein, these positions are first experienced in early infancy, but they are the basis for our engagement with the world in later life, when we continue to shift between the paranoid schizoid and the depressive positions. This story of the shifts between the persecutory anxieties of the paranoid schizoid position and the anxious guilt and remorse of the depressive position, through the development of an inner world of partial and whole objects, constitutes Melanie Klein's account of infant development and its continuing effects in adult mental life. I have suggested that this account of what constitutes normal infant development, the inner world of the infant and the implications this might have for adult mental life, is a speculative inference based on clinical observation. However, the conceptual structure that frames these clinical observations can be broken down into constitutive elements that are not dependent on, and that do not necessarily imply, the more individualized narrative aspect of Klein's theory.

The psychic defences: identification, introjection, projection and projective identification

Klein's account of the way introjective and projective processes construct an inner representational world, which replicates the infant's experience of both inner drives and external interactions, constitutes one aspect of the concept of psychic defences. However, the theorization of these psychical mechanisms also has a second aspect which supports empirical analysis. Processes of internalization or introjection are suggested where we get a sense of separate elements within the psyche, and where there is some reference to an external source for these elements. In contrast to introjection, processes of projection are suggested when we get a sense that the subject's own feelings or characteristics are being attributed to another object. So when a child talking about seeing their old primary school building being knocked down says, 'It makes me feel sad. It's not nice for the building for that to happen. I feel sorry for it', we might interpret this as a projection of the child's unwanted feelings of sadness onto the building.[2] Klein's theorization of an inner world made up of part and whole objects that represent our feelings and experiences provides a vivid metaphorical language for the development of these kinds of interpretations. However, it is not necessary to incorporate her narrative of infant development into the analysis of psychical defence mechanisms.

The psychoanalytic literature elaborates possible distinctions between the closely related processes of identification, internalization and introjection.[3] Sandler (1988) distinguishes different forms of internalization in Freud's writing: 'the internalization of external prohibitions and regulations' and the 'internalization of aggression, the turning of aggressive impulses inwards' (p. 7). In his discussion of melancholia Freud makes a distinction between the internalization of social sanctions or prohibitions and the internalization of the parents/lost object (1923). The use of either 'internalization' or 'introjection' to refer to these different psychic relations is inconsistent, blurring the definitions of the terms. Nevertheless, some theorists articulate productive distinctions, between, for example, identification, which involves an alteration in the subject's self-representation, and introjection, in which the internalized object is kept apart from the sense of self. Sandler suggests:

> From a representational point of view it is valuable to make a sharp distinction between identification as a modification of the self-representation on the one hand, and introjection as the setting up of unconscious, internal 'phantom' companions, felt to be part of one's inner world, yet external to one's self-representation, on the other.
>
> (1988, p. 11)

For example, when a child says that it is important for her to keep her room tidy to help mummy, we might interpret this as an internalization of adult praise or sanction. This internalized object might support the child in ordering and controlling her world. In such a case we might say that she has identified with the object, that a 'modification of the self-representation' has taken place. Alternatively, the injunction to keep her room tidy might act as a critical voice of sanction, pointing out when she fails to live up to the internalized regulation. Following Sandler, we might describe this as an instance of introjection without identification, where the introjected object constitutes an 'internal phantom companion', an inner voice that is not integrated into the child's self representation.

A similar range of theoretical distinctions is evident in debates over the meanings of projection and/or projective identification. In general, projection is understood as the attribution of one's own feelings or aspects of one's character to an external object. The term projective identification is sometimes used to suggest the way in which this process has effects that go beyond the subject's image of the object, into the object itself: i.e. the object of the projection will in some way either respond to, or take on the elements attributed to them. The nature of the process of projective identification is the subject of debate: is it an intense form of projection that nevertheless occurs only in the phantasy of the subject; is it a more concrete response by the object of the projection to communication of the projection by the subject; or is it a more mystical sounding movement of affect between two subjects (Sandler, 1988; Meissner, 1988, see p. 62; Jervis, 2009)?[4] Klein's own position is probably closer to the first of these. She describes the process as 'the phantasy of forcefully entering the object' (1946, p. 186), limiting its effects to the subject, and not the object, of the projection. Contemporary post-Kleinians, following the ideas of Wilfred Bion (1961), tend to adhere to the second interpretation, which suggests an interpersonal model of projective identification.

Joseph (1988) provides a useful summary of some forms of projective identification suggested in Klein's work:

> She discussed the manifold aims of different types of projective identification, for example, splitting off and getting rid of unwanted parts of the self that cause anxiety or pain; projecting the self or parts of the self into an object to dominate and control it and thus avoid any feelings of being separate; getting into an object to take over its capacities and make them its own; invading in order to damage or destroy the object. Thus the infant, or adult who goes on using such mechanisms powerfully, can avoid any awareness of separateness, dependence or admiration or of the concomitant sense of loss, anger, envy, etc. But it sets up persecutory anxieties, claustrophobia, panics and the like.
>
> (Joseph, 1988, pp. 65–66; see also Klein, 1946, p. 183)

This account suggests three different instantiations of projective identification. The first of these, 'splitting off and getting rid of unwanted parts of the self that cause anxiety or pain', is probably the meaning that is most assimilated into everyday language. If I am deeply competitive and yet ashamed of my competitive feelings, I may project this characteristic of mine onto those around me, so that, for example, I fear others' envy of my success. This is an unconscious identification in which I deny my own feelings and in phantasy project them onto the other.

Joseph describes two further instantiations of projective identification: 'projecting parts of the self into an object to dominate and control it and thus avoid any feelings of being separate'; and 'getting into an object to take over its capacities'. The first of these describes instances where the unconscious assumption of sameness can be a mechanism for control and exploitation. The second describes a different kind of merging, where the subject seeks to construct an identity from the characteristics of the other.

These processes can protect against painful feelings of separateness, but can evoke difficult feelings when the object in some way reasserts its separate identity. The documentary *Man on Wire* provides an instance where it is possible to see the interrelation between these two types of projective identification.

Man on Wire tells the story of the wire walker Philipe Petit, and his successful plot to walk on a high wire between the Twin Towers in New York. The story is narrated by Petit himself, and is told through a combination of dramatic reconstruction and interviews with the friends who helped him to carry out his plan. Petit comes across as a fascinating, seductive character, totally overwhelmed by his own desire to perform between the Towers that he feels were constructed almost for this purpose: to tantalize, seduce and finally to be conquered by his skills on the wire. However, in order to achieve this goal, he requires the support of a group of co-conspirators who will help him to enter the towers and set up his wire. The most committed of these is a childhood friend who has helped to set up his wires for previous dangerous and illegal walks. When Petit calls to ask for his help, his friend flies over from France to take his part in the performance. Petit also recruits an Australian and two New Yorkers, each of whom drops out before the wire is in place: they are scared by the mortal risk to Petit if the walk is unsuccessful. Clearly, for Petit, the necessity to walk obliterates the immensity of what he is asking of his friends. This is what enables him to persuade them to help him to put himself at risk. He projects his own commitment onto those around him, charismatically merging their desires with his own. In Petit's case, perhaps, this projection is not related to a fear of separateness, but to other aspects of his overwhelming commitment to his art. For his friend the inverse mode of projective identification seems to be taking place. He seems to find an identity of his own in Petit's desire. He becomes deeply engaged in refining the details of the plans and its final execution, and revels in his position as the member of the group who has the greatest understanding and experience of how Petit sets up his wires. We might describe his relation to Petit as a way of constructing an identity by 'getting into an object to take over its capacities'.

The walk is successful, and Petit is lauded by the New York public, who are overwhelmed and grateful for the feat he has performed for them. Petit succumbs to his celebrity, apparently oblivious to his friend's contribution, and it seems that the friendship between the two men is broken. At the end of the documentary, which is enthusiastically narrated by Petit, his friend weeps, and cannot finish telling his part in the story. This example, I think, implicitly suggests how projective identification might be understood as an interpersonal experience in which the projections of each party influence or intensify the responses of the other, rather than as a purely individual phenomenon.[5]

Within Kleinian and post-Kleinian psychoanalysis these conceptualizations of projection and introjection are used to describe individual and interpersonal relations. However these different forms of psychic defences have also been used to explore the construction of social and institutional identities. Examples from organization studies and sociology can illustrate the productivity of this usage. As I have suggested, though, it is possible to mark out a distinction within this work between studies that articulate conceptualizations of both the psychical defence mechanisms and the narrative of the internal world, and studies that substitute or supplement the narrative of ego development with a conceptualization of social structures and institutions. The conceptual tussle taking place is over the centrality, or not, of the individual as the site of psychical identity.

From psychic defence to social defence: the recontextualization of Kleinian ideas into organizational analysis

Within psychoanalytically informed organization studies, it is possible to mark out a distinction between work that continues to conceptualize anxiety in the context of individual development and work that re-conceptualizes anxiety in the context of the organization. Writing some time after the first studies published by the Tavistock group, David Armstrong suggests this distinction in his analysis of the field of psychoanalytically oriented organizational research and consultancy. He points out that work within this field can focus too much on individual or group relations, missing out what he describes as 'the organization as an independent variable':

> I am thinking, for example of the work done on narcissistic leadership, or the role of oedipal configurations, or some of the work on group and team dynamics or on inter- and intra group relations. Within this body of work, the organization as an independent variable, with its own internal logic – political, socio-technical, but also psychic – can easily get lost. Or, to put this the other way round, the emotional world of the organization can appear simply as a function, a kind of artifact, of human relations within it.
>
> (Armstrong, 2005, p. 93)

Armstrong suggests that there is a psychic logic that is specific to organizations that should not be subordinated to theories of individual or group development. In doing this he suggests the possibility of substituting or supplementing the conceptualization of the individual within Kleinian discourse with a conceptualization of the institution.

It is worth noting Armstrong's use of the term 'independent variable' to describe the logics of the organization. This maintains a sense of organization and individual as separate entities that prefigure the analysis; so he is not rejecting a notion of individual psychic development, but simply introducing the organization as a psychical entity, an 'emotional world' in its own right. It would be possible to go further than this; to begin to trouble the distinction between 'individual development' and 'organization' in the constitution of subjectivity. It is perhaps an artefact of the position of the field of psychoanalytically informed organization studies as a direct offshoot of traditional schools of psychoanalytic training, and specifically the Kleinian oriented Tavistock Clinic, that it articulates such clear continuities with traditional, individualizing psychoanalytic notions of development.

The rest of this section maps out the trajectory Armstrong constructs, from the prioritization of individualized conceptions of defences against anxiety, to a fuller recognition of anxiety as a part of the 'emotional world of the organization'. My account constructs Elliott Jaques' work as an instance of the former, and the work of Isabel Menzies Lyth as an instance of the latter. Jaques' exploration of relations between workers, workers representatives and management representatives in a wage negotiation uses Kleinian concepts to explore group processes as social, rather than purely psychical, instantiations of the defences of projection and introjection. However he does not extend his analysis to include structures or practices inherent to the institution. Lyth's study of a hospital nursing service, in contrast, focuses on ways specific practices within the service can be understood as institutionalized social defences against anxieties that inhere within the work of the hospital. She thus shifts the focus away from the individual as the source of anxiety, and away from interpersonal relations as the site of defences. The shift away from an understanding of anxiety as originating in internal drives to an understanding of anxiety as embedded within social organizations represents a move away from Klein's narrative of infant development, while still making use of her theorization of the psychic defences. Jaques' and Lyth's contrasting approaches can be understood as distinct recontextualizing strategies in relation to a Kleinian psychoanalytic discourse.

Elliott Jaques: group processes, 'social defences' and a Kleinian language of individual ego development

There are three aspects of Jaques' work that are of analytical interest in relation to the recontextualization of the concept of 'psychic defences' in organizational research and consultancy. First, his development of an understanding of 'social defences', as mechanisms that are similar to 'psychic defences', but that are common to groups of individuals, socially sanctioned in a way that is not the case with the original Kleinian concept. Second, his reiteration of both Klein's theory of ego development and her conceptual language of 'projection', 'introjection' and 'splitting'. And finally, his conceptualization of the therapeutic effects of his own analysis and interpretations.

Between 1948 and 1951, Jaques carried out an exploration of processes of cultural change and industrial conflict in the Glacier Metal Company (Jaques, 1951). He presents this exploration as somewhere between a consultancy project, a therapeutic intervention, and a piece of research. In reporting the project Jaques sometimes refers to 'the research team' or 'the researchers' and sometimes to 'the consultant', and it is clear that 'the consultant' offered interpretations during meetings that were designed to draw participants' attention to the psychical construction of their interactions. For example, when workers' representatives in a meeting to negotiate a new payment system expressed the view that 'all supervisors were on management's side', Jaques notes that this comment appeared to reiterate earlier suspicions expressed about the role of the research team. He reports: 'The consultant therefore interpreted this to them as a displacement on to supervision of suspicion towards himself and the research team, representing once again their own suspicion of each other at the moment' (1951, p. 383). The consultant suggests that the general suspicions the participants have of each other are being 'displaced' from one group to another. This kind of interpretation is understood to have a direct influence on the progress of the negotiations. Jaques' comments that the interpretation was 'vigorously denied'; but he also notes that after the denial the participants noticed that supervisors were not represented at the meeting, and they agreed to make sure they were present in future meetings (ibid., p. 383). There is an implication that the consultant's intervention might have contributed to the realization that supervisors should be invited to join the negotiations, and this constitutes a therapeutic aspect to Jaques' intervention in the Glacier Metal Company.

The consultant's intervention in the pay negotiations uses a psychoanalytic language to rearticulate what is going on in the meeting. The interpretation, noting the way feelings of mistrust or suspicion are moved from one object to another, suggests the comment that 'all supervisors were on managements' side' can be understood as an instance of projection, whereby bad or unwanted aspects of the self are 'displaced' onto the other. Within a Kleinian framework, it is possible to suggest that the workers' representatives' doubts and uncertainties in relation both to the potential change in the payment system and to their own role in the negotiations are displaced, in turn, onto the researchers, the supervisors and the managers, in order to defend against persecutory anxieties. What is of note here, for Jaques, is the social aspect of the projective process: the workers' representatives find a shared object through which to defend against their anxieties. Because the workers' representatives constitute their supervisors as a shared object of projection, Jaques suggests that the process should be understood as a social, rather than a psychical defence mechanism. In such instances, he suggests, the aggression directed at the object by the ego is sanctioned within the shared practice: 'Social sanction means that denial of unconscious hatred and destructive impulses against internal objects can be reinforced by turning these impulses against a publicly hated real external enemy' (1951, p. 427). He goes on to elaborate the psychical function of social legitimation. He suggests that the social sanction of destructive impulses is introjected, and supports the ego in its denial of aggression and avoidance of the associated anxiety and guilt (p. 427). For Jaques the social here refers merely to a similar psychical process experienced by a group of individuals. He does not elaborate more specific features of the social context, such as the differential roles of the various participants in the negotiations, which might constitute a significant aspect of these projective processes.

In addition to this reiteration of the association between the psychic defences and the individual, Jaques' account also invokes elements of Klein's developmental narrative, explicitly referring back to the paranoid schizoid and depressive positions that she theorizes as constitutive of the early stages of development of the ego. He suggests: 'institutions are used by their individual members to reinforce mechanisms of defence against anxiety, and in particular against recurrence of the early paranoid and depressive anxieties first described by Melanie Klein' (p. 420). This kind of assertion reconstructs Klein's inference from interpretations of mechanisms such as projection and displacement to, in Jaques' words, 'processes of working through the unresolved conflicts of the infantile depressive position' (p. 429). Jaques thus detaches the interpretation from the context of the institution and reinserts it into the story of the development and integration of the ego. This constitutes the role of social defences such as shared processes of displacement and projection as one of helping individuals to 'find relief from their own internal persecution' (p. 426). The repeated inference from psychical defence mechanisms back to individualized anxieties obscures the specific tensions and anxieties of the factory within Jaques' analysis.

Similar moves, identifying interactions as instances of developmental positions, can be seen in other examples in Jaques' analysis of the pay negotiations at the Glacier Metal Company. He suggests that when the workers expressed suspicion of their elected representatives, their own 'bad' impulses are first projected (onto their representatives) and then reintrojected in such a way that they can be 'maintained as a segregated part of the ego' (p. 433). This process is, again, supported through social sanction:

> In addition to defence against internal persecution, the introjection of the other workers provided social sanction for considering the internalized representatives as bad, offsetting the harshness of super-ego recriminations for attacking objects which contained good as well as a persecuting component.
>
> (p. 433)

The reference to 'super-ego recriminations for attacking objects which contained good as well as a persecuting components' invokes Klein's depressive position, and the guilt introduced with the recognition of ambivalence.

Both the managers and the elected representatives are similarly inscribed within the terms of infant development towards an integrated ego. The managers' expressions of trust in the workers are described as an 'idealization' that is interpreted as a way of avoiding the implications of the exercise of managerial authority:

> The idealization can be understood as an unconscious mechanism for diminishing guilt which was stimulated by fears of injuring or destroying workers in the day to day situation through the exercise of managerial authority – an authority which, there is good reason to believe is, at least to some extent, unconsciously felt to be uncontrolled and omnipotent.
>
> (p. 433)

This interpretation constructs the managers as overwhelmed by a sense of their own authority, and of the damage this might inflict on their subordinates. It mirrors Melanie Klein's account of the infant's sense of its destructive impulses as dangerously omnipotent, and able to bring about the death of good objects. However, there are other possible interpretations of the managers' expressions of trust in the workers; and the inference from an interpretation of mechanisms of idealization back to positions associated with early development pathologizes and infantalizes the managers' approach.

In a similar way, the 'suspicion and hostility' expressed by the workers' representatives during meetings with managers are interpreted in terms of their 'anxiety and guilt about damaging the good managers': a further iteration of the depressive position. Jaques suggests:

> The primary defence mechanism against the onset of depressive anxiety was that of retreat to the paranoid schizoid position. This came out as a rigid clinging to attitudes of suspicion and hostility even in situations where there was a conscious feeling that some of this suspicion was not justified by the situation actually being experienced by the representatives.
>
> (p. 433)

The description of 'retreat to the paranoid schizoid position' re-inscribes the participants within a Kleinian trajectory of infant ego development. In its rigid reiteration of this narrative, Jaques' analysis might be said to displace alternative interpretations that might situate the suspicion and hostility observed within the hierarchically differentiated structures of the setting.

Finally, it is worth briefly noting Jaques' claims regarding the therapeutic effects of his interpretations within the process of negotiation. He suggests that the conflict between the parties in the negotiations was 'partly resolved' by the 'open interpretation' of the suspicions and idealizations articulated by participants (p. 436). However, he also acknowledges an important social mechanism that supported the resolution. This was the setting up of a Council of workers and management with an ongoing role in determining policy within the department. Jaques describes the Council as 'an explicit social institution ... which allowed for the establishment of unconscious mechanisms at the phantasy level for dealing with paranoid and depressive anxieties'. He suggests that both the consultant's interpretations and the mechanism of the Council 'helped individuals to deal with anxiety' (p. 436). He thus conceptualizes therapeutic support as something directed at individual anxieties, rather than at the emotional configuration of the institution as a whole.

As David Armstrong has suggested, Jaques' focus on individual anxiety does not only fail to recognize the significance of the emotional life of organizations, it also pushes the therapeutic resources of the consultant in the wrong direction, and misdiagnoses the object of treatment as the emotional well being of individuals. For Armstrong, emotions interpreted in the analysis are not the object of treatment, but rather a clue in coming to understand the life of the organization: 'No emotional experience in organizational life is a suitable case for treatment. Rather, a resource for thinking, for releasing intelligence' (2005, p. 109). Emotional experience may be articulated by individuals, but the intelligence it offers relates to the structuring of the organization.

Isabel Menzies Lyth: the location of anxiety within the social system

The organizational analysis developed by Isabel Menzies Lyth (1959) references Jaques' work and at several points it echoes his recourse to the language of individual psychical development. However, Lyth's analysis also constitutes a precise articulation of the social aspects of anxiety: the production of anxiety within social systems and organizations. As we have seen, Jaques analyses the projections of parties in the pay negotiations, but he does not situate these projections in an analysis of organizational structures or of the substantive content of organizational activities. Lyth's study of the nursing service in a teaching hospital contextualizes the social defences against anxiety in a way that shifts the analysis from individuals or groups of individuals to the broader structures and purposes of the organization. The empirical basis of the study comprised observations, interviews and group discussions, which fed into more 'therapeutic' activities with five senior nurses.[6] Lyth's publications on the study focus largely on the initial analysis, rather than on the more therapeutic work. There are two stages to this analysis.

The first stage contextualizes the production of anxiety within the nursing service in relation to the objectives, or 'primary task', of the hospital. Lyth suggests that the emotions related to the 'objective situation' of the hospital 'stimulate afresh' the 'primitive levels of the mind' associated with 'early situations' (1959, pp. 46–47). The detail of her analysis foregrounds features of the 'objective situation': the nurses' relations to illness and to patients and relatives within the hospital:

> The direct impact on the nurse of physical illness is intensified by her task of meeting and dealing with psychological stress in other people, including her own colleagues. It is by no means easy to tolerate such stress even if one is not under similar stress oneself. Quite short conversations with patients or relatives showed that their conscious concept of illness and treatment is a rich intermixture of objective knowledge, logical deduction and fantasy. The degree of stress is heavily conditioned by the fantasy, which is in turn conditioned, as in nurses, by the early phantasy situations. Unconsciously, the nurse associates the patients' and relatives' distress with that experienced by the people in her phantasy world, which increases her own anxiety and difficulty in handling it.
>
> (p. 48)

This analysis gives equal weight to the 'objective' features of the hospital and to the internal objects of the nurses' inner representational world. The objective features include the 'direct impact on the nurse of physical illness' and the mixture of knowledge and fantasy in patients' and relatives' 'concept of illness and treatment', all of which constitute a part of the everyday working context of nurses in the department. The emotions associated with a nurse's inner representational world are evoked where s/he is not able to maintain a distinction between 'objective reality' and the 'phantasy situations' of her inner world. Lyth suggests that this distinction is achieved through symbolization: 'To be effective, such symbolization requires that the symbol *represents* the phantasy object, but *is not equated* with it'. She continues: 'If, for any reason, the symbol and the phantasy object become almost or completely equated, the anxieties aroused by the phantasy object are aroused in full intensity by the symbolic object' (p. 49). Lyth describes an instance when the distinction between symbol and phantasy object was not sustained: 'a nurse whose mother had had several gynaecological operations broke down and had to give up nursing shortly after beginning her tour of duty on the gynaecological ward' (p. 50). Through this analysis of 'objective features' of the setting and their relation to the 'phantasy world' of the nurses, Lyth constitutes a link between the two as inherent to her analysis of the nursing service: the anxieties experienced by the nurses cannot be separated from the organizational context of the hospital. A similar analysis in Jaques study of the Glacier

Metal Company might have foregrounded the contrasting objectives of workers and managers within the organization, and the ways in which the fantasies they constructed might be accounted for in relation to specific features of their differential positioning.

In concluding this first stage of her analysis Lyth argues that nurses' relations to illness, patients and relatives are not sufficient to account for the high levels of anxiety observed during the study. The second stage of her analysis explores the social defences established within the nursing service: the institutionalized practices constructed to alleviate anxiety. Lyth argues that institutional practices that might appear to protect against anxieties related to the primary task of hospital care can fail in this function, or can themselves become the source of secondary anxieties within the nursing service.

Lyth suggests that the members of an organization, in this case the nursing service, 'use' the organization to avoid anxiety: to do this they develop 'socially structured defence mechanisms which appear as elements in the organization's structure, culture and mode of functioning' (p. 50). For example, in order to avoid the intense anxieties likely to be provoked in personal relations with severely ill patients, the service is organized to limit the development of such relations, by dividing the care of individual patients into 'tasks' allocated to several nurses:

> The nursing service attempts to protect her from the anxiety by split-
> ting up her contact with patients. It is hardly too much to say that the
> nurse does not nurse patients. The total workload of a ward or depart-
> ment is broken down into lists of tasks, each of which is allocated to a
> particular nurse. She performs her patient centred tasks for a large
> number of patients – perhaps as many as all the patients in the ward,
> often thirty or more. As a corollary, she performs only a few tasks for,
> and has restricted contact with, any one patient. This prevents her
> from coming effectively into contact with the totality of any one
> patient and his illness and offers protection from the anxiety this
> arouses.
>
> (p. 51)

Lyth's interpretation of the 'task list' as a mechanism for organizing nurses' practice suggests that it aids 'depersonalization' and the 'elimination of individual distinctiveness in both nurse and patient' (p. 52). This contrib-utes to 'an almost explicit 'ethic' that any patient must be the same as any other patient' (p. 52), so that nurses avoid or suppress preferences for or relationships with individual patients. This ethic is also instantiated in a general denial of the disturbing feelings and emotional strain that arise in response to distressing situations nurses face within their work. Lyth reports, for example, that when a student nurse makes a mistake, 'she is usually reprimanded rather than helped' (p. 54). Thus, while the division of labour instantiated in the task list might reduce the likelihood of nurses developing relations with patients that might cause them anxiety, it also contributes to an ethos that denies support and recognition of necessarily distressing situations.

Lyth also notes an underlying fear within the service that practitioners will behave irresponsibly. This fear is instantiated in the regulation of practice by means of the task list, but also in the ways that nurses talked about each other. Lyth reports:

> Nurses habitually complain that other nurses are irresponsible, behave carelessly and impulsively, and in consequence must be ceaselessly supervised and disciplined. The complaints commonly refer not to individuals or to specific incidents but to whole categories of nurses, usually a category junior to the speaker.
>
> (p. 57)

Lyth argues that these complaints, usually targeted at a group rather than an individual, 'stem from a collusive system of denial, splitting and projection'. She suggests that all nurses have greater or lesser tendencies towards irresponsibility, and that in order to deal with these frightening tendencies they split them off, and project them onto their colleagues, so that: 'Her irresponsible impulses, which she fears she cannot control, are attributed to her juniors' (p. 57). The shared objectification of junior nurses as irresponsible can thus be understood as a social defence against anxieties more senior nurses have about their own irresponsibility. In addition, these processes of projection support a strict disciplinary regime, within which mistakes are treated as irresponsibility and suitably reprimanded. As with the task list, the effect is to suppress the justified anxiety related to the primary task of nursing, and to construct ways in which the practice of the department was likely to evoke secondary anxieties, not directly related to the primary task, but related instead to the strict hierarchical regime within the service.

Lyth concludes that the system of social defences within the nursing service 'itself arouses a good deal of secondary anxiety as well as failing to alleviate primary anxiety' (p. 65). She argues, further, that the effect of the defences is to prevent individuals from experiencing or confronting their anxieties:

> Thus the individual cannot bring the content of the phantasy anxiety situations into effective contact with reality. Unrealistic or pathological anxiety cannot be differentiated from realistic anxiety arising from real dangers ... The forced introjection of the hospital defence system, therefore, perpetuates in the individual a considerable degree of pathological anxiety.
>
> (pp. 74–75)

The suggestion is that the social defences are internalized by those working within the system and that the internalized social defences cover over unbearable feelings of anxiety, rather than addressing or coming to a more considered understanding of their source. For Lyth, as we have seen, the source of the nurses' anxieties must be contextualized within the primary task of the hospital: relations to illness, patients and relatives. Her articulation of a conception of institutionally structured defence mechanisms supplements Klein's psychic defences and at points substitutes the institution for the individual as the site of anxiety. This disrupts the individualized narrative of ego development as a progression from the paranoid schizoid to the depressive position, and places the emotional life of the organization at the centre of the analysis.

Modes of recontextualization of Kleinian discourse

As I have suggested, it is possible to interpret Jaques' work and Lyth's study as instantiations of contrasting strategies for the recontextualization of Kleinian discourse. Jaques' work articulates identifications with both aspects of Klein's theory and substitutes her conceptualization of the paranoid schizoid and depressive positions for an account of the social structure of the factory. In so far as he reiterates her prioritization of the individual over a notion of social structure, Jaques' account also constitutes an identification with the management of the factory that already functions to individualize roles and responsibilities within the workplace. We might perhaps interpret this as a form of disavowal in which he sees but does not acknowledge the differential status of managers and workers. The factory is right in front of him, but all that Jaques sees is the infantile defences of the paranoid schizoid and depressive position. In contrast, Lyth's analysis both rearticulates Kleinian concepts and at the same time introduces supplementary terms into the discourse. These contrasting strategies might be understood in terms of Laclau and Mouffe's conceptualization of the logics of equivalence and difference (2001).[7] A logic of equivalence involves the metaphorical substitution of one term for another, while a logic of difference supports multiple meanings within the signifying system. Either strategy might act either to maintain or to subvert hegemonic social formations (see Howarth, 2000b, Marchart, 2004; Lapping, 2008). In this instance, Jaques' interpretive activity constitutes a logic that equates the factory with psychodynamics and obliterates the differences between social structure and individual. This equivalence extends the authority of the individualizing discourse of Kleinian psychoanalysis from the clinic to the factory. Lyth's strategy, in contrast, introduces a differential element which might act to limit or subvert psychoanalytic authority. However, while her conceptualization of the social defences shifts the focus from individual to social organization, she does not develop this as an explicit critique of psychoanalytic orthodoxy.

It is worth noting the dangers that might be associated with an explicit subversion of this kind of a hegemonic formation. In an interview with Ann Scott and Robert M. Young, while Lyth noted that she felt it was important for people involved in work with organizations to have a background in social science as well as a psychoanalytic training (Lyth, 1988, p. 8), she also talked about pressure she came under from the psychoanalytic community in relation to her work:

> when I continued my [organizational] work at the Tavi after I had qualified in psychoanalysis, I did come under a lot of pressure from senior Kleinian analysts who felt I was wasting my time and my gifts staying there when I could have been working full-time in psychoanalysis. That subsided a bit when my papers began to appear, which showed how I was using psychoanalysis, and also when I made fairly rapid progress in psychoanalysis, becoming a full member of the Society and a training analyst pretty quickly.
>
> (ibid., p. 33)

Insofar as it is possible to interpret Lyth's lack of acknowledgment of the disjunctures between her work and Klein's ideas – and her uncritical referencing of work by other researchers at the Tavistock – as a disavowal of the distinctiveness of her own work, this disavowal should be understood in relation to the pressure to conform to the powerful regulative authority of senior members of the psychoanalytic community. Just as Paul Dowling's (1998) work on school mathematics suggests the way different modes of recontextualization both construct and limit educational opportunities, so the mode of recontextualization of psychoanalytic ideas constructs and limits professional trajectories.

The articulation of 'psychic defences' within Basil Bernstein's theory of recontextualization

Where Jaques and Lyth were both professionally located within the Tavistock Institute of Human Relations, Bernstein, like Bourdieu, held a university post as a sociologist, and therefore did not require legitimization from psychoanalytic authorities. Nevertheless, the lack of reference to psychoanalytic theorists as sources for some of his ideas is noteworthy, since in other instances he does not conserve energy in trying to establish correct interpretations of his relations to other authors and fields. He devotes a paper to an account of his relation to the field of sociolinguistics, acknowledging his intellectual debt to Hallidayan linguistics and tracing his relation to other researchers within the field (Bernstein, 2000, pp. 145–153). Bernstein also spends considerable time distinguishing his theory from that of Bourdieu, providing evidence that Bourdieu's critique of his work is based on a misreading, and rejecting the suggestion that his own work might be seen as a development of Bourdieu's ideas (ibid., pp. 175–189):

> Harker and May state that my analysis of pedagogic discourse 'starts where Bourdieu and Passeron ... left off'. This is nonsense. The basic recontextualizing model is set out in the Introduction to *Class, Codes and Control*, Vol. III, 1975, p. 31, developed in Bernstein, 1981, whilst the concepts of instructional and regulative discourse go back much earlier (Bernstein, 1965) ... I have clearly gained much from reading Bourdieu; in particular, the concept of field. But there is a considerable difference which emerges out of my development of the importance of exploring within/between relationships ... *Homo academicus* is not about the constitution of academic discourses, their systems of transmission, their formations of specialized consciousness, it is about power games and their strategies.
>
> (pp. 188–189)

It would be possible to argue that Bernstein's refutation of the overlap between his work and that of Bourdieu has the structure of disavowal. Somewhat ironically, in refuting Bourdieu's interpretation of his work, Bernstein accuses him of 'reading omnipotence', which he defines as 'a clinical condition which renders texts which disturb one's own interpretation unread, even when they are' (p. 177). This would seem to be a version of Freudian disavowal, but Freud is not referenced. Indeed, in the collection of essays in which the comment appears, Freud's name appears once, in a long list of other major sociological and psychological theorists, and Melanie Klein is not referenced at all, despite Bernstein's use of the vocabulary of Kleinian psychic defences in his account of key concepts throughout the collection. Where psychotherapy is mentioned it is as a potential object of analysis, not as a source for his ideas (p. 212).

It is worth noting Bernstein's complicated strategies in relation to the acknowledgement of individual and disciplinary origins, but I don't want to speculate further about the possible meaning of these strategies.[8] Or at least, I simply want to note the productivity of reading Bernstein's suppression of a relation to psychoanalysis alongside Steinmetz's (2006) account of similar moves in Bourdieu's writing, which might mitigate any tendency to interpret either in terms of individual pathology. Instead we might speculate on the apparently allergic relation between the disciplinary field of sociology and the acknowledgement of key authors and theories from psychoanalysis. In the remainder of this chapter, however, I want to explore the potential productivity of Bernstein's unelaborated inclusion of Kleinian terms, to see what these psychoanalytic ideas might contribute to his theorization of processes of recontextualization.

Bernstein's work within the sociology of knowledge develops conceptual models that suggest how forms of knowledge are constituted in relation to the social contexts in which they are articulated. For example, he describes how the strength of boundaries between fields of disciplinary knowledge relates to organizational structures, and how this relationship will tend to serve the interests of one social group over another. For Bernstein, the strength of the boundaries between fields of knowledge constitutes a key feature in processes of recontextualization. He refers to this feature, the strength of the boundary insulating fields from each other, as 'classification'.

Bernstein invokes the notion of 'psychic defences' in relation to the principle of classification, that which constitutes distinctions between fields of knowledge, or discourses. He suggests that the principle of classification, the basis of differentiation, is always related to power and acts to naturalize what are in fact arbitrary power relations: 'the arbitrary nature of these power relations is disguised, hidden by the principle of classification' (2000, p. 7). In its function of disguise, Bernstein suggests, the principle of classification relates not only to external social relations, but also to 'relations within individuals'. It is this internal function of the principle of classification that Bernstein describes as 'a system of psychic defences':

> externally, the classificatory principle creates order, and the contradictions, cleavages and dilemmas which necessarily inhere in the principle of a classification are suppressed by the insulation. Within the individual, the insulation becomes a system of psychic defences against the possibility of the weakening of the insulation, which would then reveal the suppressed contradictions, cleavages and dilemmas. So the internal reality of insulation is a system of psychic defences to maintain the integrity of a category.
>
> (ibid., p. 7)

What Bernstein articulates here is the psychic structuring of fields of knowledge. The order or coherence that appears to underlie the construction of disciplinary fields or systems of knowledge is achieved through 'a system of psychic defences'. The broader point is that any form of knowledge will serve the interests of a specific social group, and it is this aspect of knowledge that is repressed, both in organizational discourses of legitimate knowledge and in the individual construction of psychical objects. Thus, 'the principle of classification comes to have the force of the natural order' (p. 7).

In two of his later papers, 'Pedagogising Knowledge: Studies in Recontextualising' and 'Official Knowledge and Pedagogic Identities: The Politics of Recontextualisation' (in Bernstein, 2000), Bernstein uses the vocabulary of the defences in his account of contemporary forms of disciplinary knowledge within educational institutions. In particular, he describes disciplinary and institutional identities as constructed through processes of projection and introjection. Thus, although in the extract quoted above, he appears to associate the defences with the construction of individual rather than collective identities, in his discussion of particular modes of knowledge and institution this distinction seems to get lost, and psychical processes appear to be attributed to collective identities. However, Bernstein never explains or elaborates the meaning of these psychical processes within his theory.

In the following sections I have taken extracts where Bernstein uses the vocabulary of psychical defence mechanisms and I have attempted to elaborate possible interpretations or meanings evoked by his use of these terms. I look at his conceptualization of three modes of knowledge that he suggests are to be found within formal educational settings. These are: *singulars*, rarified forms of knowledge that are considered discrete, strongly classified and autonomous or self-legitimating; *regions*, forms of knowledge that combine knowledge from singular disciplines and apply this knowledge in fields beyond the school or university; and *generic modes*, forms of knowledge that originate outside educational institutions and are imported into educational settings, typically in the construction of vocational qualifications. For Bernstein, each of these modes of knowledge serves an economic goal and can be considered as 'instrumental' (p. 54). However, the explicitness with which the instrumental goal of knowledge constitutes a part of the identity of the field varies according to mode. Similarly, in Bernstein's account, the psychic defences associated with fields of knowledge vary from mode to mode.

Singulars

Bernstein suggests that traditional disciplines such as classics, English and history, physics and chemistry, economics and the social sciences are all examples of singulars. He associates these knowledge structures with historical developments of the nineteenth century: nationalism, the development of the empire, new material technologies, and the development of the market and its associated 'management of subjectivities' (p. 54). He suggests:

> Classics provided privileged access to the administrative levels of the Civil Service. The specialized sciences provided the basis for material technologies. However, despite these external linkages singulars are like a coin with two faces, so that only one face can be seen at any one time. The sacred face sets them apart, legitimizes their otherness and creates dedicated identities with no reference other than to their calling. The profane face indicates their external linkage and internal power struggles. Organizationally and politically singulars construct strong boundary maintenance. From this point of view singulars develop strong autonomous self-sealing and narcissistic identities. These identities are constructed by procedures of *introjection*.
>
> (emphasis in original, pp. 54–55)

Thus the 'sacred face' of singular modes reveals aspects of knowledge that appear as pure intellectual activity, while the 'profane face' represents 'external linkages', instrumental aspects of knowledge that appear unrelated to the legitimized, intellectual activity. In defining these knowledge structures as 'narcissistic', Bernstein seems to suggest the direction of libido towards specialized disciplinary characteristics, the 'sacred elements', and the repression or denial of characteristics associated with external linkages. This might be consistent with the projection of the profane 'external linkages' onto other objects/disciplines/contexts. Yet Bernstein describes these identities as 'constructed by procedures of *introjection*'. This is consistent with a Kleinian account of narcissism as 'love for and relation with the internalized good object' (Kleing, 1946, p. 204), and this formulation reminds us of the idealized and phantasmatic nature of the characteristic that is here the object of narcissistic love: idealized because intellectual values can never be abstracted from their interdependency with social contexts; phantasmatic because the splitting off of the idealized object is a product of unconscious phantasy. However, it is not clear why Bernstein wants to claim that introjection is more significant than processes of projection in the establishment of 'singular' identities. This may be related to his tendency to produce slightly homogenizing, static models. The terms 'projection' and 'introjection' are partly deployed to construct a distinction between 'singulars' and more externally oriented knowledge structures (regional and generic modes). He claims: 'If the procedures of introjection construct the identities produced by singulars then the procedures of projection construct the identities produces by the new regionalization of knowledge' (Bernstein, 2000, p. 55). But he revises this homogenizing claim a few paragraphs later, when he acknowledges both processes within the singular mode:

> The 'autonomous' [singular] mode is ambiguous as the context acts selectively upon whether autonomy is emphasized and dependency masked or dependency is pragmatically embraced. Thus the identity here is split but manageable when introjected elements and projected elements can be actualized in discrete contexts.
>
> (p. 55)

Both the tendency to construct static, homogenizing models and the inconsistency illustrated here are characteristic of Bernstein's theorizing.

It is also worth speculating a little more on Bernstein's claim that the identity of singular modes 'is split but manageable'. Splitting arises here because of the need to defend against profane elements by separating (bad) dependency from (good) autonomy. Bernstein suggests that this split is manageable as long as the institution instantiates separate sites for the articulation of these contrasting elements of the identity, e.g. teaching and research versus committees and administration. It seems plausible that the provision of 'discrete contexts' allows the de-toxification of the dependency that is otherwise likely to remain as a persecuting 'bad object'. However, some settings might support a more integrated and ambivalent understanding of these disciplinary identities. In these instances, there would be no need for the splitting that Bernstein suggests, so that a singular mode might be instantiated within a 'depressive' rather than a 'paranoid schizoid' position.

It is worth noting here that Lyth's account of the nursing service would suggest that the instantiation of the 'depressive' or 'paranoid schizoid' position might be dependent not just on institutional context, but also on individual disciplinary subjects: the combination of dependency and autonomy might be felt as an unbearable attack by some but as a bearable ambivalence by others. There is a clear distinction between the perspectives of the two authors. Lyth's account of the hospital foregrounds instances where individual psychical histories come into contact with the psychical logic of the organization. Bernstein's models, in contrast, conceptualize knowledge modes as social identities, and the individual emerges only as a type within the social, not as a subject with its own psychical identity.

Regions

Bernstein defines regional modes as fields of knowledge that relate both to the specialized intellectual field of singular academic disciplines and to external fields of practices. Examples include medicine, engineering and architecture each of which incorporates ideas from several singular disciplines for application in settings beyond the university. Bernstein suggests that one feature of regional modes is their construction through processes of projection:

> Regions are recontextualiasations of singulars and face inwards towards singulars and outwards towards external fields of practice [...] Identities produced by the *new* regions are more likely to face outwards to fields of practice and thus their contents are likely to be dependent on the requirements of these fields. Identities here are what they are, and what they will become, as a consequence of the *projection* of that knowledge as a practice in some context.
>
> (emphasis in original, p. 55)

The suggestion that regions are constructed through projection requires some elaboration. The distinction between 'projection' and 'projective identification' might help to clarify this process. One interpretation of projective identification suggests a process whereby the ego does not merely split off a part of itself and project it into an object, but, in addition, the ego then identifies with the object of the projection (Mitchell, 1991, p. 20). Another variation suggests that the object of projection takes on the identity projected onto it by the ego. If we consider the identity of regional knowledge modes, analogous processes might be inferred. Regional knowledge structures – disciplinary fields situated within higher education – might first project meanings or concepts onto external practices, and then, following the projection, they will identify with the external practice. So, for example, medical researchers might identify with doctors, or educational researchers with teachers. Or, alternatively, it might be the case that ideas and concepts from the regional mode will not just be projected onto the contextualized practice of engineering, medicine or education, but will be taken in as a part of the identity of this external object. Where professional bodies and individual professionals construct their identities by reference to knowledge developed within an academic context, when professional practice comes to be evaluated in the terms of a recontextualized academic language, we might describe this as a process of projective identification. However, there is also likely to be some movement the other way, i.e. 'regional' knowledge structures taking in (introjecting) idealized aspects of the contextualized external practice. There remains a question, though, as to the extent to which this might be understood as an individual or a collective process, and also as to the conceptualization of the unconscious within these processes.

In more Lacanian terms, we could describe both of these processes – the introjection of knowledge from external practice into the academy and also the projection of knowledge from the academy into external practice – in terms of the master discourse (Lacan, 2007). The process of recontextualisation transforms knowledge from S2, the chain of signifiers, into S1, the master signifier. Lacan describes these as 'the two aspects of knowledge', embedded knowledge or 'know how', represented by S2, and 'articulated knowledge', S1 (ibid., p. 22). The point of articulation, S1, abstracts knowledge from its context to assert it as a regulatory reference point, initiating new chains of signification.[9] This occurs when a particular aspect of professional practice is taken up to be researched within the university, but also when knowledge produced within the university is inserted into the regulatory systems of professional practice. Both processes involve the extraction of knowledge for the purposes of the master, or, Lacan says 'betrayal, of the slave's knowledge, in order to obtain its transmutation into the master's knowledge' (p. 22).

Generic modes

A third mode of educational knowledge that Bernstein distinguishes within the contemporary context is what he calls 'generic'. As this term (perhaps) suggests, this mode incorporates a wide range of practices within the category of 'knowledge'. It includes practices and experiences that do not originate within the traditional disciplinary regimes of higher education.[10] The value of these modes originates outside formal educational settings, as they are 'essentially directed to extra school experiences: work and 'life'' (2000, p. 53). He suggests that they are produced through 'a functional analysis' (p. 53) of 'a set of general skills underlying a range of specific performances' (p. 55). However, he also says:

> generic modes and the performances to which they give rise are directly linked to instrumentalities of the market, to the construction of what are considered to be flexible performances. From this point of view their identity is constructed by procedures of projection.
>
> (p. 55)

Joseph's account of Kleinian forms of projective identification can help us to make sense of Bernstein's use of 'projection' here. She suggested that one form of projective identification consisted in 'getting into an object to take over its capacities and make them its own' (1988, p. 65). If we recontextualize this idea, we can think of pedagogic identities as forced to project themselves into the values of the market. If all worth appears to be attributed to something other than pedagogic values, pedagogic identities, full of worthlessness, will, in phantasy at least, take over the capacities of the market and make them their own. This is, of course, only a phantasy, and the production of pedagogic identity through this violently defensive mechanism is likely to produce something approximating the paranoid schizoid, or, in Bernstein's reformulation, the 'pedagogic schizoid' (2000, p. 71) position.

A similarly violent psychical process is suggested in Bernstein's account of the psychical construction of the identity of higher education institutions in an era where funding is tied to performance indicators such as research output in 'prestigious' journals. He describes the way the identity of elite universities is bound up in their ability to attract appropriately productive members of the academic staff:

> Elite universities can maintain their position by buying in research leaders, and as a consequence will have *less* need to change their discourse or its organization to maintain their power and position ... [T] he identities formed in elite institutions are likely to be formed by introjection of knowledge. That is the identity finds its core in its place in an organization of knowledge and practice.
>
> (p. 70)

The suggestion is that elite universities introject aspects of knowledge found in other objects (research leaders) and incorporate these into their identities. Reading this example alongside Julia Segal's account of introjection can help us to develop a more elaborated picture of the psychical relations that may constitute the institutional identities that Bernstein is describing. She suggests:

Phantasies in which parts of others are taken into the self (introjection) are also extremely important. Where this takes place under the influence of the paranoid schizoid position the parts taken in will be split and idealized: larger than life and wonderful or excessively persecuting and dangerous. The boundary between self and other is in some way denied, and the self may be felt to be attached to or identical with a very powerful idealized other who can do no wrong. This idealization covers a conviction that this other is really frightening and aggressive, diminishing the self, humiliating and destructive....

(Segal, 1992, p. 35)

Both aspects of this account, the idealization of the object and the denial of the boundary between self and other, might be applicable to the relation between academic institutions and certain celebrated members of academic staff. The further suggestion that this relation 'covers a conviction that this other is really frightening and aggressive', and that the idealized other in some way diminishes the self is also insightful as an account of the institutional insecurities that exist within higher education.

The productivity of Bernstein's use of Kleinian vocabularies

Bernstein does not elaborate the conceptual implications of his introduction of the language of psychic defences into his account of educational practices. Apart from a joking reference to 'a new pathological position at work in education' which he terms 'the pedagogic schizoid position', there are no traces of Klein's individualized, developmental narrative in his models of contemporary forms of knowledge. The productivity of his use of Klein's terms seems to lie in the meanings associated with the signifiers 'projection' and 'introjection', and in the potential these have to articulate relations between educational identities and the 'internal' and 'external' objects in relation to which these identities are constructed. They offer a language through which we might begin to conceptualize psychical aspects to processes of recontextualization.

Bernstein's introduction of unelaborated, and unacknowledged, instances of Kleinian psychoanalytic vocabulary – signifiers without signi-fieds – into his conceptual apparatus also invites us to play, and to move beyond the models that he has constructed. I have argued elsewhere that there are congruencies between Bernstein and Lacan, especially in their shared interest in the production of codified meanings and their conceptualization of the gap that is that site of unthinkable, that which is excluded from codified knowledge (Lapping, 2004; see also Davis, 2004). So, I would argue, there is some basis for drawing on a Lacanian framework to explore possible connotations of the psychoanalytic references in Bernstein's work. A more Lacanian approach, I have suggested, might help to articulate discursive aspects of knowledge practices, emphasizing the instantiation of knowledge and subjectivity within symbolic systems of power that are not so clearly captured in the Kleinian language with its psychologizing metaphors of internal world and individual ego (see also Kracke and Villela, 2004, pp. 181–182). By tracing the articulation, extraction and substitution of signifiers across different contexts, in a re-articulation of Bernstein's models, we might begin to map shifts in the political and symbolic regulation of academic and professional contexts and the interdependencies of these contexts in the production of regulatory codes.

Bernstein's detachment of the psychic defences from Klein's developmental conceptualization of the ego and from notions of an integrated and individualized subject creates possibilities for analysing the defences as constitutive of institutional identities or discursive fields. This move expands the potential productivity of the concept for social scientific analysis. It might also be understood to take us closer to a Lacanian conception of the defences, which suggests that what is defended against is not the disintegration of the ego, but the power of unconscious meanings. Ragland-Sullivan explains: 'Because Lacan delimits consciousness and makes consciousness and language themselves defences against unconscious meaning, he is not generally understood by ego psychologists who place defences in the ego itself' (1986, p. 120).

This radically extends the notion of the defences. Rather than conceptualizing defensive mechanisms such as splitting and projection as distorted linguistic representations of real relations, language itself is understood as a distorting, defensive mechanism. Consciousness does not represent a normalized, rational relation to reality, but a necessary defence against the unconscious. From this perspective, unconscious meanings pose a threat to individualized human identities, but no more so than they pose a threat to institutional or social identities. The strong association between Kleinian theory and invocations of the psychical defences seems to set an unnecessary limit on the use of this conceptual tool in the analysis of social relations.

Conclusion: contrasting recontextualizations and the unconscious of power

It seems relatively mundane to suggest that the contrasting positioning of Jaques and Lyth, within the psychoanalytically regulated Tavistock Institute of Human Relations, in comparison with Bernstein and Bourdieu, as academic sociologists, can explain their differential articulations of psychoanalytic ideas. The sociology of knowledge provides a more precise analytical framework for exploring these recontextualizations, one that constructs disciplinary fields and concepts as social objects that are neither unified nor separate from the contexts in relation to which they are articulated. Dowling's 'domains of action' schema foregrounds the constitution of disciplinary languages in signifiers and signifieds that articulate relations to a variety of differential discourses and social positions. Bernstein's conceptualization of 'singulars', 'regions' and 'generic modes' foregrounds the economic relation of disciplinary fields of knowledge. These analytical languages help us to construct a more precise account of contrasting articulations of knowledge and of the discursive/social alliances and oppositions that they enact. The chapter has also attempted to articulate the psychical aspect of these recontextualizing strategies, suggesting that the articulation or substitution of signifiers and their relation to different signifieds can be understood as constitutive of psychical relations within discourse. Thus strategies of acknowledgement or suppression of psychoanalytic antecedents in the work of Jaques and Lyth, and of Bernstein and Bourdieu, might be understood as unconscious articulations of the complex alliances and oppositions necessary to the production of their particular professional and intellectual identities.

I want to finish this chapter with two thoughts. The first relates to the contrast between the empirically or ontically oriented conceptual frameworks within the sociology of knowledge and more abstracted, theoretically or ontologically oriented conceptual frameworks. The second relates to the notion of the unconscious.

At various points throughout the book I have set up an opposition between the empirical and the speculative, the particular and the universal; and a question remains about the relation between these two modes of investigation. This has been described by Laclau as the 'complex dialectic between particularity and universality, between ontic content and ontological dimension' (cited in Marchart, 2004, p. 57) and he refers to the impossibility of achieving either pure universality or pure particularity (Laclau, 2004, p. 310). We might consider the move between the more abstracted terms of the ontological dimension and the more particularized concepts of ontic analysis as the space within which psychoanalytic terms are recontextualized in the analysis of both clinical and non clinical material. The distinction between Laclau and Mouffe's more abstracted conceptualization of the logics of equivalence and difference and the specificity of models developed within the sociology of knowledge is an example of this kind of shift in levels of analysis. The introduction of the unconscious at the ontological level will carry through into the ontic account of the particularity of the setting, but the ontic always contains an excess that, in Zizek's words, 'eludes ...the ontological clearance within which entities appear' (1994, p. 181; see also Laclau, 2004., p. 305).

Finally, I want to reflect briefly on the shifts in the meaning of the unconscious that are necessitated when we begin to conceptualize the defences as constituted within organizational and social structures. Where for Klein the unconscious is a force that acts in relation to an individual ego, it is not clear what constitutes the unconscious in Bernstein's models of different modes of knowledge. It is certainly not an individualized unconscious. Indeed, it seems far more like the Lacanian appearance of the unconscious in the symbolic punctuations in the signifying chain. Or perhaps we might understand the very conceptualization of the force that constitutes legitimized fields of knowledge in relation to economic and social hierarchies in terms of something more like Butler's unconscious of power. If, as Butler suggests, the unconscious is 'whatever resists the normative demands by which subjects are instituted' (1997, p. 86), then the relation between fields of disciplinary knowledge and the economic field that is foregrounded in Bernstein's models can be understood as an element positioned within the unconscious. It is precisely this *relation* that resists the normative demands of objective, scientific knowledge. When this relation, then, is foregrounded within the terms of knowledge itself, within the conceptual frameworks of the sociology of knowledge, this may become something like the mobilization of subjection against subjection that Butler defines as the unconscious of power (ibid., p. 104). Where the unconscious is that which resists articulation, the unconscious of power is the mobilization of articulated terms against the normative conditions of articulation.

Conclusion
Troubling attachments

No doubt Lacan would have liked me to play this role of academic philosopher. But to take someone, me, for example, to be an academic philosopher on the pretext that he gets paid for that by an institution, to identify him with or reduce him to that function on this pretext is above all not to read. This impulsive gesture, which is as self-interested as it is defensive, is more or less symmetrical – not altogether but more or less – with the gesture that would consist in taking an analyst for an analyst on the pretext that that is what he or she gets paid for: I have always avoided that gesture.

(Derrida, 1998, 'For the Love of Lacan' in *Resistances of Psychoanalysis*, p. 57)

Derrida's judgement here draws attention to the inadequacy of institutional position as a mark of knowing, to the excess beyond these kinds of attributed identities, and to the dangers of not reading beyond the sealed categories through which we are presented, each to the other. He is writing about the ambivalence or, more precisely perhaps, the undecidability of his relation to Lacan, both in their theoretical work and in their more personal encounters. Both his account and my response to his account suggest the complexity of articulating and maintaining a unified theoretical position.

Derrida presents his initial theoretical encounter with Lacan as a 'chiasmus', an intercrossing that produces an inversion. He explains how at exactly the same time that he was identifying deconstructible motifs within philosophy, Lacanian discourse emerged making 'the most strenuous and powerfully spectacular' use of those same motifs (p. 54). He thus describes Lacan's work as both the inversion of his own, but also as a kind of absented inspiration, in relation to which he would continue to pursue his own ideas (p. 56). However, he also suggests that Lacan overemphasized their contrasting institutional positions, relating his surprise at the fact that Lacan seemed to harbour 'an intense or even avid desire' for the position of the Acadamy (p. 57), and expressing equal disappointment at the way Lacan seemed to claim a special status for the psychoanalyst. Derrida, in contrast, proposes:

The fact that I have never been in analysis, in the institutional sense of the analytic situation, does not mean that I am not, here or there, in a way that cannot be easily toted up, analysand and analyst in my own time and in my own way. Like everyone else.

(p. 68)

Derrida's particular disappointment in Lacan relates, at least in part, to two of their more personal encounters. He describes an incident where a colleague had asked Lacan for his opinion on a lecture that he, Derrida, had just given, and reports: 'Lacan supposedly replied: "Yes, yes, it's good, but the difference between him and me is that he does not deal with people who are suffering," meaning by that: people in analysis' (p. 67). Derrida describes Lacan's judgement as 'very careless', since suffering is not limited to the analytic situation, and interprets Lacan's words to imply that clinical experience is a prerequisite for speaking, or a prerequisite for speaking 'about all this' (p. 67). The second disappointing encounter where, again, Derrida was not present, he describes as a 'compulsive blunder' (p. 67). Derrida recounts how Lacan suggested, in one of his seminars, that he, Derrida, was in analysis, and he notes that this announcement was followed by laughter from the audience. Derrida points out that he had in fact never been in analysis, and wonders about the implications of Lacan's erroneous statement:

How could Lacan make his listeners laugh on the subject or on the basis of a blunder, his own, concerning a hypothetical analysand – even as he himself presented himself (and this is, moreover, one of his most interesting assertions) as an analysand, a master of truth as analysand and not as analyst? How could he insist on two occasions on my real status as institutional nonanalyst and on what he wrongly supposed to be my status as institutional analysand, whereas he ought to have been the first to cast suspicion on the limits or borders of these sites, to pay attention to the tangled knots of this invagination?[1]

(pp. 68–69)

Once again, there is an undecidability in Derrida's position. There is a suggestion that Lacan's comment might have trivialized the position of analysand, but there is also admiration for Lacan as the one who suggested that it is the analysand, and not the analyst, who is the master of truth. Derrida's indecision in relation to Lacan might also be interpreted in relation to the impossibility of constituting Lacan as a unified identity articulating a consistent theoretical position. Derrida's rejection of the institutional borders of psychoanalysis is a similar rejection of a false marker of unified identity. Both 'psychoanalysis' and 'Lacan' are signifiers that are used to guarantee certain kinds of knowledgeable identities, and our faith in these signifiers needs to be continually put into question. As Derrida points out, this is an argument that we might expect to hear from 'Lacan' himself.

I want to finish with a brief exploration of my own response to Derrida's text, in order to reflect on the relation between psychical attachments to knowledge, reflexivity and the unconscious of power. This relation has emerged, in various ways, as a central theme within the book.

On my first, quite casual, reading of Derrida's essay, I was attracted by moments that put into question the institutionalization of the knowledge of the analyst. It was the memory of these passages that led me to return to the text when I was thinking about a conclusion for this book. Then, when I read the complete text for the first time, I found the experience disturbing. What did I find discomforting about it?[2] Was it the elusiveness of Derrida's position? Was it Lacan's apparent arrogance? Or was it the anger it is possible to interpret in Derrida's response to Lacan? It is possible that on some level I identified with Lacan's gossipy misinterpretation and laughter at another's expense, so perhaps I felt as if Derrida's commentary on Lacan's 'blunder' was directed at me. Perhaps I felt threatened by a sense of angry accusation in Derrida's questioning account of Lacan's indiscretion. However, as I have argued throughout the book, there is a danger in relying on your own affective response as an indicator of the affect of an other. It might be safer, or at least, methodologically more secure, to interpret these passages as a serious speculation on the fallibility of the analyst and the institutionalization of analysis, rather than an expression of anger or resentment. Perhaps Derrida is offering, without resentment, an affectionate portrait of Lacan's fallibility.

It is also possible that I was troubled by the sense of being caught between two theorists and not knowing where to find an authoritative voice. Lacan is one of the theorists I have returned to most frequently in my research and writing. I am seduced by the reflexivity of his language, though intimidated by his apparent, if elusive, philosophical erudition, which Derrida seems to put into question, describing it as 'in the best of cases elliptical and aphoristic, in the worst, dogmatic' (p. 54). In addition, Derrida's more substantive critique of Lacan evoked a worry about my own uncritical exposition of Lacan's ideas, and also about the coherence of drawing on both authors. In fact, I think, a more careful reading of Derrida's text confirms the genuine undecidability of the extent of his appreciation – Derrida uses the word 'love' – of Lacan's work. I might have taken this as permission for my own indecision, in the same way that I felt a certain relief in re-reading a quotation from Laclau that affirms the compatibility of the two theorists. Laclau talks about the centrality and importance of both Derrida's logic of undecidability and Lacan's logic of lack, and concludes: 'I am very much against attempts of simply opposing deconstruction to Lacanian theory. The two can be productively combined in a variety of ways' (Laclau, cited in Marchart, 2004, p. 56).

What is in question, for me, is the fact that I seemed, in this particular moment at least, to be seeking an impossible affirmation to assuage some slightly unfathomable fear, of criticism, of making a mistake, or of the difficulty involved in formulating my own position. This affective nexus of my responses to Derrida's text might be understood in terms of the need to attach myself to the terms of established discourse, to a conceptual language that precedes my own interpretation. There is also a troubling reiteration of a feminized position in my search for a legitimizing authority.

What does it mean to have my attachments troubled in this way in the reading of a new text? What is the importance of holding on to this sense of dislocation, rather than rushing to reassert a consistent academic identity? Throughout the book, I have argued for the importance of recognizing the social and psychical aspects of our attachment to the terms of knowledge, in order to maintain a sense of the provisional nature of our interpretations. The implication is that we should resist the lure of these attachments, and there are several ways of conceptualizing how this might be achieved. The Derridean foregrounding of undecidability can be aligned with the Lacanian foregrounding of ignorance, as both prioritize the inaccessible navel that resists understanding, or, as Derrida has put it, in relation to which the notion of resistance loses its meaning. For both, the terms of knowledge are always suspect, as they offer a seductive illusion of clarity and order. The Lacanian unconscious is the punctuation of this order with the pulse of a symbolic relation to another order of meaning that resists the normative demands of discourse. From this perspective, it seems that it is only that which is outside discourse that might disrupt discourse, and so the space of dislocation might constitute the only position from which it is possible to avoid the risk of authoritative knowledge. Butler's account of the unconscious of power, in contrast, suggests that it is possible to mobilize the terms of knowledge against the conditions of articulation of knowledge. This re-introduces the possibility of speaking the terms of knowledge in a way that is not necessarily subservient to the prevailing order of discourse. In relation to research, the unconscious of power might be seen to legitimize our recourse to established conceptual frameworks as a structure for interpretation.

The distinction between ontological space and ontic content might help us to further dismantle the rigid opposition between the use and disruption of the terms of knowledge. David Howarth has described the ontological and the ontic as different modes of inquiry. He suggests that the ontological dimension refers to 'the implicit assumptions presupposed by *any* inquiry into specific sorts of phenomena'. The ontic level, in contrast, he says, 'designates research into specific sorts of phenomena themselves' (2004, p. 266). Thus ontological inquiry constitutes the frame, or the conceptual structure through which entities are produced as objects of inquiry; while the ontic constitutes elaborated accounts of these entities within specific empirical contexts.

This book has argued for a better understanding of the multiplicity of instantiations of any conceptual structure. Abstracted conceptual structures such as 'the unconscious', 'transference' or 'melancholia' open up an ontological space that permits multiple particular articulations. Each of these articulations constitutes a relation to an embodied practice that necessarily exceeds the limits of the structure. This productive force of conceptual structures, described by Laclau as the 'complex dialectic between particularity and universality, between ontic content and ontological dimension' (cited in Marchart, 2004, p. 57), might constitute another way of thinking about the unconscious of power. The elision of the space between ontic particularity and ontological abstraction might constitute a strategy of exclusion, as, for example, in the attempt to foreclose what might count as a legitimate use of psychoanalysis. So, for example, the elision of 'transference' as a conceptual structure with the articulation of particular embodied practices within clinical encounters closes down an important space of substitution in the relation between psychoanalysis and social research. Where, in contrast, we can maintain a sense of the excessive space between the abstract and the particular, between the ontological and the ontic, we can maintain both the mobility of our concepts and the provisionality of our interpretations. From this perspective, a reflexive position might be constituted, not in the sense of dislocation itself, but in a recognition of the differential space that is covered over in contrasting instantiations of the same concept.

My analysis has pointed to the way that the contrasting empirical projects discussed throughout the book tie psychoanalytic concepts into the particularities of the research context, shifting and elaborating the meaning of the conceptual structure that produces the entities observed in the analysis. Chapter 1, for example, argued that the conceptual structure 'melancholia' makes it possible to articulate differentiated empirical moments as instances of loss. My account suggested how each of the examples of empirical research tied the notion of melancholia into a new context, relating gendered, classed or ethnic identities to the particularities of a specified economic or historical moment. In a similar way, the examples presented in Chapter 2 demonstrate how the nodal point in an overdetermining web of signifiers can be elaborated at an ontic level in the specific alliances congealed in a key moment of national politics, or in the relation between localized institutional politics and international policy discourse. The empirical analysis in each of these instances ties the abstracted conceptual structure into the context of the research.

In Chapter 3 I argued that, for both Freud and Foucault, there is a notion of repetition inscribed into the conceptual structure of resistance. I suggested that instances of repetition within empirical data that can be interpreted as a segment of discourse might also be interpreted within more personal, individualized historical trajectories. The chapter also presented a more Lacanian account of resistance in which interpretations are themselves understood as reiterations of the intellectual, political and professional attachments of the analyst. The reflexive potential of this notion of resistance was explored further in Chapters 4 and 5: first in relation to my own use of Lacanian ideas in the analysis of empirical data; and then in relation to contrasting articulations of Kleinian theory in applications of her ideas to the interpretation of social contexts. The resistance of the analyst emerges, it seems to me, when we fail to recognize the specificities of the setting, when we apply ontological categories as if they exist, as if they are entities that persist beyond their articulation in the abstracted signifiers of a conceptual language. The ontic interpretation, in contrast, is produced in the space between the abstracted, ontological concept and embedded experience of the context. However, there is always an excess that is not captured within this interpretation, and the failure to recognize this unknowable excess also constitutes an aspect of resistance.

I am suggesting, I think, that the philosophical distinction between the ontological and the ontic might offer a way to conceptualize a mode of reflexivity. The ontological space opened up in the theorization of 'melancholia', 'overdetermination' or 'resistance', for example, produces entities in a dialectical relation with the ontic (see Laclau, 2004, p. 311). If the excess between these two modalities is elided, there is a fixing or pathologization of one version which re-emerges in the practice of both politics and research. If, in contrast, it is possible to maintain a reflexive space between the conceptual structure and the multiplicity of ontic instantiations, then we might be able to maintain mobility in our practice in relation to the production and analysis of complex social entities. However, reflexivity, in the sense that I am wondering about here, also involves a dislocating recognition of an excess that cannot be captured in the articulation between an ontological dimension and an ontic particularity.

In other words, perhaps, we should not aim or expect to conform to the frameworks provided by the apparent authors of our conceptual vocabularies. My initial response to Derrida's text might be understood in terms of my failure to fully occupy the necessary and obvious space between us: an imaginary merging with the symbolic authority. This book as a whole has tried to suggest, I think, some ways in which researchers who draw on psychoanalytic ideas, myself included, might wonder about the space between the particular settings of empirical research and the authoritative voices of social and psychoanalytic theory.

Notes

Introduction

1 We might understand this in terms of the contrast between the ontological space opened up in the conceptualization of 'transference' and 'counter-transference' and the interpretation of particular ontic instantiations that are defined by, but that also exceed, the ontological space (Marchart, 2004; Laclau, 2004; Zizek, 1994).

2 For example, in my interview-based research into academic practice, I might trace ways in which I identify with different aspects of my participants' practice. At times I might identify with their particular theoretical interests, their political commitments or cultural preferences; or I might find myself identifying with their *relation to* their institution, their writing or a particular author. By attempting to recognize exactly what object or relation it is that I am responding to, I can set aside my imaginary identification and begin to develop a more precise analysis of my participant's practice. In my view it doesn't matter a great deal whether or not I choose to label these distinctions versions of 'counter-transference'; what matters is the productivity of the conceptualization and analysis. The choice of terms merely signals an allegiance, making explicit a link that is already present in the tangle of conceptual frameworks and ideas. (See also Lapping, 2008, for an analysis of the process of interpretation that I think, retrospectively, might have been framed within a conceptualization of transference and counter-transference.)

3 The move to incorporate empirical studies of methodological practice into conceptions of research can be seen in other recent writing on methodology. In *After Method: mess in social science research* (2004), John Law uses studies from the sociology of science to draw attention to the messy hinterland of social scientific methodology and to argue against notions of scientific order and objectivity. Bourdieu (2004) also positions his conception of reflexivity in relation to work within the sociology of science.

1 Melancholia: lost objects of national, ethnic, classed, gendered and sexual identities

1 Laclau and Mouffe describe the distinction between 'sedimentation' and 'reactivation': 'Sedimented theoretical categories are those which conceal the acts of their original institution, while the reactivating moment makes those acts visible again' (2001, p. viii).

2 Deleuze and Guattari offer a trenchant articulation of a similar point in their criticism of Klein for failing to follow through the implications of her conceptualization of part objects:

Partial objects unquestionably have a sufficient charge in and of themselves to blow up all of Oedipus and totally demolish its ridiculous claim to represent the unconscious, to triangulate the unconscious, to encompass the entire production of desire. The question that arises here is not at all that of the relative importance of what might be called the *pre-oedipal* in relation to Oedipus itself, since 'pre-oedipal' still has a developmental or structural relationship to Oedipus. The question, rather, is that of the absolutely *anoedipal* nature of the production of desire. But because Melanie Klein insists on considering desire from the point of view of the whole, of global persons, and of complete objects – and also, perhaps, because she is eager to avoid any sort of contretemps with the International Psycho-Analytic Association that bears above its door the inscription 'Let no one enter here who does not believe in Oedipus' – she does not make use of partial objects to shatter the iron collar of Oedipus; on the contrary, she uses them – or makes pretense of using them – to water Oedipus down, to minaturise it, to find it everywhere, to extend it to the earliest years of life.

(1983, pp. 44–45)

3 Rosi Braidotti (2002) criticizes the emphasis on loss within feminist theory, asking 'what if the "fixer" of the psychic landscape were the over-flowing plenitude of pleasure, rather than the melancholy discourse of debt and loss?' She suggests that the orientation towards loss in Butler's work is driven by the urgency of the political context:

Admittedly, this emphasis on mourning and melancholia is motivated to a great extent by Butler's concern for the deaths caused in the gay community by the AIDS crisis. More particularly, her work is informed by the question of how to formalize a gay discourse about death and loss in the public sphere. Public rituals of mourning are needed so as to enforce the recognition of gay grief and have it accepted socially. I think this worthy and humane concern lies at the heart of Butler's investment in the political economy of mourning and loss. It also attaches her more firmly to the Lacanian tradition of thought than her own work would actually allow.

(p. 53)

4 This analysis has resonances with Lyth's conceptualization of institutional practices as social defences, see Chapter 5.
5 The mechanisms of repression, disavowal and foreclosure are discussed in more detail in Chapter 4
6 Stephen Frosh has made a similar point about his own work in the same period (Autobiographies of Gender Research Seminar Series, Institute of Education, 2007). In a seminar reflecting on his analysis of gendered practices in his early writing (e.g. Frosh 1987) he suggested that this work was significantly influenced by the approaches to feminism within the women's movement at the time, and that he would now take a less essentializing position on men's relation to sexual abuse.
7 It should be noted that there were also moments when this mournful invocation of regulative notions of femininity were disrupted. Ringrose reports the girls' more critical engagement with the dominant discourse. Gwyneth, for example, argued:

I think girls can be mean, but not like more than anyone else, they are kind of making out like, it's just teenagers being mean, kind of thing, like adults get mean, and like, babies get mean… it's like everyone gets angry… I think they are just talking about girls. like they're trying to spread it around, like all girls are horrible… like I don't reckon it's true.

(2008, p. 48)

2 Overdetermination: the conceptualization of dreams and discourse

1 This controversy – over the nature of the interaction and the extent to which an intimate form of recognition might be achieved between analyst and analysand – is embedded within a variety of current debates, e.g. over the meaning of 'projective identification' (see Sandler, 1998) and over the distinction between relationality and intersubjectivity (see Benjamin, 1998)

2 There are many critiques of Freud's specific interpretations, as well as of his general approach. For a useful discussion of ways in which Freud might be seen as imposing his theories rather than interpreting details presented by a patient, see Benzaquen (1998), on the case of Little Hans, also Verhaeghe (1997), on Freud in position of master.

3 Bruce Fink explores these issues in his critique of Winnicot's belief that it is the analyst's duty to play mother to the analysand. He says:

> The problem, according to Lacan, is that this makes the analysand ever more dependent on the analyst, and the analysand's desire (as expressed in his or her fantasy) comes to revolve entirely around the analyst's demand [...] that the analysand get better, dream, daydream, reflect, or whatever else it is the analyst demands or the analysand thinks the analyst is demanding.
>
> (1997, p. 89).

4 See also papers in Howarth *et al.*, (2000), Howarth and Torfing (2005).

5 For a discussion of the relation between 'nodal point' and 'empty signifier' see Howarth, 2004, pp. 261–622 and 267–679 and Laclau's response in the same volume, pp. 321–322. Laclau (2004) suggests that the two terms 'have exactly the same referent and the distinction is that "nodal points" makes allusion to the articulating function, while its empty character points in the direction of its universal signification' (p. 322). Howarth explains that the universal aspect of the emptiness of the signifier relates to its position in covering over 'the structural impossibility of signification as such' (p. 261).

6 This distinction is similar to Lacan's distinction between 'surplus *jouissance*', the enjoyment that is 'a result of the use of language' (Lacan, 2007, p. 66, see also Verhaeghe, 2006, pp. 33–34) and the *jouissance* that exceeds linguistic categorizations. 'Surplus *jouissance*', associated with the affects that we name, is a temporary and partial satisfaction afforded within the constraints of the symbolic order. This quasi-enjoyment, which has a symbolic origin, stands in for the *jouissance* of the real.

3 Textures of resistance: 'discourse' and 'psyche' and 'the compulsion to repeat'

1 The spectre of a unifying entity within Foucault's account of the heterogeneous micropolitics of power has been discussed elsewhere, see for example Zizek (1994, pp. 198–199) and Hook (2008b).

2 Here resistances are understood as interactions that avoid serious engagement with ideas within a session. Christopher Bollas suggests that 'the clearest resistance is willful silence' (2009, p. 122). He also describes certain types of talk as constitutive of a resistance to work: imprecise or rambling accounts of recent events, or apparently 'deep' philosophical discussions that enable the patient to avoid productive engagement within the session (pp. 123–124). The language in which the patient formulates their ideas can also be interpreted as resistance. A patient might adopt, for example, a vocabulary of inability that disavows

responsibility and externalizes agency: 'I can't talk about it', 'something is stop-
ping me from doing it' (Schafer, 1981). Many aspects of a patient's behaviour
can be interpreted as a resistance that enables the patient to avoid confrontation
with difficult material.

3 Derrida refers to Freud's enumeration of five types of resistance, associated
respectively with the ego, the id and the superego (Freud, 1926, pp. 159–160).
However, other typologies of the different ways resistances might be articulated
within clinical sessions are equally open to Derrida's critique: 'All these organized types of resistance can be distinguished by a logical, conceptual, methodological analysis, but in reality they are all tangled up with and overdetermine
each other....' (Derrida, 1998, p. 22)

4 I am very grateful to my anonymous research participant for pointing out the
relevance of Spivak's paper to this chapter.

5 Spivak's discussion of Foucault's nominalism focuses on his account of 'power'.
She suggests the importance of the connotations of different terms used by
Foucault in the place of 'power': the term 'puissance', she suggests, has implications of rationality and intentionality, while 'force' has connotations of unreason and disorganization. Thus, narrow, traditionalist conceptions of power
might be associated with 'puissance', in contrast to Foucault's attempt to evoke
an a-rational, de-individualized 'force': ' "Force" is the subindividual name of
"power" ' (Spivak, 1993, p. 31). For similar discussion in relation to Foucault's
conceptualization of the body see Hoy, (2004, pp. 57–69) and Butler (1997).

6 In volume one of *The History of Sexuality* (1979) Foucault articulates four
'rules to follow' (p. 98–102) in analysing the production of discourse within the
field of power relations, but he demurs: 'these are not intended as methodological imperatives; at most they are cautionary principles' (p. 98).

7 Butler suggests that Foucault's theorization of the body might be interpreted as
a 'substitute' for the psyche:

> If, according to psychoanalysis, the subject is not the same as the psyche
> from which it emerges and if, for Foucault, the subject is not the same as the
> body from which it emerges, then perhaps the body has come to substitute
> for the psyche in Foucault – that is, as that which exceeds and confounds
> the injunctions of normalization. Is this a body pure and simple, or does
> "the body" come to stand for a certain operation of the psyche...?
>
> (1997, pp. 94–95)

8 It should be noted that Moore was not persuaded by this gendered analysis. He
suggested that issues of class or status might be more pertinent to Bill's case.
Certainly, further theoretical and empirical elaboration would be needed to
develop this analysis. The important point is that what appears as an idiosyncratic, personal desire can be reinterpreted through the discursive requirement
to produce coherent gendered/classed/professional identities. Elsewhere
(Lapping, 2006, 2007) I have used a Lacanian framework to explore ways in
which instances of resistance can be understood in relation to the symbolic
requirement to maintain a coherent gendered identity.

9 Deleuze and Guattari's language of territorialization, reterritorialization and
lines of flight (e.g. 1983) constitutes a theoretical language to explore some of
these different textures of resistance; Laclau and Mouffe's conceptualization of
the logics of equivalence and difference also offer a way of theorizing the political effects of discursive moments (see Laclau and Mouffe, 2001; Lapping,
2008).

10 Personal communication November 2009

11 Ragland-Sullivan (1986) explains resistance within a Lacanian framework as
constituted in the opposition between the *moi* and the *je*. She explains Lacan's

foregrounding of the *moi*: 'As the unconscious subject of identifications and narcissism, the *moi* assumes a place of privilege over the speaking subject, rendering the latter opaque and discontinuous', (p. 42). It is then, she suggests, the distinction *moi* and *je* that constitutes resistance:

> Lacan's elevation of the subject of the unconscious over consciousness sheds new light on the phenomenon of resistance. It is the insistence of an unconscious discourse, which prefers to repeat itself in language and behaviour (rather than to know itself), that must be called resistance. So seen, resistance becomes an Imaginary function of the *moi*. Resistance is not a function of conscious ego defenses, therefore, but a revelation of the fact that *moi* (being) is different from *je* (speaking).
>
> (p. 121)

4 Signifying chains in academic practice: the appearance and disappearance of affect, politics and methodology

1 All names have been changes. Other details have also been changed to ensure appropriate levels of anonymity. These changes were made in consultation with each participant.

2 This has not been the case with other participants so far. Having sent detailed comments, in the interview Andy found it difficult to remember what he had wanted to say, and I felt that for the later participants it might be more productive to focus on eliciting oral responses in the interviews, rather than asking for written comments. In addition, Andy had always been extremely enthusiastic about his participation in the project, so it hadn't felt demanding to request written comments from him.

3 At some points Andy indirectly referred to ways in which the politics of cultural studies pedagogy is more complicated than the liberal humanist approach that he constructs as dominating practice. For example, in explaining why students find the species text challenging he said: 'I think, by this point, the students have mostly got used to the idea that these potty leftie lecturers are going to start challenging gender and race and class and consumption and the usual things, but I'm fairly sure, at no point, will they have had their very concept of species or humanness challenged' (Int. 2.)

4 In Interview 5 Jeff described a colleague's qualitative interviews as 'thick description', and a little later on in the interview I used the term to describe his intensive long-term engagement with Area.

5 When he read the case study that included this analysis, Jeff seemed pleased by my interpretation of his experience as constituting a part of his methodology. He said:

> You make a very interesting point that this is actually part of my methodology – I guess it depends on the definition of methodology – I don't think you'd find it in books on methodology. 'My method is to immerse myself in a country for 25 years'. But I can see what you're saying. I found that interesting, actually, useful.
>
> (Int. 6)

6 The project methodology includes a 'reflecting team': five colleagues who meet with me twice a term to support the development of the methodology and analysis. The members of the reflecting team are Tamara Bibby, Deborah Chinn, Alex Moore, Jenny Parkes and Olivia Sagan.

7 Wilfred Bion (1961) describes a parallel situation, where he was made to question one of his interpretations in his work with therapeutic groups. He uses the

example to argue that the concept of projective identification is a useful resource in interpreting experiences of counter-transference. He suggests that in such circumstances, when there is a strong repudiation or scepticism about the analyst's interpretation, the analyst needs to shed the 'numbing' feeling that they have given a wrong interpretation (pp. 147–149). However, as Bion notes, there are dangers in this position, and in the assumption that the subjective responses of the analyst should be interpreted as resistance on the part of the group rather than as resistance on the part of the analyst. It is always possible that the sense of having given a wrong interpretation is related to the fact that the interpretation is in fact wrong...

5 From psychic defences to social defences: recontextualizing strategies and Klein's theory of ego development

1 For Klein, these are not strictly speaking 'stages', but rather positions that we move between throughout our lives. However, her account of infant development does seem to specify an ordered movement through the two positions.

2 This example comes from Tamara Bibby's ethnographic study of learner identities in a primary school (2005–2007). See also Bibby (2010).

3 The distinction between internalization and introjection is also sometimes related to the distinction between 'inner representational world' and 'psychic structure' (Meissner, 1988, p. 64)

4 Sue Jervis (2009) gives an illuminating and detailed account of an interview where she experienced both physical and affective sensations that, she argues, might be understood as instances of projective identification. Within her account she is clear that researchers 'should be careful not to make any interpretations based upon the feelings evoked in them unless those interpretations are supported by other evidence within the research material' (p. 155). She suggests that 'by reflecting upon their bodily experiences or emotions, researchers might achieve a deeper understanding of respondents' experiences', but warns that 'researchers face similar problems to analysts in differentiating which feelings belong to whom' (p. 163).

5 Projective identification is usually an unconscious process. However, it has been argued that the conscious recognition of the interpersonal effects of projective identification can be used to support interpretations within psychoanalysis. Wilfred Bion has argued that in work with groups 'the most important' interpretations 'have to be made on the strength of the analyst's own emotional reactions' (1961, p. 149). While acknowledging the problems inherent in interpretations based on the subjective reactions of the analyst, he argues:

> It is my belief that these reactions are dependent on the fact that the analyst in the group is at the receiving end of what Melanie Klein has called projective identification, and that this mechanism plays a very important role in groups. Now the experience of counter-transference appears to me to have quite a distinct quality that should enable the analyst to differentiate the occasion when he is the object of a projective identification from when he is not. The analyst feels he is being manipulated so as to be playing a part, no matter how difficult to recognize, in somebody else's phantasy – or he would do were it not for what in recollection I can only call a temporary loss of insight, a sense of experiencing strong feelings and at the same time a belief that their existence is quite adequately justified by the objective situation ... From the analyst's point of view, the experience consists of two closely related phases: in the first there is a feeling that whatever else one has done, one has certainly not given a correct interpretation; in the second there is a

sense of being a particular kind of person in a particular emotional situation. I believe the ability to shake oneself out of the numbing feeling of reality that is a concomitant of this state is the prime requisite of the analyst in the group: if he can do this he is in a position to give what I believe is the correct interpretation, and thereby to see its connection with the previous interpretation, the validity of which he has been caused to doubt.

(pp. 149–150)

Bion's account seems to attribute authority to the analyst's interpretation of the 'distinct quality' of the counter-transference.

6 For further details on the methodology see Lyth. (1969) 'Some methodological notes on a hospital study'.

7 There are resonances between the logic of equivalence and the radical defences of the paranoid schizoid position, while logics of difference constitute multiple and ambiguous meanings that might be associated with the depressive position. However, for Laclau and Mouffe, there is no privileging of one strategy over another as a psychical relation to 'reality'. Klein's terms have also been used in political analysis (e.g. Rustin, 2010) but tend to psychologize political positions, rather than developing the strategic analysis offered in Laclau and Mouffe's conceptualization of contrasting logics within the politics of hegemony. (For a defence of Kleinian approaches to political analysis see Rustin, 2001.)

8 However, it occurs to me that it might be possible to interpret Bernstein's slightly allergic relation to Bourdieu in relation to Foucault's account of the hegemony of the author function, the ideological mechanisms that constitute the relationship between text and author so that 'the text points to this "figure" that, at least in appearance, is outside it and antecedes it' (Foucault, 2001, p. 9. Also Metivier, 2010).

9 The master signifier can also be thought of in terms of the 'nodal point': a signifier that is able to contain different meanings, and thus to initiate chains of meaning within contrasting discursive contexts. See Chapter 2.

10 Instantiations of this mode could be found in UK colleges of further education in the 1990s and beginning of the twenty-first century, where courses mimicked the high street: hairdressing is taught in a mock up of a hair salon and service is open to the public; travel and tourism students mimic the work of a travel agent; beauty therapy courses serve the public at cut price rates, and teach students to promote products at the end of each treatment; catering students run the internal catering service; etc. New English National Curriculum subjects such as Personal Social and Health Education, citizenship and SEAL can also be interpreted as generic modes.

Conclusion

1 The Oxford English Dictionary (1983) defines 'invagination' as the 'the action of sheathing or introverting'. It is difficult to ignore the slightly discomforting gendered connotations of Derrida's use of this sexualized term in his account of Lacan's failure to consistently question the enclosure of identity within the bounds of a legitimizing institution. It constitutes, I think, a problematic reiteration of the alignment of the feminine with the maintenance/taming of established positions of authority.

2 Of course, my response may have had little to do with the text itself. It may have been more to do with other concerns and pressures of the day, including the fact that I was trying to complete a draft of my book.

References

Althusser, L. (1962 [1990]) 'Contradiction and overdetermination: notes for an investigation' in *For Marx*, London: Verso, 87–128

Althusser, L. (1971) 'Ideology and the ideological state apparatuses', in *Lenin and Philosophy*, Monthly Review Press, 127–186

Armstrong, D. (2005) *Organization in the Mind: Psychoanalysis, group relations and organisational consultancy*, London, New York: Karnac

Benjamin, J. (1998) *Shadow of the Other: Intersubjectivity and Gender in Psycho-analysis*, New York: Routledge

Benzaquen, A. S. (1998) 'Freud, Little Hans, and the desire for knowledge', *Journal of Curriculum Theorizing*, 14(2): 43–52

Bernstein, B. (2000) *Pedagogy, Symbolic Control and Identity* (2nd edition), New York: Rowman and Littlefield

Bibby, T. (2010) *An Impossible Profession: psychoanalytic explorations of learning and classrooms*, London: Routledge

Bion, W. (1961) *Experiences in Groups*, London: Routledge

Bollas, C. (1999) *The Mystery of Things*, London Routledge

Bollas, C. (2009) *The Infinite Question*, London: Routledge

Bourdieu, P. (2004) *Science of Science and Reflexivity*, Cambridge: Polity Press

Braidotti, R. (2002) *Metamorphoses: Towards a materialist theory of becoming*, Cambridge: Polity Press

Burgos, R. (1997) 'Education in a post-modern horizon: voices from Latin-America', *British Educational Research Journal*, 23(1): 97–107

Burgos, R. (1999) 'The spectre of theory in curriculum for educational researchers: a Mexican example', *International Review of Eduation*, 45(5/6): 461–478

Burgos, R. (2000) 'The Mexican revolutinary mystique' in D. Howarth, A. Norval and Y. Stavrakakis (eds) *Discourse Theory and Political Analysis: Identities, hegemonies and social change*, Manchester University Press, 86–99

Butler, J. (1990) *Gender Trouble*, New York: Routledge

Butler, J. (1997) *The Psychic Life of Power*, California: Stanford University Press

Butler, J. (1993) *Bodies That Matter*, New York: Routledge

Critchley, S. and Marchart, O. (eds) (2004) *Laclau: a critical reader*, London: Routledge

Davis, Z. (2004) 'The debt to pleasure: the subject and knowledge in pedagogic discourse', in Muller, J., Davies, B. and Morais, A. *Reading Bernstein, Research-ing Bernstein*, London: Routledge Falmer

Deleuze, G. and Guattari, F. (1983) *Anti-Oedipus: Capitalism and Schizophrenia*, London: The Althone Press

Derrida, J. (1978) 'Structure, sign and play in the discourse of the human sciences', *Writing and Difference*, trans. Alan Bass, London: Routledge. Online. Available at: www9.georgetown.edu/faculty/irvinem/theory/Derrida (accessed 10 May 2010)

Derrida, J. (1998) *Resistances of Psychoanalysis*, California: Stanford University Press

Dowling, P. (1998) *The Sociology of Mathematics Education: mathematical myths/ pedagogic texts*, London: Falmer Press

Dowling, P. (2009) *Sociology as Method: Departures from the Forensics of Culture, text and knowledge*, Rotterdam: Sense Publishers

Eng D. and Kanzanjian D. (eds) (2003) *Loss: the politics of mourning*, Berkley: University of California Press

Eng, D. and Han, S. (2003) 'A dialogue on racial melancholia', in Eng, D. L. and Kazanjian, D. (eds) *Loss: the politics of mourning*, Berkley: University of California Press, 343–371

Evans, D. (1996) *An Introductory Dictionary of Lacanian Psychoanalysis*, London: Routledge

Fink, B. (1995) *The Lacanian Subject: between language and jouissance*, Princeton: Princeton University Press

Fink, B. (1997) *A Clinical Introduction to Lacanian Psychoanalysis: Theory and technique*, Cambridge: Harvard University Press

Foucault, M. (1977) *Discipline and Punish: the birth of the prison*, London: Penguin Books

Foucault, M. (1979) *The Will to Knowledge: the history of Sexuality: Volume 1*, London: Penguin Books 1998

Foucault, M. (2001) 'What is an author?', *Contributions in Philosophy*, **83**: 9–22

Freud, S. (1905) 'Three Essays on the Theory of Sexuality', in *The Standard Edition of the Complete Psychological Works of Sigmund Freud Volume V11 (1901–1905): A Case of Hysteria, Three Essays on Sexuality and Other Works*, Vintage, The Hogarth Press and The Institute of Psychoanalysis, 121–245

Freud, S. (1920 [1984]) 'Beyond the pleasure principle', in *On Metapsychology: The Theory of Psychoanalysis, The Pelican Freud Library Volume 11*, London: Penguin Books, 275–338

Freud, S. (1923) 'The Ego and the Id', *The Standard Edition of the Complete Psychological Works of Sigmund Freud Volume X1X: The Ego and the Id and Other Works*, Vintage, The Hogarth Press and the Institute of Psychoanalysis, 2001, 3–66

Freud, S. (1926) *Inhibitions, Symptoms and Anxiety*, London: The Hogarth Press

Freud, S. (1957) 'Mourning and Melancholia', in *The Complete Psychological Works of Sigmund Freud Volume X1V*, London: The Hogarth Press and the Institute of Psychoanalysis, 243–257

Freud, S. (1958) *Penguin Freud Library Volume 4: The Interpretation of Dreams*, London: Penguin Books

Frosh, S. (1987) 'Issues for men working with sexually abused children', *British Journal of Psychotherapy*, 37(4): 332–339

Frosh, S. (1994) *Sexual Difference: Masculinity and Psychoanalysis*, London: Routledge

Frosh, S. (2007) Paper presented at the 'Autobiographies of Gender Research' seminar series, Institute of Education

Frosh, S. and Baraitser, L. (2008) 'Psychoanalysis and psychosocial studies', *Psychoanalysis, Culture and Society*, 13: 346–365

Glynos, J. and Stavrakakis, Y. (2004) 'Encounters of the Real Kind: Sussing out the limits of Laclau's embrace of Lacan', in S. Critchley and O. Marchart (eds) *Laclau: a critical reader*, London: Routledge, 201–216

Goodchild, P. (1996) *Deleuze and Guattari: an introduction to the politics of desire*, London: Sage Publications

Hey, V. (1997) *The Company She Keeps: An ethnography of girls' friendships*, Buckingham: Open University Press

Hey, V. (2006) 'Getting over it? Reflections on the melancholia of reclassified identities', *Gender and Education*, 18(3): 295–308

Hoggett, P. (2008) 'What's in a hyphen? Reconstructing psychosocial studies', *Psychoanalysis, Culture and Society*, 13: 379–384

Holland, E. (1999) *Deleuze and Guattari's Anti-Oedipus: introduction to schizoanalysis*, London: Routledge

Hook, D. (2008a) 'Articulating psychoanalysis and psychosocial studies: limitations and possibilities', *Psychoanalysis, Culture and Society*, 13: 397–405

Hook, D. (2008b) 'Absolute other: Lacan's "big Other" as adjunct to critical social psychological analysis', *Social and Personality Psychology Compass*, 2(1):51–73

Howarth, D. (1997) 'Complexities of identity/difference: Black Consciouness ideology in South Africa', *Journal of Political Ideologies*, 2(1): 51–78

Howarth, D. (2000) 'The difficult emergence of a democratic imaginary: Black Consciousness and non-racial democracy in South Africa', in Howarth, D., Norval, A. and Stavrakakis, Y. (eds) *Discourse Theory and Political Analysis: identities, hegemonies and social change*, Manchester University Press, 168–192

Howarth, D. (2000b) *Discourse*, Buckingham: Open University Press

Howarth, D. (2004) 'Hegemony, political subjectivity and radical democracy', in S. Critchley and O. Marchart (eds) *Laclau: a critical reader*, London: Routledge, 256–276

Howarth, D., Norval A. and Stavrakakis Y. (2000) (eds) *Discourse Theory and Political Analysis: Identities, hegemonies and social change*, Manchester University Press

Howarth, D. and Torfing, J. 2005, *Discourse Theory in European Politics: identity, policy and governance*, Basingstoke: Palgrave Macmillan

Hoy, D. (2004) *Critical Resistance: from poststructuralism to post-critique*, Cambridge, Mass.: The MIT Press

Jaques, E. (1951 [1990]), 'Working through industrial conflict: the service department at the Glacier Metal Company', in Trist, E. L. and Murray, H. (eds) *The Social Engagement of Social Science*, London: Free Association Books

Jen, G. (1991) *Typical American*, Boston: Ghoughton Mifflin

Jervis, S. (2009) 'The use of self as a research tool', in Clarke, S. and Hoggett, P. *Researching Beneath the Surface: Psycho-Social Research Methods in Practice*, London: Karnac, 145–166

Joseph, B. (1988) 'Projective identification: clinical aspects', in Sandler, J. (ed.) *Projection, Identification, Projective Identification*, London: Karnac Books, 65–76

Jukes, A. (1993a) 'Violence, helplessness, vulnerability and male sexuality', *Free Associations*, 29: 25–43

Jukes, A. (1993b) *Why Men Hate Women*, London: Free Association Books

Kingston, M. H. (1976) *The Woman Warrior: Memoirs of a Girlhood among Ghosts*, New York: Vintage

Kingston, M. H. (1989) *China Men*, New York: Vintage

Klein, M. (1935 [1986]) 'A contribution to the psychogenesis of manic-depressive States', in Mitchell, J. (ed.) *The Selected Melanie Klein*, London: Penguin Books, 115–145

Klein, M. (1940 [1986]) 'Mourning and its relation to manic-depressive states', in Mitchell, J. (ed.) *The Selected Melanie Klein*, London: Penguin Books, 146–174

Klein, M. (1946 [1986]) 'Notes on some schizoid mechanisms', in Mitchell, J. (ed.) *The Selected Melanie Klein*, London: Penguin Books, 175–200

Klein, M. (1951 [1986]) 'The origins of the transference', in Mitchell, J. (ed.) *The Selected Melanie Klein*, London: Penguin Books, 201–210

Kracke, W. and Villela, L. (2004) 'Between desire and culture: conversations between psychoanalysis and anthropology', in A. Molino (ed.) *Culture, Subject, Psyche: dialogues in psychoanalysis and anthropology*, London: Whurr Publishers, 175–209

Kvale, (1999) 'The psychoanalytic interview as qualitative research', *Qualitative Inquiry*, 5(7): 87–112

Lacan, J. (1957 [1989]) 'The agency of the letter in the unconscious or reason since Freud', in A. Sheridan (trans.) *Ecrits: a selection*, London: Routledge, 161–197

Lacan, J. (1979) *The Four Fundamental Concepts of Psycho-Analysis*, London: Penguin Books

Lacan, J. (1991) *The Seminar of Jacques Lacan Book II: the ego in Freud's theory and in the technique of psychoanalysis 1954–1955*, New York: W. W. Norton and Company

Lacan, J. (1998) *Encore: the seminar of Jacques Lacan Book XX: On feminine sexuality, the limits of love and knowledge, 1972–1973*, New York: W. W. Norton and Company

Lacan, J. (2007) *The Seminar of Jacques Lacan Book XV11: The Other Side of psychoanalysis*, New York: W. W. Norton and Company

Laclau, E. (1996) *Emancipations*, London:Verso

Laclau, E. (2004) 'Glimpsing the Future', in Critchley, S. and Marchart, O. (eds) *Laclau: A critical reader*, London: Routledge, 279–328

Laclau, E. and Mouffe, C. (2001) *Hegemony and Socialist Strategy: towards a radical democratic politics* (2nd edition), London: Verso

Laplanche, J. (1999) *Essays on Otherness*, London: Routledge

Laplanche, J. and Pontalis, J-B. (1973) *The Language of Psychoanalysis*, London: Karnac Books

Lapping, C. (2004) 'Discipline, Gender and Institution: an empirical study of in/exclusion in undergraduate American Literature and Political Thought classes', unpublished thesis, University of London

Lapping, C. (2006) 'Recodifications of academic positions and reiterations of desire: change but continuity in gendered subjectivities', *Studies in Higher Education*, 31(4): 423–437

Lapping, C. (2007) 'Interpreting 'resistance' sociologically: a reflection on the recontextualisation of psychoanalytic concepts into sociological analysis', *Sociology*, 41(4): 627–644

Lapping, C. (2008) 'The ethics of interpretation: the signifying chain from field to analysis', *Discourse: Studies in the Cultural Politics of Education*, **29**: 69–83

Lather, P. (1991) *Getting Smart: feminist research and pedagogy with/in the post-modern*, New York: Routledge

Law, J. (2004) *After Method: mess in social science research*, London: Routledge

Lyth, M. I. (1959 [1988]) 'The functioning of social systems as a defense against anxiety', in *Containing Anxiety in Institutions*, London: Free Association Books, 1988, 43–85

Lyth, M. I. (1969) 'Some methodological notes on a hospital study', in *Containing Anxiety in Institutions*, London: Free Association Books, 115–132

Lyth, M. I. (1988) 'Reflections on my work: Isabel Menzies Lyth in conversation with Ann Scott and Robert M. Young', in *Containing Anxiety in Institutions*, London: Free Association Books, 5–37

Malcolm, J. (1986) *In the Freud Archives*, London: Fontana Paperbacks

ManKind Initiative (February 2009) 'Male Victims of Domestic Abuse: Key Statistics, Online. Available at: www.mankind.org.uk (accessed February 2009)

Marchart, O. (2004) 'Politics and ontological difference: on the 'strictly philosophical' in Laclau's work', in Critchley, S. and Marchart, O. (eds) *Laclau: a critical reader*, London: Routledge, 54–72

Meissner, W. W. (1988) 'Projection and projective identification', in J. Sandler, ed. *Projection, Identification, Projective Identification*, London: Karnac Books, 27–49

Metivier, J. (2010) 'Authorship and identity: a study of two fiction writing groups', unpublished upgrade report, Institute of Education, University of London

Mitchell, J. (1991) 'Introduction', in *The Selected Melanie Klein*, London: Penguin Books, 9–32

Mitscherlich, A. and Mitscherlich, M. (1967 [1975]) *The Inability to Mourn*, New York: Grove Press

Moore, A. (2004) *The Good Teacher: dominant discourses in teaching and teacher education*, London: Routledge

Moore, A. (2006) 'Recognising desire: a psychosocial approach to understanding policy implementation and effect', *Oxford Review of Education*, 32(4): 487–503

Nobus, D. and Quinn, M. (2005) *Knowing Nothing, Staying Stupid: elements for a psychoanalytic epistemology*, London: Routledge

O.E.D (1983) *The Shorter Oxford English Dictionary: on historical principles*, London: Guild Publishing

Parker, I. (2010) 'The place of transference in psychosocial research', *Journal of Theoretical and Philosophical Psychology* 30(1): 17–31

Phillips, A. (1997) 'Keeping it moving: commentary on Judith Butler by Adam Phillips', in J. Butler, *The Psychic Life of Power*, California: Stanford University Press, 151–159

Pitt, A. J. (1998) 'Qualifying resistance: some comments on methodological dilemmas', *International Journal of Qualitative Studies in Education*, 11(4): 535–553

Racker, H. (1982) *Transference and Countertransference*, London: Karnac

Ragland-Sullivan, E. (1986) *Jacques Lacan and the Philosophy of Psychoanalysis*, Urbana: University of Illinois Press

Ringrose, J. (2008) ' "Every time she bends over she pulls up her thong": Teen girls negotiation discourses of competitive heterosexualised aggression', *Girlhood Studies: An International Journal*, 1(1): 35–59

Rustin, M. (2001) *Reason and Unreason: Psychoanalysis, science and politics*, London: Continuum

Rustin, M. (2008) 'For Dialogue between psychoanalysis and constructionism: a comment on paper by Frosh and Baraitser', *Psychoanalysis, Culture and Society*, **13**: 406–415

Rustin, M. (2010) 'The psychosocial climate of climate change', paper presented at the 3rd Psychosocial Studies Network Conference, University of East London

Sagan, O. (2008) 'Getting it down on paper: mentally ill adults' use of community-based expressive literacy provision', Unpublished thesis, University of London

Sandler, J. (1988), 'The concept of projective identification', in Sandler, J. ed. *Projection, Identification, Projective Identification*, London: Karnac Books, 13–26

Schafer, R. (1981) 'Narration in the psychoanalytic Dialogue', in W. J. T. Mitchell, *On Narrative*, The University of Chicago Press, 25–49

Segal, J. (1992) *Melanie Klein*, London: Pelican

Skeggs, B. (1997) *Formations of Class and Gender*, London: Sage

Spivak, G. (1993) 'More on Power/Knowledge', in *Outside in the Teaching Machine*, New York: Routledge, 25–51

Stravrakakis, Y. and Chrysoloras, N. (2006) '(I can't get no) Enjoyment: Lacanian theory and the analysis of netionalism', *Psychoanalysis, culture and society*, **11**(2): 144–163

Steinmetz, G. (2006) 'Bourdieu's disavowal of Lacan: psychoanalytic theory and the concepts of "habitus" and "symbolic capital"', *Constellations*, **13**(4): 445–464

Trist, E. L. and Murray, H. (eds) (1951) *The Social Engagement of Social Science: A Tavistock Anthology, Vol. 1: The socio-psychological perspective*, London: Free Association Books 1990

Truong, M. T.-D. (1991) 'Kelly', *Amerasia Journal*, **17**(2): 41–48

Verhaeghe, P. (1997) *Does the Woman Exist? From Freud's hysteric to Lacan's feminine*, London: Rebus Press

Verhaeghe, P. (2006) 'Enjoyment and impossibility: Lacan's revision of the Oedipus complex', in J. Clemens and R. Grigg (eds) *Reflections on Seminar XVII: Jacques Lacan and the other side of psychoanalysis*, Durham: Duke University Press, 29–49

Walkerdine, V. (1990) *Schoolgirl Fictions*, London:Verso

Young, M. F. D. (1971) *Knowledge and Control: new directions for the sociology of education*, London: Collier Macmillan

Zizek, S. (1989) *The Sublime Object of Ideology*, London: Verso

Zizek, S. (1994) *The Metastases of Enjoyment*, London: Verso

Zizek, S. (19 November 2009) 'Post-Wall', *London Review of Books*

Index